GENERATION'S END

GENERATION'S END

A PERSONAL MEMOIR OF AMERICAN POWER AFTER 9/11

SCOTT L. MALCOMSON
FOREWORD BY GEORGE PACKER

POTOMAC BOOKS, INC.
WASHINGTON, D.C.

"September l, 1939," from *Collected Poems of W. H. Auden.* Copyright © 1940 (renewed 1968) by W. H. Auden. Used by permission of Random House, Inc., Faber and Faber, Ltd., and the Wylie Agency, LLC.

"Try to Praise the Mutilated World" from *Without End: New and Selected Poems* by Adam Zagajewski. Copyright © 2002 by Adam Zagajewski. Translation copyright © 2002 by Farrar, Straus and Giroux, LLC. Reprinted by permission of Farrar, Straus and Giroux, LLC, and Faber and Faber, Ltd.

"Qasida for a Rose" and "Ode to Walt Whitman" from *Obras Completas* (Galaxia/Gutenberg, 1996 edition) by Federico Garcia Lorca. Copyright © Herederos de Federico Garcia Lorca. English translation(s) by Catherine Brown, Greg Simon, and Stephen F. White, copyright © Catherine Brown, Greg Simon, Stephen F. White, and Herederos de Federico Garcia Lorca. All rights reserved. Reprinted by permission of Penguin and the Lorca estate. For information regarding rights and permissions please contact lorca@artslaw.co.uk or William Peter Kosmas, Esq., 8 Franklin Square, London W14 9UU, England.

Selected Poems of Shmuel HaNagid, translated by Peter Cole. Copyright © 1996 Princeton University Press. Reprinted by permission of Princeton University Press.

"The Scientist." Words and music by Guy Berryman, Jon Buckland, Will Champion, and Chris Martin. Copyright © 2002 by Universal Music Publishing MGB, Ltd. All rights in the United States administered by Universal Music—MGB Songs. International copyright secured. All rights reserved. Reprinted by permission of Hal Leonard Corporation.

Library of Congress Cataloging-in-Publication Data
Malcomson, Scott L.
  Generation's end : a personal memoir of American power after 9/11 / Scott L. Malcomson ; foreword by George Packer. — 1st ed.
      p. cm.
  ISBN 978-1-59797-540-7 (hardcover : alk. paper)
  1. United States—Foreign relations—2001-2009. 2. September 11 Terrorist Attacks, 2001—Influence. 3. War on Terrorism, 2001-2009. 4. Malcomson, Scott L. 5. Mello, Sérgio Vieira de, 1948-2003. 6. United Nations. High Commission for Human Rights. 7. Journalists—New York (State)—New York—Biography. 8. United Nations—Biography. I. Title.
  E895.M36 2010
  327.73009'05—dc22

                                                                                    2010021559
(alk. paper)

Printed in the United States of America on acid-free paper that meets the American National Standards Institute Z39-48 Standard.

Potomac Books, Inc.
22841 Quicksilver Drive
Dulles, Virginia 20166

First Edition

10 9 8 7 6 5 4 3 2 1

To my *Times* colleagues
and the firefighters of Engine 226,
and in memory of Sergio

CONTENTS

FOREWORD

Nine years on, we no longer live in the era of September 11. The events of that day have entered history: at some point, Americans stopped carrying their shock in their nervous systems and arguing their meaning around the clock with the intensity of life-and-death matters. The day that was supposed to change everything changed a great deal (not as much as it seemed then), but these new things—from airport security to the language of jihad to the constant prospect of catastrophic attack—are now ordinary features of the landscape. Two wars remain unfinished, and so do the debates about them, and their most important and permanent consequences are still not clear. But the images of American soldiers patrolling the streets of far-off Muslim countries and being hit by buried explosives have been with us for so long that their connection to the attacks that took place at the start of the millennium has grown attenuated. America's counterinsurgencies have taken on a life and momentum of their own, so that President Barack Obama, in announcing his strategy for the war in Afghanistan at the start of his term, had to remind the public that the United States was still fighting in the region because al Qaeda was still there, too. He had to give the country a history lesson.

This passage of time lends Scott Malcomson's personal chronicle of the days and weeks and months following September 11, 2001, a peculiar power. In the hands of such an unusually thoughtful and talented writer, the special atmosphere of that time comes alive again in all its vividness: the fatal smell of ground zero, the sudden sense of fragility, the vigils and poems, the temporary insanity of being able to think and talk of nothing else and yet finding no relief in thinking and talking. It was the worst of times and—in the sense that heightened consciousness is preferable to prolonged dullness and daydreaming—the best. Because Malcomson was an opinion editor at the *New York Times* and saw his job as a kind of civic responsibility, within the first hours he was professionally committed to reflecting on what the attacks meant for the city, the country, and the world; and those reflections remain provocative today. But before any thoughts, there are the author's sense-memories: the exhaustion of walking miles into the city to reach the office that morning, the swirl of business documents that fell like snow on Brooklyn, the hysterical laughter of grief-stricken firemen at the station across the street on the second day. These make Malcomson's account seem as fresh as ones written in the immediate aftermath. The first reason to read *Generation's End: A Personal Memoir of American Power After 9/11* is simply to be reminded.

But Malcomson is also writing with the advantage of history, even the short span of nine years. His book takes you from the morning of September 11, through the anthrax attacks, the overthrow of the Taliban, the turn of the Bush administration toward an aggressive new foreign policy, the lead-up to the invasion of Iraq, and its aftermath, concluding with the bombing of United Nations (UN) headquarters in Baghdad in August 2003, and the death of Sergio Vieira de Mello, the UN envoy, who had been Scott Malcomson's boss since his departure from the *Times* earlier that year. This period of not quite twenty-four months has the feel of a discrete chapter of the larger era, bookended by two disasters for the writer and his world: the first unexpected and immense, the last a more foreseeable result of American actions. These two years contain all the decisions that would set in motion the larger era, and because it was possible to imagine things taking a different course, the story unfolds and deepens like a tragedy.

The act of looking back with the passage of time allows Malcomson to make these events immediate and to give them the significant glow of history. *Generation's End* is both a memoir and a historical essay, but it's the second that separates this book from many other fine accounts of September 11. Malcomson's organizing structural principle is, in addition to chronology, the workings of his own mind, and because it's such a supple, self-questioning, idiosyncratic mind, the book becomes a page-turner: you want to know what happens next because you want to know what the writer thinks next. He takes a familiar occurrence—for example, a presidential speech—and uses it as a jumping-off point for an extended meditation, full of unexpected twists and turns and implications, on aspects of the book's central theme of how America used its power after 9/11.

Malcomson's digressions are not detours but the point of the journey, and they are always welcome because he never stops being curious about the world and subjecting it to his patient interrogations. September 11 prompted a clamor of instant certitudes and flimsy generalizations—writers raced into the fray fully armed with explanations and exhortations, as if mental vulnerability were an intolerable state. But the horrors of the day led Malcomson to ask questions, and then deeper questions. He managed to think and act even amid uncertainty— Keats called it "negative capability"—and this ability serves him well as a writer. He had a powerful moral and emotional response to the attacks (the effects on his family make for some of the most compelling passages), and yet he didn't allow it to settle into dogma. His account is faithful to the stages of unknowing that any intellectually honest person had to pass through, and these wear better and make for more truly lively reading than the louder, attention-grabbing voices of those who always purported to know the answers. Malcomson can be severe in his judgments, but his temper isn't partisan or polemical. Instead, he guards his inwardness, his love of history and literature, and follows the backstreets of his own curiosity. His tolerance and openness remind me of certain liberal writers—E. M. Forster comes to mind—who wrote in a time before instant punditry made it unacceptable and even dangerous to scrutinize an object from more than one angle.

Not that Malcomson draws no conclusions. *Generation's End* is, as its title suggests, an elegy—in some ways quite a bitter one—for members of his age group (and mine) who grew up thinking that America was, if not always a force for good, at least the indispensable center of the world, the standard by which other countries would be judged and to which they should aspire. In a few short years, the Bush administration's response to September 11 squandered this power and privilege, and it's unlikely that future generations of Americans will be able to assume the same role for their country again. Malcomson arrives at this conclusion reluctantly, after an extended argument with himself, because, although he's a cosmopolitan and well-traveled man, he also loves his country, critically but passionately. This book is the beautiful and sad record of a lover's quarrel.

George Packer
Brooklyn, 2010

I

ONE DAY

The babysitter was late. My wife's sister had phoned earlier to tell us a plane had flown into the World Trade Center. My wife, Becky, and I were eager to get to work. She was an assistant United States attorney in the Southern District, downtown Manhattan; I was an opinion editor at the *New York Times*. These were the sort of civic-institution posts where you feel you ought to be around in emergencies. Becky's dad called to say a second plane had hit the World Trade Center. Becky had just taken our daughter to her preschool class down the street. The babysitter arrived; traffic on Flatbush Avenue had slowed her down. I went to drop off the dry cleaning. The truck (Engine 226) from the firehouse, straight across the street from us, was gone.

I returned home to dress for work. Becky called her office, and the security officer answering the phone said the building was closed. At Church Street and Park Place, Becky's building was just north of the Trade Center's towers, both of which now had substantial fires burning away in their upper floors. Becky's boss, Mary Jo White, had prosecuted the bombers who had hit the World Trade Center in 1993, and I had somehow thought she would already be at her desk, sending out investigators and so on. She was proud of her antiterrorism prosecutions and expertise. But the fires were too close.

So Becky would stay home. We heard that the subways were closed. I would have to walk. As I went down the stairs Becky called out that a plane had hit the Pentagon.

I considered going to P.S. 261, the local elementary school, to vote in the Democratic mayoral primary. I didn't like any of the four candidates much. But I try to be a good citizen, and voting is the really tangible part of living in a democracy so I hate to miss it. Nonetheless, as I walked toward the school I noticed that downtown Brooklyn was being covered in ash. (The first tower had fallen, but with all the sirens, traffic, and other sounds I had not heard it.) I guessed that the election would be rescheduled. I stopped at a small shop to buy a fresh notebook and pen, then walked up into Brooklyn Heights. There was so much smoke that I thought a building had gone down on our side of the East River; but it was all from the massive cloud created by that first tower falling and by the smoke of the fires.

I walked along a path down an alley of trees in a small park dedicated to Brooklynites who had died serving in World War II. This was where I would jog on normal mornings. There were people covered with ash walking the other way and guards with shotguns by the courthouses. I was worried that I might have trouble talking my way onto the Brooklyn Bridge, but when I reached the entrance the real problem was that the walkway was filled with thousands of people pressing into Brooklyn. I jumped down to the roadway—the Manhattan-bound side was already closed to nonemergency traffic—then climbed back up to the walkway when the crowd there had thinned some. Ahead was the north tower, burning at about the ninetieth floor.

On the roadway, below me now, cars with sirens raced by every thirty seconds or so. I saw a fireman on a small motorcycle, almost a scooter, going as fast as the little motor could take him, into Manhattan; and another fireman walking in the same direction by himself. It occurred to me that these men were off duty and had heard about the fire and were simply trying to get to it by whatever means. Walking ahead of me—we were pushed up against the right-hand barrier by people going the other way—were three people in civilian clothes with sidearms on their belts; off-duty cops, I supposed, heading toward the disaster.

I was relieved to be going their way. Whatever this disaster was that was happening around us, I felt lucky because I had a job to do. Whatever this disaster was, there would be a debate on it, and public debate was what my job was all about. I had to see what I could see and get to the paper; it gave me a feeling of resolve, a peaceful feeling.

There was an old man in a dark suit, coated with white ash. He was nearly round—a creation, I suppose, of decades spent sitting in chairs and moving only his hands. He conveyed himself steadily forward in a rhythmic, rolling, heaving walk, carrying one of those distinct red-brown accordion folders that lawyers use to hold their papers. It was full to bursting (they always are), clutched in his left hand. In his right hand a briefcase. Ash covering his bottle-thick glasses.

A young man with a ripped T-shirt. Everyone, just about, with ash on their clothes. Very few people crying. To say this was an orderly procession is somehow an understatement. It was as though people were commuting away from death; that was their point of departure for the day. A handful of people ran, I imagine out of simple anxiety or because they might have thought the Brooklyn Bridge could be attacked, too. (And why not? Why not kill us everywhere? Why was I not falling into the river?) But the great majority walked away from death at a prudent, if quick, pace.

A young man jogged past me toward Manhattan, in his running outfit, headphones on. He was not going to let a little disaster interrupt his exercise routine. He was, in his way, the most surprising sight on the bridge.

I was halfway or so across when a rumble sounded and the second tower collapsed. A thousand people turning around for a moment; some screams. I checked my watch: 10:30 a.m. The building came straight down like a waterfall (like a pillar of water). It seemed unbelievable that something so huge could drop that way. It took maybe fifteen seconds.

A thousand people turned back to resume their walk toward Brooklyn. Some had cried out and friends or strangers had braced them up. The helpfulness of people was striking in that it was so unsentimental, quick, and practical. We had just seen hundreds of people exactly like us die.

A man appeared beside me. I could not tell why he was going into the city. He gestured up at the open air where the towers and the people in them had been. "Somebody's going to pay for this," he said.

"Somebody already has," I said. I'm not sure what I meant. It's just what I said. I had the dead in mind. The lightness of that new open air above the city, the heaviness of these newly dead.

As the bridge ramped down into Manhattan, the smoke thickened and there were even fewer people. I could breathe, more or less, but not well. The air had a distinctive smell, with burning plastic in it and something like wet clay.

I considered turning left and heading toward the towers, but to reach the *Times* I needed to go right. Responsibility took me uptown, past City Hall, and up around the courthouses on Center Street. Most of the police officers and firemen were rushing toward whatever remained of the World Trade Center so the streets were clear; the civilians had fled, the officials had not yet taken over. I felt I had the run of the city, that sense that comes when the streets have emptied during emergencies or very heavy snows. I felt, *I can go anywhere, and I am alive.*

Security people had already cleared a space around the Javits Federal Building, which is attached to the New York headquarters of the Federal Bureau of Investigation (FBI). I thought, almost involuntarily, of old Senator Jacob Javits, son of Lower East Side immigrants, a good-hearted Republican who did not mind having his name put on big buildings. I was glad he had not lived long enough to see this happen to his city. I'd never thought of death in quite this way before—as something that could happen just in time, fortunately; as something you would not want to do too late.

Walking north through Chinatown I tried to reach Becky by cell phone, but the phone system had ceased working. At pay phones people were lined up, waiting so patiently in their ash-covered clothes to phone in and say they weren't dead. Two men in Chinatown pulled the grate down on their commercial-sign store. What else to do but close up? Who knew what would be happening later that day? Who could possibly have even the slightest idea? North through Chinatown, the news became less clear, less emphatic. Maybe on this block of SoHo they could keep the shop open? Even though so many people were simply standing in the street with their mouths open, staring downtown, waiting? And already around Prince Street I looked a bit odd, because of the ash coating. It's in my eyes, nose, mouth, and hair. It is, it was, the pulverized remains of two tall buildings, also in some tiny part the last powdery remains of several thousand people, which I tasted on my tongue and around the rim of my mouth and swallowed. Good-bye.

By the time I reached the Village I was brushing the ash off my shirt and face because people were looking at me strangely. On Bedford above Houston, not far beyond the fire station, a woman bounced on the balls of her feet in physical anticipation of a grief that was coming her way. She just knew it, she said to the woman standing before her, a friend, "They say to wait because they still don't have no information." The second woman began to cry and totter, saying something; the first woman braced her up, yet bounced even more rapidly. She held her friend by the shoulders, at arms' length, screaming, "No, don't say that! Don't say that! They don't have the information yet!"

I found my sister-in-law nearby, in the West Village. I was tired of walking and had thought to borrow her bicycle. She was at the deli around the corner from her apartment, stocking up on food to get her through whatever calamities lay immediately ahead. She had a colleague with her, a young woman who hung back while we talked. The woman (my sister-in-law told me quietly) had got to their office early, before the first plane hit. Their office was on Church Street below Chambers Street. When the plane hit, and then for some time afterward, she had observed people falling from the sky. Or not falling, exactly, because they were not pushed. They were flying.

Straight down to death on the sidewalk.

My sister-in-law's colleague had fled from this sight, hurrying north; now she was here at the deli counter, furtive, hardly able to speak. She could not get back home to New Jersey because all the routes had been closed. She would spend the rest of the day at my sister-in-law's tiny apartment in silence.

I rode the borrowed bicycle north, coughing up the ash I had taken in downtown.

At the *Times*, on East Forty-third Street between Broadway and Eighth Avenue, I headed to my office on the tenth floor. When I got off the elevator Gail Collins was there with a warm embrace. Formerly a columnist, she had become the editorial page editor five days before. She appeared relaxed and confident, but she also needed help. My immediate superior, the Op-Ed editor, Terry Tang, had been unable to make it in from New Jersey, with the bridges and tunnels being closed and the ferries either moored or being used for rescue. Other colleagues were missing, too.

At Op-Ed, it was just Mary Suh and I out of our normal staff of five editors. The decision had been made already to have columnists fill our page, unless some piece came in from outside that was so perfect it would have to run. But we could not be certain the columnists would come through, and in any case there was the rest of the week to plan. So Mary and I set about trying to find contributors and thinking of angles that would become relevant two, three, or more days ahead. We called former secretaries of state, terrorism experts, engineers who understand big buildings, specialists in airline security. We tried to contact fiction writers and historians and others who had a more general expertise in the human condition, with the idea that they could illuminate, somehow, what was happening to us.

I had been hired by the *Times*'s Op-Ed page for several reasons, the main one being to shape its coverage of foreign affairs. I had spent years working abroad, writing articles and books in South America, Africa, Europe, Central Asia, and the Pacific islands. I had covered election campaigns and disease outbreaks and murders, business stories and cultural stories, and all this added up to a sort of professional expertise—not least of which was an expertise in how the United States was seen from outside. There was no one at the Op-Ed page with similar experience and hadn't been for some time. This may seem odd—it did to me—but it makes sense within the *Times*'s industrial-democratic business model. The basic idea is that a journalist develops a skill set that exists independent of expertise; he or she can be moved from Rome to the Newark school board to sports to business without a dip in quality. The bargain for the journalist is that he doesn't have to develop (or be limited to) a particular expertise; the bargain for management is that the journalist is replaceable. Within Op-Ed, this democratic gravitational force did not apply to the writers we reached out to—they had to be experts—but it did apply to what they had to say, which needed to be comprehensible and useful to the average reader. As editors, we both had to know more than the average reader and to be able to imagine what it was like to not know much at all. (The ultimate power, then, rested with the editor rather than the writer; the story was sometimes told of an exasperated editor shouting into the phone, "When we want your opinion, we'll give it to you!") The editor who could most forcefully put across the point of view of the uninformed often won the editorial arguments. It was a peculiar balancing act and took some getting used to.

Before this morning, foreign affairs were, from the page's perspective, of only modest interest. American power and leadership were secure and essentially unquestionable, and foreign topics were localized: Middle East negotiations, North Atlantic Treaty Organization (NATO) expansion, Irish republicanism, Hutus and Tutsis. This was about to change.

It was difficult for people to phone into Manhattan. It was difficult to get a line into Boston or Washington, as well—the two cities that, along with New York, provide most of the commentators one sees on television and Op-Ed pages. There is something of a master media Rolodex: we kept seeing the people we were phoning show up on CNN; sometimes we saw someone on CNN we had not thought of or didn't know and proceeded to hunt the person's numbers down. George Shultz, who had been Ronald Reagan's secretary of state, phoned back when I was away from my desk; then a half hour later there he was on CNN, from a studio in San Francisco. Gen. Wesley Clark was on, appearing uncomfortable, with his soldier-in-the-spotlight look. I had met him not long before, at Richard Holbrooke's apartment during a party. I was struck at the time by his good humor, by his nervousness, and by what he said about America's future of waging optional wars—what would come to be called wars of choice—because there would be no real necessity for fighting, only possibilities for fighting, and America, as the indefinitely hegemonic power, would be free to select among them.

President George W. Bush was off somewhere, flying around, though he had announced from Sarasota, Florida, that he would hunt down "those folks who committed this act." Holbrooke appeared repeatedly on CNN, talking about Osama bin Laden and states that shelter terrorists. He appeared reasonably confident that the author of these attacks—we knew that four planes had been taken, and there were rumors of more—was bin Laden, together with his group, al Qaeda, or "the Base." The bin Laden group worked out of Afghanistan. What they were doing boarding planes in Boston, Newark, and Dulles, Virginia, then somehow flying them into the World Trade Center and the Pentagon, was anyone's guess. It hardly seemed plausible. Pushing a raft full of dynamite against a ship in Yemen was one thing. It seemed quite another to take control over and fly four commercial jets. And how could bin Laden, somewhere in Afghanistan and (as the country's Taliban leaders had been saying for well over a year) forbidden from even using a telephone, possibly be the "mastermind"?

Yet Holbrooke and others felt confident he was, mainly from a process of elimination. There were, incredibly enough given a world population of 5 billion, not that many people one would think of as having the means, desire, and opportunity to kill on such a spectacular scale. Of these three requirements, the desire was by far the most important. The desire, or perhaps the "motive," or the "will." Or a word that captures each of these three senses and could have answered our question of the day: why?

What little we knew could indeed be walked backward, so to speak, to the person of Osama bin Laden. He was, at the least, a helpful place to put what was immediately apparent, namely, that these attacks demonstrated a real hatred for the United States and, in particular, a hatred for our military and economic power, the substance of these symbols the Pentagon and World Trade Center.

The hatred as such did not surprise me. I had traveled many places in the previous twenty years. Anti-Americanism had long since become familiar, and of course the number of Americans killed by terrorists was already high before this morning. From the suicide bombing of our embassy in Beirut in 1983 to September 10, 2001, there had been eight major terror attacks with the United States as their principal target and 1,066 people dead as a result, a majority of them American citizens.

To me, what seemed truly new in the post–Cold War decade was a widespread pro-Americanism, or at the least an acceptance of the American victory; admiration of the American model; hope for American attention, esteem, or help; and dependence on America to make sense of the world's future. The reality of Americanism seemed to have shaded into its inevitability. You could deal with it, or you could go away.

American culture, in the same ten years, grew, if anything, more isolationist. The nation itself became more diverse, and in that sense less isolated, than it had been in the 1960s. But this diversity was not widely perceived—unlike in the 1920s, when a still higher percentage of Americans were foreign-born—as a dire threat. Many of us saw it as a low-key and pleasant reminder of our specialness among nations: unafraid, we welcome others; they are happy to be here among us. This mild drama of diversity went perfectly well with increased isolationism. America could take the world into itself in a way that only increased American self-regard; the world outside presented no challenges whatsoever to anything that mattered to us. No wonder we had been so unafraid—in facing the future over this past decade—without being noticeably brave. There were no serious challenges in the world, just occasional problems among which we could select the ones we wanted to solve, or not.

This day brought something almost entirely new: a serious and effective attack on the physical body of our country. What I found surprising was how unamazed people around me were that someone should come to slaughter us, specifically, how I did not hear anyone saying that the killers were simply insane. So we would find reasons for what they did. And if they had no reasons, or none we could understand, we would supply some ourselves.

I had this terrible notion that the killers were an entirely self-contained group, all dead now, therefore leaving no testament and no surviving member to explain their thinking. A self-erasing group. Then we could never even pretend to know why so many of us had been killed.

By eleven thirty that morning, the Pearl Harbor analogy had appeared on television and in the articles that began to come into our office by fax and e-mail. This idea took over the conversation: both attacks were by plane against Americans on American territory; both were sudden and massive. Both got people talking about war. War? It had been such a gorgeous morning, clear as could be; the loveliest of mornings in autumn, our city's loveliest season, the one people sing about. War. Nothing could have been further from our minds before nine o'clock.

By noon there were lines, hours long, to donate blood. At about the same time, the dead started getting names—the likely dead, as there was not time yet for identifying bodies. Distinctions could be made, though. Anyone on the floors above where the planes hit was presumably dead, because the fires had been such that no one could get past them. This was why people had been jumping rather than waiting for it, oh, . . . they wanted to feel they had a *choice.*

The television stations had footage of bodies falling. They showed a little but soon stopped. To show it would have been disrespectful and indecent.

Yet this was the indecency we were in.

Mary Suh heard at last from her husband, who had been taking pictures downtown for the Associated Press. He had been poking around in the rubble since the towers fell and had finally been able to locate a live phone cable in a destroyed pizza place and used alligator clips to upload his digital images. He saw bodies everywhere and parts of bodies. There was an expectation that at least one and possibly more tall buildings would be coming down soon. He compared what he was seeing to an urban war zone; but that comparison didn't quite work.

When Mary got off the phone she was crying. "I've never heard him like that," she said. He'd sounded shattered. She mentioned some of the horrible places he had worked before and some of the horrors he had seen, that he was a pretty tough guy. But this was different from the other places.

Maybe it was just the scale and the completeness. He was seeing no survivors and neither was anyone else. If more buildings came down there might be survivors, but from the initial two collapses, it didn't seem possible. Each of those people had had 110 stories of building fall on top of him or her, or had fallen that far, or some combination of these that added up to the same thing. When you saw it, the conclusion seemed inevitable: thousands of people snuffed out in two moments, each perhaps fifteen seconds long.

On television they were getting more video in. A long segment showed one of the towers coming down, as seen from the street below. The cameraperson started running away from the cloud of smoke and debris as it unfurled down the canyon of a street. Soon we had the definitive murder images of the planes hitting the towers. The newest image was the harshest, somehow, that of the second plane hitting the south tower. It was flying at such a speed that the image was very hard to absorb; it kept being unexpected, like a sudden punch from nowhere, which was how it felt in my body, too. So after a while I couldn't watch it anymore and had to stay alert to look away, or close my eyes, when that picture was coming, because I was getting punched up here, and I had to keep my focus and get the information in.

You could sense them editing the tapes. There were a few people in a few rooms around the city who got the tape. They saw the whole tape. They took out the bits that seemed to work, the bits that had the most information plus some allowance for texture—the pause interrupted by the offstage scream, then the ghostly figure running camera left. Five seconds of the bleeding survivor screaming. But not ten seconds or a minute and a half. Not the mutilation. Not the humiliation and the indecency. Not the people flying, not the same people hitting the ground, flattened, destroyed, skin smashed, blood and hair. You could sense them editing the tapes as they were groping, finding the story, and making the story something they thought they could tell and you could bear to watch. The planes hit the buildings (the action); the buildings come down (the result); the people run away (the reaction). The people run away! They made it! Just like you!

But now we were getting the messages by audio—the cell phone calls and voice mail messages—which were absolutely fresh information: I might not make it out. I'd better go now. Always remember that I love you.

The Pearl Harbor analogy was going full throttle through the early afternoon. People didn't have much else to work with. Pearl Harbor also provided a phrase— "Day of Infamy"—that could be turned to a new purpose. Today was a New Day of Infamy, part of a pattern, if only a pattern of two.

The debates were truncated, though, because once the idea was expressed, the next step, in normal times, would be to disagree about interpretation. This type of debate, shouting and one-upmanship was simply not appropriate at 2:00 p.m. on September 11, 2001. So ideas could be stated, then an awkward pause, and the same ideas could be stated again, then you could return to fresh footage or check the wire services for something new.

We had begun getting Op-Eds by fax and e-mail. There was nothing we had to use. Some were urging support for the president (wherever he was). Some, the most decent, simply expressed rage and sorrow, often in a poem. The rest tried to put what had just happened in the context of something the writer had been thinking about previously: military readiness, Muslim fundamentalism, the effects of globalization, American policy with regard to Israelis and Palestinians, overreliance on electronic surveillance rather than human intelligence gathering (spies), the treatment of terrorists as criminals rather than as enemy soldiers, the Bush administration's unilateralism with regard to honoring treaties, and its (now, apparently, mistaken) focus on defense against missiles. One early submission was rather long and appeared to be a text that had existed before the morning's events. A new lead paragraph, concerning the killings downtown and elsewhere, had been added, and other references dispersed within the text, to be gathered again for restatement at the end, all supporting the author's preexisting argument, namely, that American-led globalization had been a moral and economic disaster for much or most of the world. The recent attacks simply-merely-regrettably confirmed this trend in global affairs and should serve as a wake-up call.

To explain is not to excuse.

I told you so.

All the silent dead confirm what I have been saying for some time, namely that— (If we can assume that they are all, in fact, dead—)

The Op-Ed format seemed to have come up against its limits. What were Mary and I looking for? I found myself somewhat mesmerized by Holbrooke on the TV. He was uniquely appealing, not for what he was saying, but for his tone, deep and slow, unafraid—unafraid, even, to show his bewilderment. Most of the people I saw or whose words I read or with whom I spoke on the phone showed an inability to adjust their manner to the scale of what was happening. As a result, they had to make the events get much smaller. A person could not really rise to the scale of such a day, but one could rise to show recognition of the scale, not through words exactly but through one's manner. Holbrooke seemed to come close.

But Holbrooke was just an infant when the Japanese attacked Pearl Harbor. Most of the people who now had the interest, opportunity, and stamina to lead the United States were too young to remember World War II; whatever Day of Infamy this day was, they would be facing it alone. In previous months the phrase "the Greatest Generation" had entered common speech. It was the comparative part that gave the phrase life: the World War II generation was greatest not in comparison to the World War I generation but in comparison to the generations that succeeded it and, in particular, to the present generation of leaders—let's call it the Bill Clinton generation, which (according to the generation's own pundits) had scraped its way to some new low of louche tawdriness and historical insignificance. This generation seemed to view itself as comically shrunken in the face of any large task. It was going to have to grow now.

I wanted to hear from George Shultz, someone like that. I remembered seeing him at a state dinner in Majuro, the capital of the Marshall Islands, in 1988 or so. I think he had been a Marine during the battle against the Japanese for Majuro—not one of the more celebrated Pacific campaign battles but still a bloody one—an early victory in the westward island-hopping strategy.

I had this in mind while watching him say on television that day whatever he said, generalities. *Come on, Greatest Generation, help us.* Mary Suh and I agreed—we were the same age, around forty—that our world had changed greatly, and irreparably, in a few hours. We wanted someone who could see our new world more clearly than we could and tell us what it looked like, so we would know and could let our readers know. But we weren't finding that person.

I wanted Shultz or someone like him to make sense of what was happening from the perspective of an American who had fought ashore in a tough battle in World War II. He rang around 6:00 p.m. We chatted briefly. My heart stuttered and I said something about the Marshall Islands, and he said something like, "Yes, well, I don't know." He sounded old and tired and easily irritated.

And he was angry. He had been angry on television, angry like an old man who couldn't do anything, who felt so helpless he couldn't even imagine his way out of it.

Yes, well, I don't know, either.

A counterterrorism expert I spoke with remembered being in rough situations in Latin America, but he always knew he could get out of them and return to the safety of the United States. Now, he said, the one safe place was no longer safe. Part of me was glad that he could no longer prescribe for those in bondage to terrorism without thinking of his own situation. Another part of me was just terrified. I'd been in those situations in Latin America, too.

The counterterrorism expert, like nearly everyone else, asked if my family was all right and whether I had lost anyone close to me. I asked the same of him. These conversations took place all day long between total strangers, who used such phrases with each other as, "I guess you're holding up all right?"

By early evening the video had settled into its pattern. It appeared that no more buildings would come down—Seven World Trade Center, burning since morning and fully evacuated, collapsed at 5:20 p.m.—nor was anyone going to attack us any more today. So it seemed.

The Pearl Harbor analogy had become a cliché, at least by the *Times*'s clock. My immediate superior, Terry, had e-mailed from her home in the early afternoon: "much talk on news about this being the second pearl harbor. is there a way to go with this that is not a simplistic groping to find past experience—and therefore an experience that [because it had been gone through before] can be survived?"

Phil Taubman, number three in the editorial page hierarchy, told me in mid-afternoon that he didn't want to see any more pieces comparing the day's attacks to Pearl Harbor. We were already moving on to comparing our new American life to Israeli life, the phrase being, "We're all Israelis now." There would be time tomorrow to work on that historical analogy until it was carrying all it could, then watch it collapse when a bit too much was stacked on it. At that point we would move on to a new one.

For today, it was a TV story. The correspondents and even anchors had their rooftop positions staked out. The video followed its pattern, interrupted by rooftop commentary to the effect that what had happened was terrible and there was no news yet of survivors. There wouldn't be. You hoped, and you hoped, but I knew already that that part of our city was simply a tomb.

People I knew had called and e-mailed all day to see whether my family and I had survived—people of all kinds, from across the globe, and including people who had fine reasons to dislike the United States. I began to think that the terrorists, whoever they were, might have miscalculated by hitting New York, because our city was a beloved city. More human beings had New York City in common than any other place in the world. Hitting the Pentagon was different. It symbolized American military power, which by definition is something we don't really share with the rest of the world, though we do lend it. The Pentagon was not a place everyone who came to the States had visited or even wanted to see. Nor was nearby Washington an open, international city. There was no outburst of grief for the city of Washington. Most of the people in the Pentagon, in all likelihood, did not live in the city or identify with it; their identification would have been with the military. The city of Washington itself was not much loved by its most public faces. Washington was government office space and a parade ground, but it was not a hearth—at least not for those to whom the airplane-missiles were meant to Send a Message. Since the 1970s, for politicians, Washington had been a place to run against even when they were in it. The nation's government happened to operate in Washington but it could have operated from anywhere. The city represented the nation, not itself.

New York was the opposite: whatever happened here came with the stamp of the city. The terrorists may have miscalculated when they attacked our beloved city, the most peculiarly wide-open city in the world. Even some of America's enemies would grieve for New York City, because it was their city, too.

(I remembered the Taliban representative, young Rahmatullah Hashemi, who had come by the *Times* months before, how his eyes widened and his slight, coiled body gained energy when he described his car ride into Manhattan. He'd never seen anything like it.)

At 8:30 p.m. the president finally appeared:

The pictures of airplanes flying into buildings, fires burning, huge structures collapsing, have filled us with disbelief, terrible sadness and a quiet, unyielding anger. These acts of mass murder were intended to frighten our nation into chaos and retreat. But they have failed. Our country is strong. A great people has been moved to defend a great nation.

"America," the president said from the Oval Office, "was targeted for attack because we're the brightest beacon for freedom and opportunity in the world. And no one will keep that light from shining."

He looked scared. He looked as if he was worried that you did not entirely believe that he was president of the United States. And it *was* hard to believe. George W. Bush—fifty-two, a son of great privilege, reformed heavy drinker, former part owner of a baseball team, governor of the government-hating state of Texas, a person almost wholly and almost proudly ignorant of the world—was president mostly by coincidence. But he was president. We would have to make do with him.

By now, all the nonmilitary planes across the country were on the ground. Chaos at the airports and the airport hotels, silence in the sky.

I spoke with Becky after she put the kids—not yet 2 ½ and 4 ½—to bed. The children had only a vague sense that something was wrong. Becky had tried to keep their spirits up (hers too) by distracting them and keeping the TV off. She told me she saw a fire department sedan pull up in front of the firehouse across from us around 9:00 p.m. It was coated in white ash. She put a picture in my mind: so this was our messenger of death, a four-door covered in white ash driving around the emptied streets, calling.

We finished editing the columns around 10:00 p.m. I went around the corner to have a drink with a colleague. We talked for a while about who might have carried out the attacks. Although we knew little about Osama bin Laden, it still seemed hard to believe that he had been responsible. Rather, the events reminded me of the Red Brigades or another Western group from the 1970s or '60s because the attacks were so antibourgeois. The hatred felt like a secular hatred, that is, a hatred for secular things—power, money, perhaps the American people—rather than a hatred of secularism, much less a hatred born of religious rivalry. And to fly those planes would have required education, financing, solidarity, secrecy, a very steady and somewhat intellectual contempt for the rich and powerful, and a confidence in the power of shock, or, most precisely, a sustaining ability to imagine how shocking one's act would be to the master class. All this together made that morning's killing

The woman at the center did not survive. *Roberto Rabanne*

seem like bourgeois killing, in particular because poor people know from daily life how unimpressed the prosperous are by the deaths of the poor. To believe that one's death, even one's spectacular death, would be of any interest to the upper classes would require a confidence in one's own social significance, which is simply not a feature of poor people's lives. The poor don't feel entitled to attack the rich. Only people closer to the top class would really feel entitled to attack it.

We would need to learn more about Osama bin Laden.

Outside the bar, at Forty-fourth Street and Eighth Avenue, hardly anyone was about. The televisions inside had been blaring the terror news; outside it was close to silent except for distant sirens and the occasional person lurching up with an unfocused look or something odd to say, because the usual tide of people you would see at that hour in that place, leaving theaters and entering bars, had never come in. What remained were the late shift, the rejected, the mad, and the addicted tottering in the city—the left-behind people, left behind again.

I took the train home to Brooklyn. It was not my usual train, because that train normally went near the World Trade Center; those tunnels were dangerous. But other trains were working, which felt like a miracle of organizational grit. I got off in downtown Brooklyn and walked along Atlantic Avenue to my usual deli. Atlantic Avenue was the main street of Arab retailers in Brooklyn. We had a large mosque (one associated with the first Trade Center bombers) four blocks from our house; I could hear the call to prayer from my kitchen in summer when we had the windows open. The avenue had many shops selling Korans, collections of Muhammad's sayings, wall clocks with pictures of Mecca. The delis were mostly Muslim owned, and mine was no exception. The workers there were from Morocco, Lebanon, and Palestine. The next deli along in one direction was Yemeni; in another direction, Tunisian.

As a result, there were plenty of police officers around, and I was glad to see them. I stopped in at the deli and asked the man at the register whether there had been any anti-Muslim incidents. "Not yet," he said with a smile. I had seen him and his colleagues every day for four years. I hoped they weren't feeling too afraid.

And then the firehouse. I didn't stay long. I learned Engine 226 had gone over the Brooklyn Bridge around nine o'clock that morning. The guys parked near the south tower. Tom stayed with the truck. Brian, Stan, Dave, and Lieutenant Bob went into the building. When the south tower came down, the engine was crushed. Tom was in the hospital, getting one of his eyes cleaned up. Brian, Stan, Dave, and Lieutenant Bob were missing. There had been no word about them.

"I think you know Brian," one of the firemen said. I remembered all five of these men—even Lieutenant Bob, who was a visiting commander—because I saw them every day, going to and fro in their fire engine, standing in front of the firehouse in good weather. When I was fixing up my house, they would come over to help when they saw me carrying too much. They had watched my daughter grow from her sixth month and my son from birth. Both kids referred to them as "my firemen" (even when there was a woman working at the firehouse) and the engine as "my fire truck." They would always wave when they saw the truck coming back and call out, "Hi, firemen!" And the firemen would wave back, which was sweetly comical and even wrenching sometimes when they would come back covered with dirt and grim faced only to force out smiles and a wave to the kids. I knew Brian and he was a terrific guy. His eldest two children were a little older than mine, the other two younger.

Across the street, then, and into my house, into my little world. Hello, little world.

II

FINDING THE CONFLICT
WE WERE IN

In the morning I looked out the living-room window across the street to the firehouse and saw what was left of the company. They were putting on and taking off boots. Their truck was somewhere under rubble; they were at loose ends, waiting for lifts to go downtown and look for Brian, Stan, Dave, and Lieutenant Bob. That did not explain this strange behavior with the boots. Some of the guys were laughing. It looked hysterical.

The day before, at this time, two planes hit the World Trade Center, evidently an act of terrorism, its goals still unclear. No one had taken responsibility. There were no demands made. What we had at this point were acts of massive physical destruction and somewhere between three thousand and ten thousand dead people.

It was possible the firemen were losing their minds. Maybe that was what we would all be doing today. Given yesterday, it was hard to believe that life would be following much of a regular schedule.

After breakfast I dropped by the firehouse. By now everyone was sitting, silent, on the cement floor where their truck should have been, their energy all gone. Was there news about the guys? No news.

I walked up into Brooklyn Heights, which was dusty, smoky, and littered with papers. I smelled that smell again: wet cement and smoke and plastic. The papers all around were from the Trade Center: old bills, business correspondence, personnel information, legal documents. Someone would have spent minutes, hours, or weeks of his or her life thinking each of these scraps was very important to keep track of. This was the way many of us passed the days, of course, earning our time among the living by moving such papers around. A clutch of pages whipped down Joralemon Street and stuck to my legs. *Greetings from the pulverized dead! Here was what was so goddamned important before we were killed! So what's important now, survivor?*

This morning was a better time than usual to lose one's mind. As I got nearer to the Promenade I noticed more joggers. The air could not have been good for them to take into their lungs so deeply. The Promenade itself was crowded. The half-mile railing along the Promenade's edge, facing downtown Manhattan, was lined with people, all staring at the same thing. This was the single most famous view of Manhattan: the Brooklyn Bridge spanning the East River up to the right, downtown in the middle, the Statue of Liberty off in the far-left distance. The cityscape seemed so close, glittery at night and inspiring desire, and oddly toy-like, given its immensity, on a bright and clear day, like today and like yesterday. At the railing we all looked at a constant cloud issuing from what remained of the buildings and of all the people buried in them. This cloud, a burning hole in our world, blue skies.

I wondered when it would happen again. That was still a new feeling in New York City. I wondered who was coming to kill us again and when. This was the fourth time in less than ten years. The first was in '93 (at the Trade Center); the second and third tries failed; now this. Even with the unplanned crash in Pennsylvania, apparently owing to the suicidal bravery of some passengers, this latest mission had to be counted a success by whoever planned it. It would be surprising if no one thought to try it again. New York City was, as for so many things other than terrorism, the place to take your big acts, to show the world what you had.

The newspaper was hard to find. This was not a television story anymore. American big-time television is good at finding events and displaying them. It is a wire service for visual news and official statements. But that is about all it is. People wanted to know what was really going on, and for that they needed a quality daily newspaper. New Yorkers wanted to feel the object itself, the texture and weight of the paper, to see the name of the paper across the top looking just the same as it had Monday, Sunday, Saturday, and all the other before days. I also suspected many people would want the paper so that in years to come—one assumed we all had a future—they could bring it out and be able to remember September 11 with some accuracy. I was sure the publisher, Arthur Sulzberger Jr., would have ordered extra runs, but the trucks would have had a hard time making deliveries.

I waited to get my copy until arriving at Forty-third Street. Volume 150, issue number 51,874: "U.S. ATTACKED; HIJACKED JETS DESTROY TWIN TOWERS AND HIT PENTAGON IN DAY OF TERROR." The left-hand lead headline: "A Creeping Horror; Buildings Burn and Fall as Onlookers Search for Elusive Safety." Then N. R. Kleinfield's lead, "It kept getting worse." The right-hand lead, in larger type across two columns: "President Vows to Exact Punishment for 'Evil.'"

On page 2, the left-hand piece described how firefighters had rushed into the buildings and headed upstairs. "Then the buildings fell down," Jane Fritsch wrote. "The firefighters never came out." The right-hand piece, despite the headline "Survivors Are Found in the Rubble," was about the lack of survivors. Across the top was a picture of downtown workers walking across the Brooklyn Bridge. How long ago it seemed. The photo must have been taken after I crossed over, because in the background both of the World Trade Center's towers were already gone.

I turned the pages at my desk: a diagram on page 3, showing how the buildings collapsed; President Bush on page 4, his remarks below a photo from the Oval Office; the Pentagon, a gash in its side, on page 5, with stories from Washington; page 6 had a reaction story and a column, but they were hard to focus on because page 7 had a color photo of a man flying down the side of the north tower, head first, his arms at his side, his legs curiously bent. Not to die in secret—maybe that was the idea. No one in the towers yesterday would have had to jump suddenly, without thought. There would have been enough time to really think it through and decide to take your death out of the hands of your killers and perhaps of chance and to put it in your own hands, as if to say, "I am my own."

At the back of the A section was the editorial. I had seen Verlyn Klinkenborg struggling to write it the day before. Verlyn was the member of the editorial board who would get sent out into the rain; he described changes of season, public moods. "Remember the ordinary, if you can," he began. "Remember how normal New York City seemed at sunrise yesterday, as beautiful a morning as ever dawns in early September."

Today was beautiful too, just as beautiful as yesterday and wonderfully quiet: there were no planes. Fewer people walked the streets. Manhattan was closed below Fourteenth Street.

In the subway coming into work I had passed beneath Greenwich Village, my old neighborhood. But now I could not go aboveground without identification proving I resided in the area. The main memorial and gathering place in the city were, not surprisingly, right at the edge of the forbidden zone, on Fourteenth Street at Union Square Park. I can remember the park from the mid-1980s, when I moved here from northern California; it was a seedy place then, still with something of the late-seventies' inner-city-crisis feel. I found work just down the block, on Broadway and Thirteenth, at the *Village Voice*, a weekly newspaper.

Union Square in the eighties, like much of Manhattan, was spruced up at public expense. Private investors reconsidered an area once written off. Economic prospects improved to such a degree that the ground beneath the old *Voice* building (as I thought of it) became valuable, and the building was knocked down and dragged away. All that graffiti crumbled, the notes we had scrawled to each other. Up went a multiplex movie theater and the Virgin Records megastore that today (I mean September 12, 2001) looked over hundreds of candles burning through last night and the putting up of photocopied notices made by sisters, parents, best friends, asking whether anyone had seen Lizette Mendoza, who worked on the ninety-fourth.

Oh, this is not going to be an easy day. But let's keep going here, and, remember, this is our *city* and *they* are not going to ruin it.

The neighborhood continued gentrifying (as we said then) into the nineties. The area where I lived—off Tompkins Square Park, in the East Village—withstood this process only a little longer, as drugs and the police wore out one working-class generation. We bohemians waged a doomed but not unhappy battle against bourgeois values (as we said then) that was operatic enough to inspire an opera, *Rent*.

In and out of the seasons, finally across town to the West Village with my later-to-be wife and two months spent putting up walls and ceilings on a rental. The previous tenants had spray painted rebellious writings on the walls and left them as they were, buckling and crumbling down. I took almost all the walls down and all the ceilings except the stamped-tin one in the square corner room that was just wide enough to fit our couch. I broke through the recent patches to the thin, hard original plaster, then to the brown "mud," which was reinforced by animal hair and clung to the wooden laths. Where the interior walls reached the exterior brick there were some interesting curves that (I was told) could be explained by the use of jail labor in putting up tenements like ours around 1910. When the walls and ceiling were finally done, we attacked the floor, pulling up layer after layer of carpet and linoleum, each separated by a wafer of newsprint that told you when the flooring above it had been laid down. There were the seventies (my youth come back!); the space probes of the early sixties; Tojo, a shipwreck, and a plane downed in World War II; and the interwar years, which to my surprise seemed to feature melodramatic serials, with lithographs of round-shouldered women being braced up with a draught after a bit of unexpected news had given them a nasty shock. After all the layers were gone, I caressed the darkened soft wood (no hard oak for this tenement) trimmed with a simple design that some person had painted, on hands and knees and using stencils, around 1910.

A creek, Minetta Brook, ran beneath our building. The name sounds Italian but is said to have been Indian and meant "devil's water." The Minetta had once (after 1633) drained the tobacco farm of Wouter van Twiller, as a century and two later it would drain the cemeteries that are beneath Washington Square Park. When Becky and I went jogging together in the mornings, we followed, roughly, the drainage of the creek down to the Hudson River, then headed south along the shore to what was gradually becoming a park and new buildings, just upriver from Battery Park City and the World Trade Center. New York City had been arthritically slow to make any postindustrial use of its waterfront; this development was among the pioneers, and we watched it inch forward at a pace even slower than that of our so-called run in the mornings.

The best view of all this was from the water. There was a tiny kayak club operating from a pier at North Moore Street. (When the Trade Center fell yesterday one local woman grabbed her husband, and they ran to the club, stole a kayak, and paddled across to New Jersey. Hundreds of people yesterday morning, in their fear of what was to come, jumped into the river with the idea of swimming to safety or just somehow getting away.) But Becky and I were not enthused about kayaking, not least because, in the early nineties, we were unsure about the quality of the river water. Instead we took the Port Authority Trans-Hudson (PATH) train from Christopher Street, in the Village, to the Pavonia-Newport station on the Jersey side and joined a sailing club. The club used twenty-four-foot J-class boats, fast little water bugs that were hard to tip over. Becky and I learned to sail on New York Harbor. It was, as you would expect, the kind of water where if you can sail there, you can sail anywhere, dodging the massive cruise ships and zipping around freighters and the Circle Line tour boat that always leaned worryingly to one side because everyone crowded over to look at Manhattan—the Jersey gunwale, friendless, waving up in the air; the Manhattan gunwale slicing the water under its load of admirers.

We would sail upriver to the George Washington Bridge. We would sail downriver and along the Hudson River Park, then into the miniature harbor at the World Financial Center. It was a tricky entrance: the river current could be very fast, and the harbor's mouth was tiny. The harbor held a few luxury yachts and a little fleet of J-24s, like ours, which were used by another, somewhat fancier sailing school. Around the harbor were cafés, and straight inland was the Winter Garden, a vault-like glass atrium with palm trees inside. You could look up, with your back to the water, look so far up and see—

But still I think the best view of the World Trade Center was from a boat. For me, the absolute best view was after a Saturday of golf on Staten Island with my friend Caz. The public courses there, especially Silver Lake, are pretty good. The only thing that ever marred our golfing on Staten Island was that the island attracted many white people of the middle classes who were there in part to get away from the nonwhite surroundings of, say, Brooklyn—and many of these people were police officers and firemen, people on whose side the law always was, regardless of circumstance—such that, Caz being black, and not a little black either, the Staten Island golf scene was sometimes slightly tense. We could forget that, though, at dusk, after a day of golf, while crossing the water on the Staten Island Ferry. Standing right at the edge of the car level, the water only feet away, I could drink a tall Budweiser in a paper bag, smoke a cigarette, and look at the reds and pinks and oranges on the World Trade Center towers—buildings so tall and flat they're like canvases for the sun's colors—and the purple sky behind them. With a friend. A summer's day.

Today I heard that some jumpers had crashed through the Winter Garden atrium yesterday morning. I could not figure out how they would get that far. They would have had to cross West Street. I don't know how to think about such physics. . . .

When our daughter was old enough, Becky and I would push the stroller across the Brooklyn Bridge, along Chambers Street to the end, and into the park above Battery Park City. It had finally opened. We'd have a picnic. On the paths, we'd worry about getting hit by skaters on Rollerblades. When Hannah was old enough I bought a kite, a blue one. I got it up in the air and had her hold onto the string, which she did with concentration. She might have let go at any moment; the kite tugged and twisted like a puppy. She watched the string in her hand because she knew that if she looked at the kite she might forget about holding the string. Back home I drew a picture of her, tiny in the lower-left corner, then a long string curving upward to the upper-right corner where her kite was flying. We had gone down that day to the Winter Garden to use the restrooms and get something to eat. It was nice there and relatively cool in summer, with those mad palms—

And people crashing through above. Was that just a rumor? Because on September 12, 2001, there was that feeling, overpowering, that all that atrium's glass must have been shattered because everything else had been. . . . *The planes were aimed, the buildings were hit, the killers killed us, yes, but you know you did not kill all of us, the glass is shattered and you have made these towers a clumsy crematorium but we're still here, you motherfuckers, and this is* our *city and these are* our *memories and you are not going to get them even if you have covered them with our ashes.*

Anthony Lewis wrote in his *Times* column this morning: "Terror is what the attackers wanted to arouse, and they succeeded."

I remembered our happy sailing days this morning only because Becky and I, in approaching this Day 2, were wondering how we might escape, if need be. We aren't much good at sailing, but all boats are about the same. We would have to steal one. We could get anything with sails out of a slip, bumping our way out and into open water and onward to the sea. Grab the kids, steal a boat, get away. Were we losing our minds yet?

People lit candles in Tirana, Albania; in Moscow; in Tehran; in German cities. And people from other American towns and cities, people who have built sensible lives away from the corrupt and degenerate murk of our city, away from its immeasurable condescension and conceitedness—at least, that's often how you hear other Americans talk about New York City—they too lit candles.

At a national security meeting this morning, the president said,

The deliberate and deadly acts, which were carried out yesterday against our country, were more than acts of terror. They were acts of war. . . . Freedom and democracy are under attack. . . . This enemy attacked not just our people, but all freedom-loving people everywhere in the world. The United States of America will use all our resources to conquer this enemy. We will rally the world. We will be patient. . . . The freedom-loving nations of the world stand by our side. This will be a monumental struggle of good versus evil. But good will prevail. Thank you very much.

The commentaries we were getting at the *Times* all agreed that Nothing Would Be the Same. Terry had been able to get in from New Jersey and Nora Krug made it in from Brooklyn, so we were only one person short. Part of Nora's job was to monitor the unsolicited submissions. They were coming in more quickly than she could read them, and she had to catch up on yesterday's. Many were poems. I had had no idea that hundreds of Americans would think the right response to catastrophe was to create rhythmic rhyming sentences. It was surprising, too, that they sent them to the *Times*'s Op-Ed page, which had published perhaps half a dozen poems in the past decade; in essence, the *Times* did not publish poems. And here we were with hundreds written in the hot moments of grief and fear.

The poems tended not to address how Nothing Will Be The Same except in that they viewed September 10 in the light—maybe I should say darkness—of September 11. Many read like this: Our precious place, America, good and friendly, innocent in its heart, its only sins those of indulgence; the attackers came in their silent planes; screams, blood, metal, and fire; disbelief; yet the flag still waves; what does not destroy us makes us stronger; and now, the terrible swift sword of vengeance?

It amazed me (and I'm a Protestant) how Protestant the American mainstream was, how redemptive in adversity.

We didn't know what to do with the dead. We could not make any sense of their deaths. Any kind of "sense" would have been a concession to the killers; it would have given them the power to attach some meaning to their act and therefore the power to give *their* sense to *our* deaths. Having killed, they could have stolen the significance of their victims' deaths as well.

So we couldn't make sense of these deaths.

But if that was the case, then how could Nothing Ever Be the Same? We said that nothing would be the same because we wanted to recognize the significance of the dead and their value; but giving them any significance other than complete innocence would have felt as if we were giving yet more power to the murderers, or justifying their act. So in the end we found ourselves saying that the innocent lives of the dead should be our only guide to making sense of this calamity. That meant, not that everything had changed, but that everything, or almost everything, had to be exactly the same—the dead would be back, nothing would change—otherwise, we would have Let the Terrorists Win, as the new phrase of the day went.

But everything did change, and in that sense they had already won. They had left us without any choice but to make sense of what they did.

The Op-Ed page would again be all columns. In his offering for tomorrow, Thomas Friedman announced "World War III" in his headline. Columnists normally wrote their own headlines and "blurbs," the brief passages in large type that broke up the body copy. Friedman's blurb was "From Beirut to Jerusalem to New York," which linked the events of the past forty-eight hours to his own first book, which was called *From Beirut to Jerusalem*. This new war, he wrote,

> pits us—the world's only superpower and quintessential symbol of liberal, free-market, Western values—against all the super-empowered angry men and women out there. Many of these super-empowered angry people hail from failing states in the Muslim and third world. They do not share our values, they resent America's influence over their lives, politics and children, not to mention our support for Israel, and they often blame America for the failure of their societies to master modernity. . . . It will be a long war against a brilliant and motivated foe. . . . It will require our best strategists, our most creative diplomats and our bravest soldiers. Semper Fi.

Semper Fi. "Always loyal": the motto of the Marines.

For tomorrow William Safire was writing of his conversation with Karl Rove, President Bush's political strategist, who had called to protest the criticism of Bush's seemingly odd travels on Tuesday and of the lack of White House direction that day. It seemed that the president had wanted to return to Washington, demonstrate his lack of fear, and reassure the public. But the Secret Service and senior members of his administration would not let him. I don't know quite what I wanted from our president, but I was not looking for a display of obedience.

At the Arab deli on Atlantic Avenue, still no violence. At the firehouse, still no news about Brian, Stan, Dave, or Lieutenant Bob. Becky stayed with the kids at home. Her office, like many offices in the city, was closed. She went out for supplies: water, dust masks, candles. She said she had noticed some of our neighbors on their stoops—only not quite on the stoops, but lingering in the doorways, a subtle change. One did not want to be alone with the television inside, yet one was frightened to go outside. So a number of people spent much of the day in their open doorways, neither inside nor out, waiting.

9/13

Again a pretty day. Poetry came to the *New York Post*, though it might not have meant to. The tabloid started the morning wound up with rage and a type of patriotism. It had an editorial on page 3, in a box, superimposed on a photo of a screaming fireman being carried away by colleagues. It was spread over three columns. Whether by accident or design, the typesetting, given the one-sentence paragraphs, broke the lines such that the text looked like a free-verse poem.

> America digs its dead and wounded from smoldering rubble in Lower
> Manhattan and
> in Washington.
> Osama Bin Laden exults in the Afghan desert.
> Mobs cheer in Cairo and on the West Bank, and
> Saddam doubtless dances a victory jig in
> Baghdad.
> America bleeds.
> This is war.
> It needs to be prosecuted as such.
> The men behind the men who rained havoc on
> New York and Washington need to be called to
> account.
> The heavens need to fall on their heads.
> They need to bleed.
> Not next month. Not next week.
> Now.
>
> Who are they? Who cares?
> Cast a wide enough net, and you'll catch the
> fish that need catching.
>
> So locate them
> Pinpoint them.

Bomb them.

And then bomb their smoldering rubble—one

more time!

The anonymous *Post* writer further urged the use of American "military might—just short of nuclear oblivion." Then the piece continued:

America needs to strike hard—and as often as it takes to impose peace.

But if peace doesn't take, then America

needs to do it again.

Until its enemies finally get it.

They believe they are on a fast track to

heaven. Which is fine.

Dispatch enough of them on the journey

with no return, and this war will end quickly

enough.

Bombs away.

I read this on the train going in to work. It terrified me. I did not need to be terrified any more than I already was. My children had begun to regress, as children seem to—although the phenomenon was not limited to children—in times of great stress. My daughter seemed to me about six months younger: less articulate, more prone to crying, desperate to hold onto me. At home it felt very much as though we were animals pushing as far as we could into our burrow. The helicopters overhead were very loud at night.

I read the *Post*'s poem as we passed beneath downtown Brooklyn. At the High Street stop, cops were posted at the western end of the platform—where the tracks begin to head underneath the East River—to dissuade terrorists from carrying explosives into the tunnel. An attack there would severely disrupt transport and cause more death than the same explosion elsewhere in the subway system.

When the train emerged in downtown Manhattan, the doors opened at the stops in Chinatown, then farther west at Houston Street. And each time they opened I got lungfuls of warm air with the rich, moist smell of everything that was burning downtown.

In the office on Forty-third Street we were still taking in poems by the bushel. But on the Internet the poem everyone had was by W. H. Auden, a famous poem called "September 1, 1939," made famous again. It was written to mark the outbreak of World War II.

> I sit in one of the dives
> On Fifty-second Street
> Uncertain and afraid
> As the clever hopes expire
> Of a low dishonest decade:
> Waves of anger and fear
> Circulate over the bright
> And darkened lands of the earth,
> Obsessing our private lives;
> The unmentionable odour of death
> Offends the September night.
>
> . . .
>
> I and the public know
> What all schoolchildren learn,
> Those to whom evil is done
> Do evil in return.
>
>
> Exiled Thucydides knew
> All that a speech can say
> About Democracy,
> And what dictators do,
> The elderly rubbish they talk
> To an apathetic grave;
> Analysed all in his book,
> The enlightenment driven away,
> The habit-forming pain,
> Mismanagement and grief;
> We must suffer them all again.

> Into this neutral air
>
> Where blind skyscrapers use
>
> Their full height to proclaim
>
> The strength of Collective Man,
>
> Each language pours its vain
>
> Competitive excuse:
>
> But who can live for long
>
> In an euphoric dream;
>
> Out of the mirror they stare,
>
> Imperialism's face
>
> And the international wrong.

Hangdog but tough, Auden went on to present, in a few stanzas, a picture of somewhat depressed normality from the vantage of that bar on Fifty-second Street—a this-is-all-there-is-to-life look around the room, resigned, as "helpless governors wake / To resume their compulsory game." It was a 1930s voice, that of someone who had a few strong ideas about the First World War and figured the coming new one would be like it.

> . . . Defenceless under the night
>
> Our world in stupor lies;
>
> Yet, dotted everywhere,
>
> Ironic points of light
>
> Flash out wherever the Just
>
> Exchange their messages:
>
> May I, composed like them
>
> Of Eros and of dust,
>
> Beleaguered by the same
>
> Negation and despair,
>
> Show an affirming flame.

It seemed like a beautiful and silly poem, gorgeous in its sound, tinny in argument. Politics and the coming war would only be dreary repetition: "The enlightenment driven away, / The habit-forming pain, / Mismanagement and grief;

/ We must suffer them all again." I was sure Auden honestly thought there must
be a place where "the Just exchange their messages," but his evocation of it and of
them lacked conviction. God knows we had opinions coming in every minute from
people certain they were points of light whose clever minds could see beyond our
present stupor. It made me fear for the reality of the dead as I tried to do my peculiar Op-Ed job, listening carefully as "each language pours its vain, competitive
excuse."

The 1990s probably had been a low, dishonest decade, though I don't know
how many bright and shining decades you can point to for meaningful contrast.
What hypocrisies there were in the nineties were mostly on a small scale, so much
so that social critics in that very self-critical decade hissed in disappointment at the
lack of grandeur around them. The superlative prosperity and technological innovation of the decade were consolations. But even these, looked at a certain way,
could be seen as further mockery directed at an unimpressive generation. The birth
and growth of the Internet, the information revolution, and the march of globalization could be portrayed either as miraculous—like the virgin birth dramas of nerds
in their garages inventing the personal computer—or as owing to transformations
so great in scale that even Americans could only hang on for the ride. (The biggest
uniquely American contribution to the great changes of the nineties was, in many
different ways, our astounding military budget. Without American military spending, the information revolution and globalization would not have occurred on the
scale they did. But we should only take so much pride in the consequences, mostly
unintended, of the Pentagon's lavishness.) The generation that led us through the
nineties had not won the Cold War or any other conflict. The political figures that
dominated the decade were more likely to have evaded military service when it
mattered and to have avoided any risky form of engagement, on any side, in the
conflicts of the sixties and seventies. It really was a somewhat low decade for Americans, soft in its demands.

In that day's paper, page A15, Eric Schmitt and Thom Shanker reported from
Washington: "The stunning loss of life in Tuesday's terrorist attacks and the sense,
expressed by President Bush, that these were 'acts of war,' have freed the admin-

istration to broaden potential retaliation beyond the low-risk, unmanned cruise missile strikes of the past, military and civilian officials said today." This one sentence summarized so much. "Low-risk, unmanned strikes" could be taken as the essential military expression of a low and dishonest decade: they were the sort of actions preferred by a bully, a timid one. Such strikes were not merely "of the past." They were specifically of the Clinton administration when it struck at Osama bin Laden and his supporters by firing missiles into Sudan and Afghanistan in 1998. This had seemed at the time, even by murky military standards, a mystifying and forlorn action. It was just the thing George W. Bush could define himself against, much as Ronald Reagan had defined himself against Jimmy Carter by pointing to Carter's failed attempt to rescue American hostages in Iran, another case of military hardware crashing in a dry, distant place to little effect.

But what hit me hardest was the use of the word "freed": this new administration could feel "freed" from the lowness and dishonesty of missile lobbing by the numbers of the dead on Tuesday and by the president's private sense that the attacks were "acts of war." The terrorists were supposed to have attacked us because of our freedom, and all freedom-loving people were supposed to be on our side; but surely the exercise of our freedom could not mean the freedom of our armies to use more freely their powers of destruction. And I could not accept the idea that the unusual height of the corpse mound downtown was freeing anyone in any way.

The articles we were getting in—other than the poems—had mainly to do with why we were attacked and what we should do about it. Most writers seemed to feel we should be slow and very deliberate in retaliating. First, we did not know against whom we should retaliate. Administration sources talked about the Osama bin Laden group, but actual evidence was not forthcoming, and we Americans had every reason to be suspicious of the White House's ability to name our enemies with accuracy. The Defense Department had revealed itself as highly manipulative of information in the Persian Gulf War, for example, and several of the people who had run that war were now in the White House and cabinet. The American public had been whipsawed more than once during the Balkan conflicts as to who was our ally and who wasn't—a question never quite settled with regard to the

Kosovo Liberation Army, say, or the government of Montenegro. It was also still unclear what we hit in that strike on Sudan, and why, based on what information. Finally there was one overwhelming security issue that had been looming since Tuesday morning: whoever was responsible for gathering information about terrorists—whether it was the Central Intelligence Agency (CIA), FBI, National Security Agency (NSA), Immigration and Naturalization Service (INS), Defense Department intelligence, or the State Department—they had failed. As citizens we spent more on these outfits annually than the entire United Nations' (UN) budget, and they had failed to prevent nineteen (at least) men from hijacking four planes from American airports in a carefully timed and coordinated operation, then flying them into three particularly important buildings, and killing thousands of us at a stroke. So we Americans had good reason to be suspicious of White House announcements "based on intelligence information."

A second reason to be slow in retaliating was our tendency to identify an outsider group as our enemy and attack it without reason. Evidence of this tendency could be found in American history from the mid-seventeenth century, but you didn't need to look that far back. The most recent and quite bitter case was after the 1995 Oklahoma City bombing—which had been coming up again in commentary since Tuesday—after which various angry Americans attacked mosques and threatened people they believed to be Arabs or Muslims, thinking that Arabs or Muslims were responsible for the bombing. It was a reasonable suspicion at the time, particularly given the World Trade Center attack two years earlier; but it was spectacularly wrong, as the arrest of white, Christian, Persian Gulf War veteran Timothy McVeigh proved, and not a moment too soon, either.

Already on Tuesday, at two thirty in the afternoon, I had received an e-mail from the Council on American-Islamic Relations that mentioned, parenthetically, the Oklahoma business while urging Muslims to do everything they could to help victims of the 9/11 attacks and advising, for example, that those who wore "Islamic attire should consider staying out of public areas for the immediate future." Several people across the country were being beaten up because they looked Muslim or Arab. Many attacks had been on Sikhs, who wear turbans but are not Muslim— indeed, two of the defining conflicts in Sikh history, in the Punjab, were specifically anti-Muslim—and are in no way Arabs. (Such pure and perfect terrorism: people attacked other people not because they truly were enemies but because they *looked like* enemies.) But meanwhile, out in Seattle, some non-Muslims had the idea of posting themselves outside mosques as interfaith human shields; Jews and Christians and others placed their bodies between the street and the mosque, just in case. And in my neighborhood today, while we were awaiting news about our own people whom we feared might have been killed on Tuesday, calls went out from the public elementary school—my daughter would start there in a year—to all the Muslim parents, saying that they should not be afraid, their children were still as welcome as they had been on Monday. If they needed something or had a problem, there was a number to call.

So taken as a whole, by today, Americans seemed to recognize that we had to carefully check any tendency to demonize a particular religion or people, including, as many writers emphasized, the people of Afghanistan.

The third reason for hesitation was more complicated, because it involved our attackers' motives. And because our attackers were dead and had not, it appeared, left anything behind to explain themselves other than, possibly, some generic exclamations about Muslim martyrdom, we had very little to go on. We had so little to go on, it being just Thursday, that the reasons we were coming up with—"we" being the people sending in Op-Eds and commentators and others at the paper, as well as TV commentators—said more about us than they did about our attackers, since the reasons being produced were coming not so much from them as from their actions and how those actions fit into our own pre–September 11 notions.

In fact, it seemed likely to me that the motives we attributed to our attackers were more sensible, sophisticated, and mature than their actual motives were. What they had done was so low; showed such an asphyxiated, monotonal singleness of purpose; and was so stupidly destructive that, pending much further information, I couldn't see how their life stories as such would be of much use or their motives very illuminating. They did seem to want to go to their deaths as martyrs to Islam (as eccentrically interpreted by them). This would, by definition, make the meaning of their acts useless or inaccessible to most people, including most Muslims.

The story of a purposeful suicide is a historical orphan; the hero's trajectory ends at the apex, so there is no denouement, no follow-through. The suicidal protagonist ends his presence in the story just at the point when his story will begin to have importance—that is, when his great action will start to have results, when it will take on meaning. No doubt many a suicidal killer thinks he already knows all the meanings of his act before he commits it. He may well believe that his intentions and imagined effects on the world are the same as the meanings of his act; therefore, he doesn't even need to stick around to find out what will happen. He already knows! Such narcissistic confidence, however, may be the only thing in life that is always wrong. The suicide-with-a-purpose will never learn this because, thinking he knows best, he is already dead when his actions take effect. There's something arrested and childlike about him. I think this is what people have in mind when they describe such political suicides as cowards.

One could, of course, simply take these nineteen suicidal men and use them to illustrate some larger point of which they might well have been unaware—a point or two about oneself and one's own enemies and one's own power, innocence, guilt, beliefs, passions, hopes—perhaps in much the way that whoever prepared them as single-minded weapons, and sent them to their deaths, had also used them.

Now that would be a brutal martyrdom indeed for a godly man—to have his religion not taken seriously, his sacrifice to God transformed into a sacrifice to almost anything but God; to have his sacrifice to something he loved turned into a sacrifice to something he had despised, ignored, feared, or never heard of.

Stories in the air. Why the hell should I make sense of this grotesquery?

Well, that's what we do. It's a way of talking to the dead.

The third, most complicated reason, then, for urging caution in retaliating against our enemy was that the attackers might have had something important to tell us, probably in spite of themselves. Some lesson other than "we plain hate you and will kill you whenever we get the chance." One lesson, immediately taken, was that security had been lax. No more pocketknives in the carry-on luggage. A loss of the presumption of innocence, but a loss we'd try to share democratically, as when in the future Senator So-and-So gets frisked before boarding, "just like anybody else." The feeling was that civil liberties were a bit of a luxury.

Another lesson commonly taken but nearly impossible to articulate was that we had always been vulnerable to attack, but we just hadn't known it. We had been in a fool's paradise; now we were in a wised-up hell.

Other lessons? It was time, once again, to get to know Islam. The killers clearly had something Muslim on their minds; though, if they were feeling anti-infidel, they might have tried to hit a church.

———

Also there was the question of wealth and power in the world—that is, whether we Americans had too much of them and therefore brought this destruction on ourselves, as some kind of retributive justice. Leaving aside actual evidence—taped conversations, correspondence, biographical detail, ties to the still-worth-blaming (i.e., the living)—the bulk of commentary on the killers and the meaning of their acts circled around this question of retributive justice.

There was no evidence—not a scrap—that any of the killers were poor or oppressed. They had left nothing behind to indicate that they were. Most of them seemed to have come from Saudi Arabia, one of the most absurdly wealthy and, for its size, absurdly powerful nations in the world and an American ally. They had made it to America (a chance for which people die every day). Some among them had the education to be able to enroll in flight school and learn to maneuver a jetliner.

Despite all this, many of us went right ahead and wondered whether the attacks weren't on behalf of the poor and oppressed beyond our borders. This said little if anything about the killers, but it probably said a lot about us: we suspected that we did not deserve what we had, that we'd been going through life thinking that the many miserable people in the world had a just claim against us, and that we were greedy and deserved punishment.

———

Another, related lesson: the United States had been ignoring the rest of the world, and now we had paid a high (but somehow, also, deserved) price for that ignorance. This idea usually came via the Afghanistan parable, which held that the United States had armed and used Afghanistan's holy warriors in the fight against Soviet communism, then abandoned them once the fight was won. Such abandonment, combined with an ambient militarism, led to chaos, the rise of the Taliban and a general vogue for terrorism, and then the killings of earlier this week. The implication was that the United States had neglected its obligation to take care of the rest of the world, at least those parts (pretty much everywhere) that had played some supporting role in the Cold War. Whether it was truly possible for the United States to satisfy the material and psychological desires of so many non-Americans, now defined as potential terrorists or their sponsors—whether it was possible to be something like a perfect imperial parent—was a question that could not be answered, the theory went, because the United States had never come close to making a full-hearted effort in this direction.

There was truth in the parable of Afghanistan. In Afghanistan and so many other places, American foreign policy idealism tended, in the event, to involve 90 percent aggression, questionable allies, and arms sales and 10 percent trade preferences, good-governance assistance, and food aid. (The United States was, through last week, the largest single national giver of food aid to Afghanistan.) Our predisposition to see religious expression of almost any kind as politically neutral—a critical factor in ensuring the stability of our own political culture—also caused immense challenges abroad that a more secularist approach might have avoided. Yet there was also a misapprehension at the core of the parable: the way to improve upon a weak and partial American role always seemed to involve a much greater American role, and the United States had simply never shown an appetite for such intensive and long-term commitments. Whatever the reasons might be for such reluctance, the reluctance itself was pretty consistent. The United States was a lousy sheriff, and it was unrealistic to wish otherwise.

The final leading reason for hesitating in taking righteous retribution was simple terror at the prospect of using American military power, along with a natural reluctance to go off killing. We knew that our forces could kill more and faster than anyone else's could. You have a natural fear of the gun in your hand, a fear and even a hatred of your power to destroy, in part because you know that power is also, however obscurely at times, self-destructive.

Deputy Secretary of Defense Paul Wolfowitz said today that the Bush administration would be "ending states who sponsor terrorism." What was he talking about, *ending* states? Can you "end" a state? And this was Paul Wolfowitz, the earnest idealist, who had once longed to intervene on behalf of the besieged Bosnians. Yet here he was talking like some geostrategic gunslinger.

It seemed as if the city was papered over with notices of the missing and mulched with candles, flowers, and wax. Our new garden. The missing notices usually had a photograph of the person who was gone, most often a snapshot from a party or one taken on vacation—a picture of a happy person. There were height and weight statistics and indications of race or skin color and of hair and eye color. Distinguishing marks: scars, birthmarks, deformities and disfigurements, piercings, tattoos. Even in our city of self-display this was a lot of revelation. People were being made nearly naked before us on every lamppost and fence to increase the chances of their being recognized, plucked from the milling crowd of bodies. *You—5'10",* *with a long scar on your lower back, 53—look, please call Lisa or Bob to let them know* *you're OK.* People were still putting these fliers up. Also, I saw people correcting them and adding more details. They had got the flier out too fast, and the eye color wasn't really right—they were really brown not green, though there was green in them—so that was corrected on the flier. One by one each flier had to be updated with the new information. Alternatively, someone made a new, corrected flier and posted it, being careful to take down the old one. And this went on even though everyone pretty much knew by now that practically none of the people in this, our citywide family photo album, was alive.

We began to learn who from the families of *Times* employees was killed. It appeared that no actual *Times* employees had died. We were grateful for that. Though I did not know to whom I should be grateful, and (how to put this?) I shuddered to see the process of measuring begin. This was how humans reacted. We were not points of light. We measured our distances from the dead and from each other, creating an infinite map of distinctions, each of which only made complete sense to the individual who had measured it out from his vantage point at the center of the world.

It wasn't a brother she lost, it was a nephew. I guess that's better.
She would have been there except she was late.

No one's going to say it now, but he really was an asshole.
And they shouldn't say it. I mean, what's the point?

Turns out she wasn't pregnant.

I still can't believe how close I came, I, I.

Anyone close to you? No, no one close to me. Thank God. I mean, not really close.

And I, wouldn't I have liked to have been one of the Just sending out their messages, measuring with smart precision all my closenesses and distances.

Down into the subway I went at Forty-second Street, my customary stop, but of course, they'd rearranged the trains and even, it seemed, come up with some new letters. I couldn't be certain where I was going even if the train appeared to be just as it always had been before Tuesday morning. But I could be certain I was not going to the World Trade Center, which was at this moment being erased, along with the subway lines that went beneath it and the stops they made, from the quick revision of the subway map with its new emptiness.

Walking through the station I saw a poster of Moira Smith. She was so beautiful and full of good cheer, seeming altogether happy yet in no way naive. According to the brief text below this picture of her, Moira Smith, in her capacity as a police officer, had heard an early call about the Trade Center attack and headed downtown immediately. Was last seen tending to the wounded, something like that. I couldn't take my eyes off her, even after I realized that I was singling her out from the other people on this wall of missing posters in my station (with those candles burning below) only because I thought she was pretty.

I must have looked beat up as I waited for the train. I was in uniform—dress shirt, tie, jacket, slacks, loafers, clean shaven—in sum a middle-aged, white, professional man straight out of the catalog. And the woman two seats down on the worn wooden bench, waiting with me and not very many others at this hour for the mystery train to take us home—will it call itself an F train tonight or an E?—she was from an altogether different page in the catalog: dark skinned; poor, though keeping herself up; a church lady, perhaps; about my age or younger. I hadn't noticed her (I was staring at the floor) until she said to me, "It's going to be all right."

"Pardon me?"

"It's going to be all right."

9/14

Rain fell last night. Maybe that was enough to kill someone somewhere under the rubble: rain, slurry, a shift in weight. The rain would make the rescue work harder.

———

Still no news across the street. They'd put up a handwritten sign, Pray for Our Missing Members, with a picture of each of the missing men below their names. People came by and wrote messages beneath the pictures. Flowers and candles were silted up against the corners of the wide doorway through which the truck would have passed if they'd had their truck.

Still no violence at the Arab deli or the mosque or elsewhere along Atlantic Avenue.

The urgings toward normalcy gained momentum today. Mayor Rudolph Giuliani had already told us to go shopping—that was Wednesday, I think—in order to keep the retail economy ticking over and to show that our normal lives would not be disrupted just because some terrorists killed a few thousand of us, destroyed our tallest buildings, and touched off what might indeed prove to be World War III. Remember the man on the Brooklyn Bridge that morning, jogging into the ash cloud until he disappeared? We should just Go About Our Business.

Many people had been praising the mayor for his leadership at a time when we were, in effect, still waiting to hear from our president. This praise came, it seemed to me, much more from some powerful desire on the part of the praisers for leadership rather than from anything Giuliani did. Because the moment for him to fulfill his primary responsibility—to protect us—was long gone. All he could do was roam from firehouse to precinct, reassuring his employees. He and the municipal government he headed disciplined themselves not to break down in public. He appeared from time to time with casualty lists.

I imagined that people out of town, watching it all on TV, thought the mayor was an important part of the week's events because he was on screen so often. But he was not very important. We New Yorkers were not experiencing these days on TV, we experienced them on the street; and the mayor was not leading much of anything. He was, as he had been for years, come rain or shine, telling us to Go About Our Business in an Orderly Fashion.

Today we had three articles on the page. The lead piece was by Ronald Steel, a professor of international relations. He began, "This is the end: the end of an era, the era of our invulnerability." He described the attack on the Trade Center as a battle in the war between traditionalists and modernizers:

> Even though we cannot yet be sure who directed and carried out the attacks against us, we do know that there are those in the world who hate us. Trapped between the traditional world in which they were born and the confusing world of modernity in which they inescapably live, they seek a single cause for their confusion, their resentments, their frustrated ambitions and their problems of cultural identity. It is perhaps not surprising that they would focus on the world's most powerful state as the object of their resentment.
>
> They hate us because we champion a "new world order" of capitalism, individualism, secularism and democracy that should be the norm everywhere. We orchestrate a global economic system that dictates what others shall produce, what they shall be paid, and whether or not they will find work. We proudly declare that we are the world's undisputed Number One. Then we are surprised that others might hold us responsible for all that they find threatening in the modern world. . . . It is a war in which the weak have turned the guns of the strong against them. This is a war that is showing—despite the proud claims of the globalizers—that in the end there may be no such thing as a universal civilization, of which we all too easily assumed we were the rightful leaders.

It was not hard to link this to shopping. Mayor Giuliani had suggested that we should take our (justifiable) grief, put it in an envelope, and send it to the church or another appropriate charitable institution; then take the rest of our energy and apply it to September 10–type activities, especially retail. The terrorists would then see what a resilient and steady-nerved enemy they were up against. The key was making a demonstration of our indifference, an indifference that Steel might have identified as one of the sources of our vulnerability and of the hatred we inspired.

The photo caption for a weekend arts piece read, "Cultural institutions now see a role in helping the city return to normal." Normal? Why the rush? It seemed perverse. I could not think of a single good reason to return to normal, and there were many reasons not to, our dead being the main ones. The dead terrorists, too, and their allies and intentions.

Steel, trying to figure out those intentions, almost had me hating America, and I had been feeling such a love of my country. I had always been fond of it and head over heels in love with certain aspects. I usually drifted away when it came to the "God shed his grace on thee" part, because the exclusivity of it—the idea that we were singled out by God for a better providence—seemed cruel and stupid in its dismissal of the relative worth of humanity outside our borders, both now and in the great train of history before our tiny moment. The bulk of human life was not American. This fact made me, to be honest, even more fond of our eccentric little patch; and all this week it had felt very eccentric, little, and vulnerable. Democracy, freedom from fear—why had we ever thought these were normal, natural, and to be taken for granted? The danger made things precious, and we could never know whether that farewell-for-now intensity was really the truth of the matter revealed at last—dust of daily life removed—or a romantic lie whispered through a reflex of human nature.

For now, we were swearing never to take anything for granted again.

Yet no reasonable person in normal life could have loved the World Trade Center towers, precisely because they really had symbolized just what Steel had aptly described as what many people hate: "a global economic system that dictates." Featureless and far too big, indestructibly indifferent, maybe they had had, at moments, a dandyish quality, a very remote yet still pulsing eagerness to please, and some sense of reciprocity with their audience; or maybe they had been just pure, spiritless power. Certainly by today I could hear people saying that they should not be rebuilt because they had been a mistake in the first place, when they went up in 1970. They had been an insult to human nature, not (as a 1960s optimist might have thought) a compliment paid by human ambition to the clean lines of its own intentions.

I was struck that Steel seemed to agree that the "'new world order' of capitalism, individualism, secularism and democracy" was an American order. Here was another reason why some people hated us Americans: we tended to believe that, if there was a common human project, it had to be an American project; and that if America (or an idea of it) was not universal, then the idea of universality was itself lost. This worldview was present in Steel's article and in almost everything else we received. It existed well beyond any distinction between pro-American and anti-American feeling or between American and foreigner. To see America as being at the center of the world was not—this week, very much not—a pro-American position. Many of us were suddenly dead this week precisely because our enemies thought we were at the center of the world. The center of the world was what they wanted to hit. Our dead had not done anything other than happen to be at the so-called center of the world that morning. Our power and even our vanity as Americans did not console us; the opposite was the case.

I suspect our attackers also needed us to sit huge, cold, and modern at the center of the world. That way their suicide could reach as close as humanly possible to the cosmic, and their mission could shine with the greatest possible luster.

Of course, the rain put out all the candles around the city last night. The cut flowers all drooped and—with the various messages, prayers, and missing notices—formed wet heaps on top of hardened wax. The candles were most often round and in glass, of a votive type, loosely speaking, so the rainwater accumulated in them as in a rain gauge. You had to pour the water out, then wait for the soaked wicks to dry in the sun before you could light them again.

I should be more generous to Rudy Giuliani. It was true he could not affect matters too greatly, the worst being done already. But he did give you confidence; he was like a prince, anxiously and angrily pacing the city walls, bucking up the night watchmen, and by day comforting the afflicted. He was quite tireless despite his cancer (recently diagnosed). He was eating all the quick and greasy food that his doctor (as we knew from the tabloids) had warned him against, and his constant motion through the city had become a devotional procession.

This morning Howell Raines, the editor of the *Times*, sent around a message by e-mail: "Your magnificent work speaks more eloquently for itself than any words I can muster. Now, let's take a deep marathon runner's breath, thank our teammates and get ready to put out distinguished papers over the weekend." He had been sending messages almost every day this week, always striking a note of admiration and even wonderment at the newspaper staff's abilities. It was his first full week on the job.

Howell told one of my colleagues earlier in the week, "I'm glad this happened on my fifth day as editor. If it had happened on the fourth day I wouldn't have been ready!" Not everyone could have kept his charm up like that.

His fourth day on the job had found him in the newsroom standing on a desk to announce appointments. The new team put out its first paper Tuesday the eleventh, with leads on stem cell research and "Possible Deals to Revive Economy"; a page 1 montage about the mayoral election ("City Voters Have Heard It All as Campaign Din Nears End"); below the fold, two soft pieces, one on morning TV and the other on what kids were wearing to class these days ("School Dress Codes vs. a Sea of Bare Flesh").

The bottom of the page referred to a piece on the suicide bomber's assassination of Ahmad Shah Massoud in Afghanistan ("Afghan Rebel's Fate Unclear," page A15) and what would turn out to be our last piece on shark attacks for quite a while.

I set that issue aside today because I wanted a reminder of what we were like when we were normal and didn't understand what normal meant.

I sent out invitations to friends to come to a party on Sunday. I'd make some food. *Just bring something. I want to see you.* Though that was not the whole story, because I wanted to smell them, too. You can see people, including dead people, in pictures; indeed, our city was presently coated with pictures of dead people. But to smell people in their uniqueness they have to be alive and right there. Each person has his or her own scent. I didn't mention this in the invitation—that would have been off-putting and alarming, wouldn't it!—but the fact was I wanted to empty my lungs out and take in great drafts of the scents of my friends to be completely animal certain they were alive.

I also put aside copies of the pre-Tuesday magazines to help recall the brightnesses, the obsession with product detail (how many threads per inch, how many feet down it can withstand water pressure), and the thick ambient narcissism of a time when one could shop happily.

One of the reasons I was loving my country was that the newspaper I worked for, an important newspaper, would publish just seventy-two hours after a terrible attack on our city an Op-Ed piece (the Steel piece) that went some way toward enumerating reasons why we would have been attacked, why we were hated. He, an American, was not afraid to do that, and neither were we.

An Afghan and longtime resident in the United States, Tamim Ansary, published a letter in *Salon* today. It had been written to friends, who picked it up and sent it on; now the online magazine had posted it. Ansary said that Afghans hate the Taliban, "a cult of ignorant psychotics who took over Afghanistan in 1997." But he believed bombing Afghanistan would be useless, since everything was already destroyed. He thought ground troops would be necessary—which would make involving Pakistan necessary. Ansary didn't think Pakistan would go along. He thought other Muslim nations would be outraged. "We're flirting with a world war between Islam and the West," Ansary wrote. "And guess what: That's bin Laden's program. That's exactly what he wants."

We closed the Saturday, Sunday, and Monday pages on Friday so we could have the weekend off. Now we were in a realm of extreme unpredictability, of course; we'd have to come in if war were declared or if we were attacked again. The front pages today made war seem imminent. But we could not count on any of that, one way or another, so the best thing was to proceed as if everything was about normal. This *proceed-as-if* course marked our introduction to the social comedy of extreme crisis: we were in a pantomime of normality.

The pantomime extended to our product itself, as we pretended to find the "answers" to post-9/11 questions and recommend courses of action. Op-Eds, as commonly understood, are meant to advocate a course of action. We often experienced difficulty with this part in a given piece of writing. Sometimes a writer would lay out a situation or problem with admirable clarity, then recommend a course of action that tilted into insanity. More usually, the writer would lay out the situation in a muddle, rhetorically inflate the enormity of the problem—so much so that we had a ban on using phrases involving "high stakes"—then call for a mild and clearly inadequate solution.

These shortcomings are not necessarily the writers' fault. It's hard to find solutions to large problems. The world has plenty of such problems. We had to put something on the page each day that addressed one or more of them.

There were some obvious things to cover, and we had articles about them: better airport security, quicker information coordination among the many branches of law enforcement, investment in language education and area studies, just as after World War II. (Reportedly the CIA had no one who understood Pashto, the language of the people from whom the Taliban had emerged.) However, even these fairly straightforward Op-Eds could themselves run wild. You might be reading along in a calm manuscript when, all of a sudden, an author would begin arguing that everyone on Earth should have a retinal scan and the results should be fed into a centralized data bank that would be accessible via handheld devices by law enforcement officials posted at every point of embarkation and debarkation and every point in between those points, enabling us to Stop Terrorism in its Tracks. We would try to moderate these opinions.

I worked for a while on a piece by Shibley Telhami, a scholar and commentator on Middle East matters whom I had been trying to encourage. He worried that Israelis and Palestinians would frame the killings in the United States in terms of their own relative political positions. Telhami hoped they might take a different lesson:

the paths they were on led merely to death, not advantage. The attacks in America would sober them to the reality that the ends do not always justify the means. Telhami also hoped that we Americans would bear this in mind as we considered our means of retaliation.

I don't know that any of us in my department believed Israelis and Palestinians would take a fresh look at outrageous violence as political method just because of what had happened on Tuesday. Too many voices from the region had already been telling us, in so many words, how unexciting our lives still were here in New York compared to theirs in Ramallah and Tel Aviv. But Telhami's article was a good piece of wishful thinking, which is itself a valuable type of opinion.

I also worked on a piece I had solicited from Edward Luttwak, a longtime counselor to the defense and intelligence establishments but with a broader worldview than is common in them. I wanted him to speculate about future alignments of power. His sense was that a new set of great powers—India, Russia, the United States, China, Europe, Japan—would realize a collective self-interest in fighting terrorists. This would provide a bright line of distinction in international relations; a state like Iran, for example, if it were verifiably tolerating or sponsoring terrorism, would face a clear choice between being accepted by the great powers or being isolated by them and effectively debilitated. Such great-power solidarity seemed the most likely way to ensure that terrorism did not become a habitual political form for growing numbers of people. Luttwak's was a strong opinion, also wishful in its way: coordinating those great powers would not be easy. But they would at least be organized against a worthy enemy in alliances of a reach that truly would end the Cold War.

In the early afternoon two friends of mine wrote in. Adam Shatz was worried that the nation would rush into war hysteria. The Senate today had unanimously granted President Bush considerable powers to fashion the American response. The president had been speaking rather easily of good versus evil in a way that seemed frighteningly similar to that of a terrorist—an abstracting of human relations that might clear the way for further inhuman acts. The enthusiasm for what Adam called a gigantic police operation was growing; he feared that pursuing it exclusively would lead people to forget that terrorism, like anything else, does have causes, and in this case he believed it was "based in faith, driven by desperation, and grounded in conflicts between our government and much of the Islamic world." The attacks,

Adam wrote, had "introduced a new, terrifying kind of insecurity into our lives, and stirred an understandable desire for revenge. But they should also provoke sustained reflection on America's relationship to the world, especially to the Middle East."

The other friend was George Packer. What he wrote was really not an Op-Ed. It was about kindness, companionship, helpfulness, and futility. These were not usual Op-Ed themes, particularly futility. When you express a sense of futility in the Op-Ed or column format, it may be in the form of anger, bitter retrospect, sarcasm, or even whining, but not as the straight-up emptiness that most people feel when they are experiencing utter futility. An experience we had been having now for four days, because the deed was already all done and its smoking, stinking monument already made.

George wrote about giving blood. His note to me at the top said his piece was "about the feeling of uselessness, which everyone I know has had, and what some tried to do about it." The story focused on one Lauren Moynihan, who on Tuesday had decided to give blood. "By noon," George wrote, "there was already a four-hour wait for donors at St. Luke's Hospital, on Amsterdam and 59th." Moynihan signed a form and was told to come back later. After other frustrations, she "found her way home to Brooklyn. The F train was jammed with riders trying to get home, but there was a strange calm and order and even kindness on board—people gave up seats, and called out the next stop."

The next day, George wrote, Moynihan hoped to give blood in downtown Brooklyn.

That was where I met her, at 9 in the morning on Wednesday. By that hour the line ran down Lawrence Street, made a right on Willoughby, and traveled halfway up the block. Within an hour it had reached the end of Willoughby and turned right on Jay. I guessed there were over 500 people, from all the proverbial walks of life, waiting in bright sunlight.

People formed groups, started conversations. "We were far from the wreckage and smoke, sitting on a Brooklyn sidewalk, standing up to move four feet every half hour. Yet it felt like usefulness." A young man on line said he would probably fight if war came. Moynihan herself wondered whether she might serve "in one of those strategic units." George wrote,

Civic feelings were breaking out up and down the line. "This is like a little bit short of volunteering to go for the French Foreign Legion," said Dave Lampe, a computer technician from Jersey City who was wearing suspenders decorated with brightly colored workman's tools. "People who go volunteer for the French Foreign Legion don't complain when they get on line."

A teenage girl whose high school was blocks from the World Trade Center came by with cookies and juice and said,

> I wanted to do some kind of volunteer work because I was like, we were like watching from our school and there was all this dust and concrete falling. This is the time when we need to be, like, pulling together and doing as much as we can for each other and not, like, sitting at home watching it on T.V. and saying, like, "Oh, there's another bomb."

Then, George wrote, "a volunteer named Luke Geissbuhler told me that the phlebotomists were exhausted and unstorable quantities of blood were piling up, 'like having too much milk in your fridge.' Hospitals were turning away the blood that was coming in. They simply lacked the patients to receive it."

Meanwhile President Bush had spoken at last, at an interfaith prayer service in the National Cathedral in Washington. First an imam, Muzammil H. Siddiqi, gave a Muslim prayer, and Reverend Billy Graham offered a Christian sermon. President Bush spoke at one o'clock, from a side lectern, raised up.

> We are here in the middle hour of our grief. . . . On Tuesday, our country was attacked with deliberate and massive cruelty. We have seen the images of fire and ashes, and bent steel. Now come the names, the list of casualties we are only beginning to read. They are the names of men and women who began their day at a desk or in an airport, busy with life. They are the names of people who faced death, and in their last moments called home to say, be brave, and I love you. They are the names of passengers who defied their murderers,

and prevented the murder of others on the ground. They are the names of men and women who wore the uniform of the United States, and died at their posts. They are the names of rescuers, the ones whom death found running up the stairs and into the fires to help others. We will read these names. We will linger over them, and learn their stories, and many Americans will weep.

President Bush had already decided—and, politically, there was no one to oppose him—that the attacks had been acts of war. Therefore, we were in a war. "War has been waged against us by stealth and deceit and murder," he said in the cathedral. "This nation is peaceful, but fierce when stirred to anger. This conflict was begun on the timing and terms of others. It will end in a way, and at an hour, of our choosing." He continued:

Our unity is a kinship of grief and a steadfast resolve to prevail against our enemies. And this unity against terror is now extending across the world. America is a nation full of good fortune, with so much to be grateful for. But we are not spared from suffering. In every generation, the world has produced enemies of human freedom. They have attacked America, because we are freedom's home and defender. And the commitment of our fathers is now the calling of our time.

When he had finished he returned to his seat. His father reached across Laura Bush's lap and clasped the president's elbow. The elder Bush gave his son a faint smile, as did the president's mother, Barbara. President Bush looked away from them. As a son I felt for him, since he seemed to be trying to keep his dignity intact in the shadow of his parents. President Bush was fifty-two years old, yet he still appeared to be trying to get out from under his mom and dad. And you could see— just as a practical matter, leaving aside any questions of individual character—why that would be difficult. President Bush, unlike President Clinton (who was seated next to Barbara Bush), was far from being a self-made man. He often seemed to be primarily an emanation of his inheritance, of certain families, places, and institutions; his individual characteristics were arranged atop this basic armature.

Given the crisis we were in, you just hoped that armature was solid. It was what had got him to the presidency, and it had better come through. So it was, to a degree, good to see the father reassuring his son that he had given a fine speech. These days, informally, I heard people thank God that the elder Bush was around. I heard people thank God for Dick Cheney; his heart, over the summer, seemed at the point of giving out altogether, but he had been through the Gulf War and various administrations and so inspired confidence in a way his (very physically fit) boss did not. I heard people, depending on their political views, thank God for Secretary of State Colin Powell and for Defense Secretary Donald Rumsfeld, for National Security Adviser Condoleezza Rice, for Paul Wolfowitz, for Deputy Secretary of State Richard Armitage, and even for Federal Reserve chairman Alan Greenspan. I heard people thank God for the Bush family advisers Brent Scowcroft and James Baker III. I never heard anyone say, "Thank God George W. Bush is in charge right now."

Why should they? The voters in the last election did not vote for strong leadership. None of the candidates even sought to offer strong leadership. Bush had himself emphasized, several times, that America should be more "humble" in its foreign policy. The candidate who had most made an issue of strength was John McCain, and he had an ironic distance, to put it mildly, on the idea of strength. (He was a warrior famous for having been a prisoner of war.) Strong leadership was not an important aspect of the campaign simply because, for the majority of Americans who voted, there was not much leading to be done. This was so much the case that many thoughtful voters cast their ballot for someone they knew could not win; it was so much the case that the price of prescription drugs had been a defining problem in campaign debates. Americans voted for many things—a friend, an easy-going fellow, a protester, an interesting man, a happy or amusing man—but we did not vote for a strong leader because we did not, back then, think we would need one.

Just after 3:00 p.m., an e-mail came through from the news desk: "We are beginning to do mini-profiles of the victims with the goal of doing everyone. All reporters who are out on various stories should try and grab any extra leaflets being circulated by the families of victims, or at least get the names and numbers and any other details. The SPEC2 directory in ATEX will be used for all the victim feeds, lists and stories. Currently, there are two lists: menvic and femvic, which will be lists of everyone we know about, divided by sex, listed alphabetically."

After his speech, the president left Washington to come see our city. Soon we on Forty-third Street heard planes, killer planes, fighters. These were the only planes we heard anymore in New York City.

The president arrived in Manhattan a little before five o'clock, coming by helicopter from New Jersey. The smell of the burning site seeped into the helicopter even before it had landed at Wall Street. A motorcade of twenty vehicles made its way west: the president emerged to say a few words. He was not a good extemporaneous speaker. He had only recently ceased referring to al Qaeda and the Taliban as "those folks," a choice of words that confused even his admirers. His speechwriters had hoisted him into "the middle hour of our grief" and "busy with life," beautiful phrases we needed. It was about time, too.

"On TV he looked like a scared mouse," one New Yorker told the *Times*'s columnist Clyde Haberman. "Now he's four days late showing up." The plumber Al Demchak, at ground zero for Bush's visit, said to Haberman, "When they first showed him on TV, he looked, and I hate to say this, but he looked scared, like, 'What am I supposed to do?'"

We did not know what to expect of our leaders. There they were—Senators Chuck Schumer and Hillary Clinton, Governor George Pataki, Mayor Giuliani, Congressman Jerry Nadler, President Bush—all kind of milling around in the smoke. All helpless. President Bush climbed atop a burned fire truck and grabbed a bullhorn.

"We can't hear you!" some men yelled.

"I can hear *you*," the president shouted. "The rest of the world hears you, and the people who knocked these buildings down will hear all of us soon!"

"U.S.A.! U.S.A.!"

The president looked pleased, having sworn us to vengeance in his own way and been cheered.

Around six o'clock I received a piece from a former secretary of the army. He believed that we should find who was responsible for attacking us and punish them as part of an all-out campaign against terrorism. He also believed that this "will not root out the hatred that arises from a sense of neglect and despair over the condition in which many people on this planet live and which breeds angry remorseless zealots completely indifferent to the taking of human life." He emphasized that "human suffering on distant shores can easily reach out and touch America." He wrote about foreign aid, economic development, humanitarian assistance, and diplomacy. The former secretary of the army noted that the United States benefits more than any other nation from globalization, and "thus being interconnected and looked to for leadership in world affairs, we have no choice but to provide it. We must make the efforts it will take to build a world in which there are fewer places for hatred to take root."

I lose the thread of this day. It was such a long week. At some point we finished our work and I went downstairs and around the corner to Emmett's on Forty-fourth Street, not quite a dive—that would be Smith's, kitty-corner from here—and no Auden in sight to mark the day. The TVs at either end of the bar were all terror, just like at work. The president again on TV—"We are in the middle hour of our grief"—as though we were halfway through, as though (come to think of it) we were a little bit *past* the halfway mark and soon enough this thing would be done. I was beginning to tire of being told which way my grief was going.

I looked around and thought that the forgetting must be getting under way about now. Wasn't there a play back on, *The Producers*, about forty feet from here, on the downtown side of the street, that was getting every laugh that could be got—out of Nazism? Yes, at *The Producers* and all up and down Broadway, they had their "moment of silence" today to remember, which meant to start forgetting. So we were reckoned to be halfway through to that full forgetting, that reconciliation, that many people thought was the right thing to do and a sign of health. But it seemed to me that this healthful idea was one reason why terrorism is spectacular: because we are so quick to heal, the wound must be made plenty big to Send Its Message. It was not enough to kill a little. No, in this frenetic exchanging of messages the senders couldn't just kill a little; they had to plow the dead and reap the dead. All that healthy, coping memory loss makes life cheap. You forget the dead, you diminish the living, too.

I didn't want to hurry. Hadn't we been told Everything Has Changed? Let's not be in too much haste. On TV the president gave his beautiful prayer again and his silly-boy remark downtown, for all of which we were grateful, grateful for anything. There was Peter Jennings on the screen, then a group of people singing. I lose the thread of this day; I vowed to start taking notes on all that was happening because I wasn't ready for the forgetting. The people on TV were singing "God Bless America" or "Amazing Grace" or possibly "The Star-Spangled Banner." Whichever it was, I was starting to shake enough that I couldn't look up at the TV anymore. I practically had to cover my ears. But I heard Peter Jennings's voice again as the singing stopped. He was looking at his monitor and trying not to cry, too, so there we were—*another drink, please*—me and goddamn Peter Jennings, weeping.

Down in the subway more fliers were coming to keep the beautiful Moira Smith company. There were also consolation cards appearing, much more colorful than the usually black-and-white missing posters, more spring-like and often from children. Back home in Brooklyn the deli guys had passed another day without violence. At the firehouse, Engine 226 was back, crushed in parts, its glass shattered, a white hulking thing out beneath the streetlights, white because it was covered in dust and ash. The firemen had picked off the bigger debris during the day.

9/15

I might have caught the president's press conference on TV this morning but Becky wanted me to do my fair share of the hoarding. She had found a list somewhere of things to get. No doubt President Bush already had all those things as he, along with Colin Powell and John Ashcroft, addressed the world's press at Camp David in Thurmont, Maryland.

"We're going to meet," the president said, "and deliberate and discuss—but there's no question about it, this act will not stand; we will find those who did it; we will smoke them out of their holes; we will get them running and we'll bring them to justice. We will not only deal with those who dare attack America, we will deal with those who harbor them and feed them and house them."

I was used to following current events, but I was not accustomed to having them pervade every instant of my waking life along with most of my dreams, at least the dreams I could recall. I could recall them because they were the ones that woke me up, damp and rigid, to wrench myself around and make sure Becky was still there, dreams of planes, of course, and of falling.

We needed more batteries and water. Saline solution for her contact lenses. A radio that could be operated on batteries. Canned foods. It couldn't hurt to have more face masks and another box of Band-Aids. Candles and matches, diapers and wipes for Ben. We wouldn't want to have to rush his toilet training *and* deal with fighting (or fleeing) terrorists. That would be too much.

Colin Powell came to the mike right after the president: "We should also take note, it's not just Americans who lost lives in the World Trade Center—dozens of countries lost lives and they realize that this was an attack against them, as well. We are receiving expressions of support from around the world—and not just rhetorical support, but real support for whatever may lay ahead in this campaign that is ahead of us to win the war that the president has spoken of."

Walgreens was the place for all this stuff, and we had one nearby. They were running short on water so I stocked up with six gallons. Walgreens even had a battery-powered AM/FM radio with a clock! What luck! I carried it all home. I felt like a burro. We stowed it all under our bed.

So what was this war that the president had spoken of? President Bush said in response to a question this morning at Camp David:

> The message is for everybody who wears the uniform: get ready. The United States will do whatever it takes to win this war. And I ask patience of the American people. There is no question in my mind we'll have the resolve—I witnessed it yesterday on the construction site. Behind the sadness and the exhaustion, there is a desire by the American people to not seek only revenge, but to win a war against barbaric behavior, people that hate freedom and hate what we stand for.

But I did not want revenge. And, by the way, it wasn't a construction site, either. Instead, I wanted to know why my neighbors were across the street from my house with candles, kneeling, trying to find sad songs that everyone knew the words to, trying to remember the names of the firemen so they could say how sorry they were in a way that was personalized.

Someone asked the president whether we should be worried about additional attacks. "I would think," the president said, "the American people need to be—go about their business on Monday, but with a heightened sense of awareness that a group of barbarians have declared war on the American people."

Clearly this was not going to be easy. How I was supposed to go about my business while responsibly tending a sense of imminent barbarian attack was just a mystery, though that was, more or less, exactly what I was doing this morning.

I didn't go to the not-quite-yet-memorial service my neighbors were holding at Engine 226 because I was at a loss as to how to explain matters to my daughter, Hannah. More than a year prior, there had been a gas leak six doors down the street from us. We had just been heading that way to take a walk when an extremely loud explosion occurred, and we were caught in a cloud of smoke and debris. We learned through the waning hours of the day and then the night—all through the night into the next morning and on until the last body was dug out around nine o'clock—that our neighbors and friends Harriet, Leonard, and Khay had been crushed to death after the gas exploded. Hannah had been something of a favorite for Harriet—who had no children of her own and was one of those people who brighten the world wherever they are—a feeling that Hannah, in her three-year-old way, had more than returned.

We'd had memorial services then, too, with many of the same people as today. We had sung many of the same songs and I suppose said the same prayers. This had been my daughter's introduction to sudden death. Less important, but entirely real, it was my introduction to the limits of a father's chances for protecting what was most precious to him.

I couldn't think of any reason to put her through all that once again with her firemen. She knew already that two planes had hurt the big buildings and everyone was as a result feeling sad. She'd heard talk about it in her preschool down the street. All the kids all over the city and, for that matter, across the country and over much of the world had heard about it. Therefore, we had a moment of parental convergence that reached into hundreds of millions of homes: what to tell the kids?

Honey, come here. Let's play with these blocks for a while. Let's build a building. That's just some singing outside. I don't know why. I guess Fran and A. J. and them just felt like singing.

Today Balbir Singh Sodhi, a Sikh, was killed in Arizona, apparently because (to his killer) he looked like the people who had attacked us in New York and Washington. He worked at a gas station and was forty-nine years old.

I picked up the paper and turned with gratitude to Frank Rich's column, headlined "The Day Before Tuesday." Frank's office was near mine but he came in infrequently. I hardly knew him but was gladdened when he was around because he had a habitual jollity. He was arguing this morning that we had been living, before Tuesday, in a two-part dream: "The dream was simple—that we could have it all without having to pay any price, and that national suffering of almost any kind could be domesticated into an experience of virtual terror akin to a theme park ride."

Yet he also believed we had been looking for a disaster of some kind, a "national test of character," but one with "few casualties" that "could readily be brought to 'closure.'" This "desire for vicarious battle . . . ," Frank wrote, "explains the fetishization of World War II." That desire came from a yearning for some national enterprise grander than the refinement of consumerism and of personal health. He mentioned a new TV series, "Band of Brothers," whose advertising pitch ran, "There was a time when the world asked ordinary men to do extraordinary things." Frank wrote: "In a way, the pitch enshrines the complacency of the day before Tuesday, with its assumption that the prospect of civilians having to make any kind of extraordinary effort for a national good was as far in the past as the knights of the Round Table."

Now it appeared we might have to make some extraordinary effort. It also seemed that we were supposed to simply go about our business, in part so as not to

Give In to Fear, in part to keep the economy going, in part because there was nothing else to do except, of course, to be consumed with anxiety. "Though polls show
that we overwhelmingly support the idea of going to war," Frank wrote, "they don't
indicate whether we understand that idea." They certainly didn't. It looked to me
as if we'd be making it up as we went along.

Frank was not the only person trying to extract something like hope from this
past week. He seemed, in so many words, to be hoping the attack would bring an
end to our triviality. There was an implicit hope also that we would cease gazing pa-
thetically upon the Greatest Generation and make of ourselves a great generation.
Similarly, others saw the attacks as proving that we Americans do, in fact, stand for
something, contrary to the generally held opinion—differently but strongly held
on the Left, Right, and center—that we had not stood for much in years. (The
conservative magazine the *Weekly Standard* this week had featured on its cover,
which had been printed before Tuesday, an article called "Farewell to American
Greatness.") But if we had not stood for something, they would not have tried to
knock us down.

One of my errands today was to buy a flag, but all the stores in my part of
Brooklyn had already run out of American flags. I had never thought that I would
want an American flag. Why did I want one now? I hardly knew, but it had something to do with the spectacular nature of the attacks on us. It seemed clear that
the attacks were meant to be seen, that they were visuals. One wanted to respond
to them visually, even knowing that the enemy, in all likelihood, was not looking. This flag display was a demonstration to whoever cared to see that there was
something irreducible or indivisible among us here, and that we were not going to
hide. Showing the flag also seemed to me, obscurely but intensely, a way of showing
solidarity with those who had died, of stepping into the place of a person who had
been ripped from our society. I didn't care which person in particular; not one of
them had been killed because of what he or she individually was or did. The flag in
one's hand seemed to say, "Come and get me, too." It was almost a way of making
the dead not as dead.

I did not find all the flags flying around me oppressive at all, though I might have expected to. I might have thought they represented an attempt to silence or smother, or to pull me into a too-easy delirium of angry hurt. I might have thought all these flags were there to tell me to behave. But that was not how it felt, mainly because that is not how Americans, on the whole, think about their country. Americans are not slow to self-criticism and do not, as a basic proposition, consider it unpatriotic. The sector of society most often considered patriotic—the conservatives or "right wing"—had been, for decades, the most relentlessly critical of American life. But the Left, and the liberal Left, have not been much less critical than the Right has been. The common thread is disappointment at our nation's failure to live up to its own standards. American political culture across the spectrum is at once liberal (in that it seeks change and improvement) and conservative (in that improvement is nearly always seen in terms of moving closer to a uniquely American core that is itself changeless). Because of this characteristic blending of liberal and conservative, American political culture can be self-critical yet stable. The hopes that Frank Rich expressed, for example, were premised on a criticism: he felt the national culture had become trivialized. Early in the week we got in a piece from a fully paid-up member of the foreign policy establishment who felt the attacks should make us "wake up" from "a decade of what can only be called delusion," the delusion having been "to imagine that we can intervene in other societies with impunity." The press had been full of "wake-up calls" of many kinds, all of which at least implied that some error, mistake, or shortcoming on the part of the United States was, tangentially perhaps and only to a degree, "responsible" for the attacks, or that the attacks might cause the United States to improve in some way that it otherwise would not have.

Maybe this merely showed an American, perhaps human, desire to take even massive murder and turn it to a useful purpose. Maybe it was a roundabout form of self-aggrandizement, since to accept fault can also be a way to assert control, particularly when you keep for yourself the power to define your fault. Maybe it was a type of self-hatred. Or maybe it was a way to deny the real possibility that every single thing about us did not matter in the least to our killers, that we really were just collateral damage in their argument with God, and that the only way to modify their opinion on this matter was to kill them.

9/16

The feeling was settling in that something like war was imminent, in part because the newspapers and TV shows would play up whatever rumors and indications came their way. Also the polls had 85 percent of Americans in favor of military action against whoever was responsible for the attacks on us, and 75 percent endorsed military action even if innocent people were killed as a result. The polls also showed a broad willingness to pursue a policy of assassination. It appeared that modern warfare (including terrorism) had advanced to a point where the old taboo against assassinations was being lifted. Perhaps this was in response to the cheapening of civilian lives and of the lives of those who expressed their fervors about public life (their politics and public faiths) through suicide. Since everyone was going about murdering for political reasons anyway, why not go ahead and try to assassinate leaders?

I went jogging early through downtown Brooklyn and up onto the Brooklyn Bridge. Across the river the fires were still burning. There was hardly a soul on the bridge. Partway across, at the first pylon, a couple stared at a molded iron plaque that gave the names and locations of various notable buildings on the skyline. The man and woman were trying to use the plaque to determine where the World Trade Center towers had been. I helped them with it; the confusing bit was that, with the towers gone, other buildings once hidden from view now appeared and made the plaque's skyline seem well off the mark. Besides, the plaque was poorly done. It had long bothered me, because the proportions made the buildings too squat. The towers, in particular, were flattened to an absurd degree. I'm sure the artist had limited space and had made what compromises he or she had needed to make; the towers were, inescapably, so out of proportion to their surroundings, each being at least twice the size of any other building downtown, that the artist had to flatten them to allow the other buildings some prominence. Otherwise, the skyline would have been two immense buildings with a gaggle of also-rans at their feet.

This man and woman were tourists. They hadn't been here when the buildings were "alive" (as I found myself saying, like a fool). It made me somewhat angry—I suppose because it displayed the bumptious arrival of the ignorant future in our present—that I would need to explain just how large the towers were (since you couldn't tell from the iron plaque, which was built to last, by the way), to explain they were so high that sometimes the upper floors of the towers were in clear sky while the rest of the city was covered by clouds.

Friends began arriving at our house around noon with bottles of wine or a covered dish. Soon we heard singing: the parishioners of a church around the corner were coming down to the firehouse with their hymns. Theirs was a black church—self-consciously so, under the leadership of an old civil rights man and race activist, Herb Daughtry—which made their assembly before the firehouse more textured than it might have seemed, because the firefighters through their union had long kept their jobs for fellow Irishmen and Italians. This remained largely the case.

The singers sang of consolation, not of justice, retribution, forgiveness, or peace.

We did not sing of peace, either, in my house across the street. With a few exceptions, the opinions of my friends would have been on a narrower band than those of the worshippers, firefighters, and neighbors in front of Engine 226—our band stretching only from liberal to socialist. My friends, several of whom were not American, did not have any taste for war, and some knew from experience what it can be like. We were all sworn enemies of American arrogance abroad and knew the grievance list by heart. Not that the list was our secret: I had edited a piece (by Lamin Sanneh) on the subject in this morning's paper, which also carried a lengthy article by John Burns on reasons for hating America. (Burns started his piece by noting that probably no power "has ever so dominated the globe as America does now." Among the reasons he mentioned for hating America: "the United States's support of Israel; its troop presence in the 'holy land' of the Arabian peninsula; its military encirclement and economic strangulation of Iraq; and its alliances with governments across the Middle East and Asia that are widely perceived as corrupt.")

One of our friends, a correspondent for the London *Guardian* who was staying temporarily in our home while reporting, had already been out looking for anti-war protesters. He found them last Friday night in Union Square Park, which had become a rallying spot. A well-organized meeting took place later, and further demonstrations and other peace actions were planned.

But I don't think any of the several dozen people who came by our house that long, wine-soaked Sunday afternoon had gone to an anti-war demonstration for nonprofessional reasons.

Matt, Jowa, and some of the others peeled off around 4:30 p.m. and went over to Atlantic Avenue, where a rally was starting to show that this conflict we were in, whatever it might be, was not and should not be a conflict with Muslims as such or with Arabs. The rally was, in its inspiration, a Muslim and Arab event, but there were many non-Arabs and non-Muslims who went along to show their affection for their neighbors and an understanding of their predicament.

I wanted to go but stayed to look after the remaining guests. I had been worried that it was tasteless to have a party (if that was the word) so soon after the attacks, but people seemed grateful to have an excuse to see other people and even talk about something other than war. And I was just swept up by gratitude at being able to see my friends alive.

The march went down Atlantic Avenue, then up through Cobble Hill and Brooklyn Heights to the Promenade, where the Arabs and Muslims (about five hundred in number) and their friends prayed and lit candles around dusk while looking over at the smoking skyline. They also held American flags, chanted "Allah Loves America," and sang "The Star-Spangled Banner."

9/17

The stock market reopened this morning. Expectations were high for a patriotic rally to American equities. The assembled brokers, Mayor Giuliani, Governor Pataki, Senator Schumer, Senator Clinton, and Paul O'Neill, the secretary of the treasury, observed two minutes of silence. As part of a brief ceremony, Richard Grasso, chairman of the New York Stock Exchange, said, "Today, America goes back to business. We do it as a signal to those criminals who inflicted this heinous crime on America and all Americans: they have lost." A Marine, Rose-Ann Sgrignoli, thirty-nine, led everyone in singing "God Bless America." A firefighter, several police officers, and an emergency services worker came forward to ring the opening bell. They were cheered wildly. Traders readied their telephone headsets. The politicians and the treasury secretary gave the thumbs-up signal to the cameras. The opening bell was rung at 9:30 a.m., and stocks set a new record for the biggest single-day point loss. By 9:44 the sell-off had triggered a trading curb that prevented the use of "program trading," in which computer programs take over in order to keep up with a market that is moving too fast for humans. So now we could look forward to a depression.

At some point yesterday President Bush was speaking to reporters and said, "This crusade, this war on terrorism, is going to take a while." A fearful person— and much of the Middle East and Central Asia was at this point just waiting for the shelling to begin—would have thought the Bushes came not from Connecticut but from fourteenth-century Normandy. A crusade?

That same Sunday Father Lorenzo Albacete was helping with the service at St. Mary's, "a congregation of Puerto Ricans, Dominicans and other Hispanics living in lower Manhattan," as he wrote in a piece that came across my desk. Lorenzo is a rarity in every way—Falstaffian in build and disposition, a priest who would never let an irony go unnoted. On special occasions, Lorenzo wrote, the parishioners of St. Mary's would "walk in procession up the streets of the neighborhood, dressed like the people of ancient Jerusalem, or so we believed. At every other turn I would notice *las torres gemelas* [twin towers]."

Lorenzo had often thought the parishioners must resent the twin towers, be- cause the people of St. Mary's were mostly poor and the towers symbolized wealth. However, Lorenzo wrote, that could not be the whole story, and during these spe- cial processions, at least, the parishioners "were focused on living life at a level deeper than that of economic conflict and desire."

The terrorists had lacked this focus, Lorenzo suspected, and viewed the towers differently. His impression was:

[they believed they were] acting in the name of God, on behalf of the world's poor. This is what happens when the religious sense is derailed, I thought. It binds with political ideology and quickly becomes deadly. Watching the events on television and trying, in vain, to find out the fate of the parish- ioners, I could not help feeling somehow personally accused. I imagined how terrible this must be for Islamic religious leaders devoted to their faith's love of peace—to witness the attack, to witness the celebrations around the world, to see that endlessly replayed clip of a woman in East Jerusalem trilling at the camera. In her long dresses and headscarves, I couldn't help noticing, she could have been a costumed member of one of our church's processions.

The parishioners of St. Mary's seemed to reject the various explanations for what the terrorists had done, explanations based on religion, American policy mistakes, poverty. ("I am poor!" one man said. "The poor are not like that.") "In front of the altar," Lorenzo wrote, "the parishioners had put a framed old, newspaper-sized picture of the downtown skyline lit up at dusk. Many came up to it and crossed themselves and said a silent prayer. It reminded me of how often for a funeral Mass they put there a really old picture of the dead loved one, trying to show him at his best." They also wanted the United States to be at its best and were worried by the calls for violent retribution; so they sent a letter to President Bush, suggesting that he "surprise the watching world by leading us in the incredibly difficult task of working for peace with justice."

President Bush sensibly stayed away from commenting this morning on the market or the spirit of American capitalism. He visited the Pentagon instead and said he wanted Osama bin Laden "dead or alive." At midday, Carl McCall, New York State's comptroller, announced that the state pension plan he administered had bought $250 million worth of the stocks that made up the Standard and Poor's 500 Index. He meant this as a show of patriotic faith in the economic system.

In general, the best that could be said of the market was that some patriotic investors were not yet selling off.

Around three o'clock President Bush arrived at the Islamic Center in Washington. The attacks last Tuesday, he said in a short speech, "violate the fundamental tenets of the Islamic faith." President Bush then cited the Koran: "The English translation is not as eloquent as the original Arabic, but let me quote from the Koran, itself: 'In the long run, evil in the extreme will be the end of those who do evil. For that they rejected the signs of Allah and held them up to ridicule.'" The president continued:

> When we think of Islam, we think of a faith that brings comfort to a billion people around the world. Billions of people find comfort and solace and peace. And that's made brothers and sisters out of every race—out of every race.
>
> America counts millions of Muslims amongst our citizens, and Muslims

make an incredibly valuable contribution to our country. Muslims are doctors, lawyers, law professors, members of the military, entrepreneurs, shopkeepers, moms and dads. And they need to be treated with respect. In our anger and emotion, our fellow Americans must treat each other with respect.

Women who cover their heads in this country must feel comfortable going outside their homes. Moms who wear cover must be not intimidated in America. That's not the America I know. That's not the America I value.

President Bush had begun his talk by referring to the group of Muslims gathered around him as "good folks." I winced at the return of "folks." His administration's unilateralist approach to most foreign policy issues—this had been the administration's distinguishing mark before last Tuesday—was not a folksy approach. It was an imperious one that cast all its opponents, here or abroad, as "political" or otherwise morally or historically enfeebled while everything the administration did was presented as though based on simple, timeless home truths. Bush's folksiness was a patrician, unforgiving, increasingly thin-skinned folksiness, another variation on this very particular semirural, kind-of-Southern-but-not-really, anti-intellectual, and insecure populist folksiness that had permeated American politics ever since the 1960s and Richard Nixon's reinvention of himself (and the Republican Party) as the working white man's friend. George W. Bush's presidential campaign had tested the limits of this hokum and come within a whisker of failing. His unique contribution to folksy political theater was to communicate to voters that he was simply not bright enough to be dishonest or insincere—and was too prosperous to be crooked. He had no need for personal gain. He had no ambitions. He had no needs or hungers of any kind. He presented himself as just a guy whom chance had happened to put on the path to becoming president.

Through pure political alchemy, the almost indescribable privilege and jolly satiety of this man had become the virtues of an American Everyman. See how far, President Bush had exclaimed in a commencement speech at Yale, you can get with a C average! Of all our folksy leaders from the past forty years, George W. Bush was the least likely. Unlike almost all his predecessors, he did not have even one moment of experience that could be considered "average American." Yet there he was, sunnily convinced of his averageness, and therefore able to convince many voters that he was genuinely unremarkable enough to be trusted.

And now I could see the beauty of it in a way I had not before. I could see that it was not entirely hokum. First, because of how he had said, "Our fellow Americans must treat each other with respect." When Bush talked about respect in this way you just knew he was also talking about humiliation and hurt, about being picked on, being bullied; you knew this was something he understood deeply. He was not talking about respect for a person's contributions or achievements. He was not talking about respect for anything that might be considered earned—anything that could be taken away, lost, traded. He had a more primitive idea of respect than that, and probably a more honorable one.

Second, because he had said, "Moms who wear cover must be not intimidated in America. That's not the America I know." Moms! Other politicians would have said "mothers"; most would have said "mothers, with children, and homes to look after," adding a string of modifiers to make up for, or cover up, the fact that they didn't think you really could ever imagine that woman with the veil could be your own mother. They wouldn't have had that much faith in you. They might not have had that much faith in their democratic selves or the America they knew. But George W. Bush reached right out and pulled you into the kitchen. Have a cup of coffee, mom-who-wears-cover! Be not intimidated! Because that's not the America I know.

And somewhere in America, say, at the front desk of a motel that did not (as so many did) have "American Owned and Operated" on its sign to attract guests, a scared, isolated, somehow-Arab-looking woman saw the American president say that about moms. The woman with her cover knew the president had meant it. He helped her.

———

While President Bush reassured the veiled moms of America, the disappointed head of the New York Stock Exchange was telling a reporter, "The message we are sending to the world is that you don't measure the market by one single day's performance." Investors had not been patriotic. They had dumped stocks all day long.

———

At the end of the day, the papers and TV stations were focused on the market and Bush's statement about wanting bin Laden dead or alive. Some efforts were made to reassure the public that our investing class was not entirely indifferent to the nation's fate. The dead-or-alive remark was good copy. It confirmed a certain cowboy cool, a lonely preparedness that many Americans as well as foreigners expect to see in a president. The remark also had the virtue of resembling a policy statement. We had had few enough of those. The president had simply announced last week that we were at war and said he would give us the details later. We did not even know with whom we were warring. Now at least we knew the war would include trying to execute Osama bin Laden.

Bush's remarkable mosque speech hardly made the news at all. It was not an easy fit with journalistic norms.

Before I left work the wires carried the news that Reverend Jerry Falwell had apologized for saying last week that the attacks were God's judgment on the American Civil Liberties Union, abortionists, supporters of gay rights, and federal court rulings against prayer in schools. He said that "no human being has the knowledge that any act is an act of God's judgment. . . ."

Meanwhile, envoys from our new and desperate ally, Pakistan, held their first meetings with Mullah Omar, a one-eyed preacher from the town of Kandahar in southeastern Afghanistan. He had led the Taliban to power. He had even brought out the (alleged) cloak of Muhammad the Prophet from its hiding place in Kandahar, draped it over himself, and proclaimed himself a particularly important Leader of the Faithful, an extraordinary act that had clearly registered powerfully on the minds of believers in his region. The Taliban had a sense of theater, wrapping themselves in black, exploring the fearful pleasures of ritual public violence, putting on magic cloaks.

The Pakistani envoys sought to convince Omar to give up his friend, colleague, guest, and financial backer, Osama bin Laden, or face terrible consequences. "You want to please America," Omar reportedly said as he bade the envoys farewell, their hands empty, "and I want only to please God."

9/18

There was a peace rally today in Boston with about two hundred people whom the *Boston Globe* described as a "subdued lunchtime crowd." Many had been alarmed by President Bush's dead-or-alive phrasing. "War may be very attractive to our cow-boy president," said one activist at the rally, "but we believe that justice, coalition building, and getting at the root causes of violence and hate are the answer." Several hundred people had rallied for peace in Madison, Wisconsin, yesterday, sounding similar themes. I could hardly imagine attending a peace rally. This was agonizing. There are many ways to be happy when advocating peace, but in accepting war the most pleasant sensation I craved was relief and the dominant note was misery.

People were still trying to give blood. There had not been a survivor recovered from the wreckage since last Wednesday. Mayor Giuliani announced, "We have to prepare people for the overwhelming reality that the chance of recovering anyone alive is very, very small. We still hope and pray, but the chance is very, very small."

He took some members of Congress and Kofi Annan, the secretary-general of the United Nations, to the site today. This place where the towers were, which was now a kind of burning heap, a few stories high in places and below ground level in others, we called ground zero or the site. (At the *Times* we proudly resisted neologisms, but ground zero had forced its way into early acceptance.) Mayor Giuliani said, "It's enormously important for them to be able to view it directly. . . . I do believe there is something very, very different that happens when you actually get to see it."

Colin Powell was trying hard to put together a coalition. (He was helped by the fact that other countries also suffered high numbers of casualties in the attack. About fifty nations seemed to have lost citizens; apart from Americans, the greatest number, estimated at up to three hundred, had come from Britain.) Coalition building meant talking to almost everyone except Osama bin Laden. It was clear that Russia would play a crucial role—Russia, which the administration had been hanging out to dry in previous months, explaining that all those treaties intended to prevent nuclear war seemed outdated now and we would just "unsign" them or something like that. The administration reached out to China, which had, over the spring and especially in the summer, been portrayed by experts at both the Departments of State and Defense as the big enemy of the future, successor in that role to the Soviet Union. Powell and his team reached out to Cuba and to Sudan, both long featured on the State Department's sponsors-of-terrorism list. (Sudan had been bin Laden's haven before Afghanistan.) The administration sought the help of Saudi Arabia, home to a majority of the killers of a week ago and sponsor, if not always officially, of various jihads and the Wahhabi educational system that had formed the beliefs of many al Qaeda members on the Arabian Peninsula and abroad. Finally, Powell continued to cement our alliance with Pakistan, which just over a week ago had been at the point of receiving (and certainly deserving) State Department certification as a state sponsor of terrorism thanks to its steady support of several groups in Kashmir, of the Taliban, and, via the Taliban, of al Qaeda.

So who was our enemy?

About two hundred Sikhs in America so far had reported frightening incidents to a Sikh watchdog group. Today I worked with a woman named Anika Rahman, a lawyer, on a piece for tomorrow's paper. (The headline would be "Fear in the Open City.") Rahman wrote, "My best friend, a turbaned Sikh who is a professor at Princeton University, was harassed as he walked in Chelsea because he was mistakenly viewed as being 'Palestinian' and looking somewhat like the men we suspect are the authors of our horror."

Rahman looked somewhat like them too. "I feel myself losing the power to define myself," she wrote, "and losing that wonderful sense of belonging to this city. In a way, the open city becomes closed. If the fear of attack causes America to turn on its people, these terrorists will have been spectacularly successful, more successful, I believe, than they could have expected or even understood."

We were so deep now into the land of unintended consequences. This attack, if it was a consequence of something we had done, was certainly not an intended consequence. The attack also seemed certain to have unintended consequences for our enemies, the "authors of our horror." The Bush administration, characteristically, was stingy with evidence about who these enemies might be. It had become clear that withholding information was a reflex with this White House, in part because it expected to be as mean-spiritedly attacked as its predecessor had been.

The Clinton administration had been subpoenaed and investigated so many times that people had stopped taking notes at meetings, preferring to trust their memories than leave a scrap to be exploited by their opponents—or by the press, which had also steadily lost its generosity of spirit in the final Clinton years. (One popular journalistic book of that period, written from the political Left about Clinton, was titled *No One Left To Lie To*.) All of this led the Bush administration to be extremely wary from the beginning.

The wariness was sharpened by the administration's knowledge that it had a weak political mandate. The Senate was split, and the Republicans' majority in the House was not strong. The popular vote had, of course, gone to President Bush's opponent, Al Gore, and Bush had not run a strong policy-oriented campaign at all. Taken together this meant that a significant majority of the voting public probably opposed most Bush policies that departed from the policies of Al Gore and the Democrats. However, the Bush administration did have many policy ambitions that contradicted those of Al Gore. Therefore, and given the Clinton experience, the Bush White House had an extraordinary commitment to keeping its workings secret, and its goals opaque, even before the attacks a week ago. The administration's major early policy initiative (on energy) had been formulated in extreme secrecy, so much so that the White House would be willing to have a federal agency (the General Accounting Office) hound it for months rather than give up information about the vice president's meeting schedules.

So the White House was not forthcoming with its evidence about Osama bin Laden and al Qaeda, and bin Laden had issued three denials so far—the last one over the weekend—while being careful to praise the attackers. It was frustrating; as a journalist, I always thought first of the sources and quality of the information and only later about interpretation. And the evidence of al Qaeda's connections was pretty solid, more so than you would have thought given the administration's reluctance to present its "proof" (the word being used) or even talk about it. Bin Laden was hardly an obscure figure. Since around 1996, the CIA had had a special group dedicated to following his movements. His declared goal, for several years, had been to attack Americans whenever possible. His efforts and those of groups and individuals allied with him were reasonably well known; any Arabic reader could have followed them in the London newspapers *Al-Hayat* and *Al-Quds al-Arabi*, or by dropping by the Finsbury Park mosque or the prayer meetings where the Palestinian Abu Qatada, one of al Qaeda's spiritual guides, publicly shared his thoughts.

Western Europe, after the Afghan jihad had wound down in the early nineties, had become home to many Muslim militants, and their activities were watched by intelligence and law enforcement agencies. For example, a man detained in Dubai weeks before September 11, Djamel Beghal, had been linked firmly to Abu Zubaydah, a trusted lieutenant of Osama bin Laden, and to a planned set of attacks in Europe. Beghal had been based in Paris and London. By July of this year, at least, he was well known to the CIA. Beghal knew Abu Qatada and had attended the Finsbury Park mosque. One member of his circle was Zacarias Moussaoui, who was also in custody before September 11 in Minnesota. Moussaoui was known to French intelligence agents (who had warned their American counterparts about him) and was connected, mainly via the al Qaeda financier Ramzi bin al-Shibh, to a circle of militants around the Al Quds mosque in Hamburg, Germany.

One member of that circle was Mohammed Atta, believed to have been a leader of the hijackers. He and his group had long been known to Western intelligence officials, not least because another member, Mamdouh Mahmud Salim, had been in American custody since 1998. (He was held on terrorism charges in connection with the bombings of two U.S. embassies in East Africa in August 1998.) Salim led investigators to Mohamed Heidar Zammar, who brought them (via wiretaps) into Atta's apartment, which Atta shared with the moneyman al-Shibh. Atta and al-Shibh were then put under surveillance. American agents made their own investigations in Hamburg, showing particular interest in the Al Quds mosque and Zammar. This was in early 1999.

It was, in great part, because such ties were known prior to September 11 that the White House could be fairly confident that the attacks were carried out by al Qaeda; electronic surveillance already in place picked up jubilant conversations among suspected al Qaeda militants in Germany, including an alarming reference to "the 30 people traveling for the operation" that suggested there were ten or eleven militants still at large. In many cases, European magistrates and American authorities were now willing to permit arrests of politicized Muslims long under surveillance by police and intelligence agents. The slow indictment and prosecution of al Qaeda members and associates for the 1998 East Africa bombings had turned up, and organized, a great deal of information, including interviews with Wadih el Hage, who said he had been bin Laden's personal secretary, and with such former aides to bin Laden as Jamal Ahmed al-Fadl and Ali A. Mohammed. Court documents for the trials of the first World Trade Center bombers likewise illuminated how widespread and interconnected Muslim militants had become.

By today, American investigators had already tracked the hijackers' bank accounts in the United Arab Emirates, observing deposits and withdrawals over a period of at least one year, information that suggested the all-important bankers would soon be found. Such intelligence, organized within a week, also pointed onward to the fresh fields of information held by semi-allied security services in Saudi Arabia, the Gulf emirates, and Pakistan, countries whose citizens had provided most of the personnel, money, and expertise that enabled al Qaeda to exist. Beyond that, perhaps there was some still valuable information from the days when the United States had considered bin Laden an ally against the Soviets in Afghanistan.

Yet the administration was being shy about proof. It was naturally wary of missteps. President Bush's press secretary, Ari Fleischer, had had to appear today and say that Bush had not meant anything religious by using the term "crusade" on Sunday, a choice of words that our Muslim opponents saw as a gift. The press was not quite lying in wait for the president's next misuse of English—not anymore— but Bush remained, as one presidential scholar put it in a news article, "a uniquely inarticulate man." Others among his top people, particularly Donald Rumsfeld, had their own communication quirks. But beyond that, the administration seemed to have decided—to the evident torment of Colin Powell, whose job it was to attract allies—that it would not talk about our enemies. Nor would it be drawn into giving proof.

Odd to think that this was, in part, a consequence (unintended) of Republican attacks on the previous president.

I wondered whether this secrecy wasn't also a sign that the administration lacked confidence that the people trusted it to do the right thing. It might have lacked confidence in democracy, too; there had already been signs of that.

Perhaps also the administration worried that presenting all this evidence would make people wonder why, if so much was known, the attacks had happened anyway. Many in government must have been asking themselves this crushing question: what did we fail to do?

Another reason for secrecy might have been that our current enemies all had the Islamic faith in common, and the administration was going to great lengths to ensure that its war was not perceived as anti-Muslim. Everyone understood that was what our enemies wanted: they wanted to have us attack them for their religious beliefs, thereby revealing ourselves to be what they had thought and said we were.

How people long for their enemies to perform according to plan! How we hope our enemies won't let us down! How we depend on them!

An article came in, unsolicited, by a man who had defended one of the bombers in the first World Trade Center case. His client and his client's friends were, to be sure, Islamic terrorists. He said that they did, indeed, hate Israel. They hated the United States for its support of Israel and its continued attacks on Iraq. They hated Arab leaders perceived as American puppets. However, despite being imprisoned, they liked America. ("They seemed delighted by the fact that they actually had constitutional rights.") They all admired Abraham Lincoln. They felt, however, America had not lived up to its promise.

Now *there* was an unintended consequence of American "exceptionalism"—to have the disappointed, but sincere, affection of our killers.

The attorney said his client and friends rarely said a religious word. He believed Islamic fanaticism was something of a camouflage for them. He felt their deeper motivation was a sense of humiliation and of having been disrespected, on the world's stage, as Muslims and Arabs. This had combined with some overlarge individual portions of hate to create a handful of murderers.

At nighttime, one more unintended consequence (they were beginning to pile up): catastrophe sex. Evidence was anecdotal but strong that quite a few people in our city were having sex with people whom they might have left alone prior to the attacks. This cannot have been Mohammed Atta's intention. There was also a reported upsurge in public drinking, along tomorrow-we-may-die lines.

Attacked by puritans, the public reacted with fornication and boozing.

But I felt these phenomena would soon pass, because we are a rather disciplined society. Major-league baseball returned yesterday, as did something other than terrorism to the televisions in public spaces. Articles appeared about "trauma-recovery" rates. I was afraid again of forgetting, and hoping that this fear of forgetting was not merely a personal obsession.

9/19

The updated subway map came out at last, "Revised Service Effective 9/19/01," giving order to what had been catch-as-catch-can transport. The colored lines, when they reached downtown, snaked over in a bunch to the right (east), avoiding the blank spot that now just said "World Trade Center," like the Unknown Lands on old maps. My C local, which I took to work if it came before the A express, had disappeared, as had the R Broadway local. The mapmakers had hurried and had forgotten one R symbol, which was listed for Fourteenth Street/Union Square, indicating, I thought, a ghost train; the R's replacement was called the W. The 9 Broadway local train's old path below Franklin Street—with stops at Cortlandt Street and Rector Street before the terminus at South Ferry—was gone. The 9's route companions, the 1 and 2, dodged east after Franklin Street with just two more stops to go before slipping under the river and into Brooklyn. The 9, not so lucky, had ceased to exist. "Service suspended," the new map said.

There was nothing on the map that explicitly acknowledged why we had a new map or what had happened in the big blank spot. In the middle of the Hudson was an errant footnote: "Lower Manhattan bus service is subject to change."

At least we A and C riders were no longer traveling on the F train's tracks. We were back on our old line, except there was no C now and there was no stop at Chambers Street/World Trade Center (WTC). Earlier this week we had been on this line a few times and passed through Chambers/WTC; the conductor had kept silent as we drifted slowly through the darkened station. I imagined him or her staring straight ahead down the tunnel, trying to believe that this was not really happening—that down here really was still safer than up there.

But for some reason today the conductor announced that the train would not stop at the Chambers Street/World Trade Center station. He was, for the first time, permitting himself to note its existence, as though some inhibition had receded. We were no longer rolling through it in complete silence, although we passengers were still quiet during this underground crawl through dark emptiness. Why had the conductors begun to admit the existence of the Chambers/WTC station at just the moment when the station had been erased from our map?

Laurie Goodstein and Tamar Lewin reported on page 1 of the paper this morning that the person who killed a Sikh man in Arizona had "then fired on a Lebanese clerk at a nearby Mobil station and into the home of an Afghan family. 'I'm a patriot,' the suspect, Frank S. Roque, said as he was arrested. 'I'm a damn American all the way.'"

The Pentagon announced Operation Infinite Justice. Ships left for the Persian Gulf. The aircraft carrier USS *Theodore Roosevelt*, with seventy planes, left port in Norfolk, Virginia, as a band played "New York, New York." It looked as if we were getting ready for a bombing campaign. President Bush announced he would tell us something tomorrow night at nine o'clock. He said, "I owe it to the country to give an explanation."

The weekly magazines began to arrive in the mail. I hoped to get a longer view from them. So much had happened and (it now seemed) all so quickly. The longing to find a pattern to events was gaining ground on my wish to reject all the patterns and live like the dead a while longer, without pattern. I kept thinking of the angel in the ninth of Walter Benjamin's mystical "Theses on the Philosophy of History." Benjamin was a left-wing German literary critic and essayist, and this particular paragraph of his was popular among my generation of undergraduates. Some of

Benjamin's political friends dismissed his "Theses" after his early death (in 1940), disparaging them as sentimental, possibly hysterical, as symptoms of the stress of the political moment and untrue to his otherwise ideologically clear mind. (Auden had dismissed his own poem written from the dive on Fifty-second Street for being sentimental and politically unclear.) Benjamin, being dead, could not defend or repudiate his writings. Certainly the "Theses" were composed under the stress of an all-enclosing European war. This might make them more true than not; coolness is not necessarily the most truthful of states for a writer. (And is there really a politics entirely separate from sentimentality?) The "Theses" meant something to my generation in part because of their strong sense of helplessness.

So the one I kept thinking of was the ninth:

A Klee painting named "Angelus Novus" shows an angel looking as though he is about to move away from something he is fixedly contemplating. His eyes are staring, his mouth is open, his wings are spread. This is how one pictures the angel of history. His face is turned toward the past. Where we perceive a chain of events, he sees one single catastrophe which keeps piling wreckage upon wreckage and hurls it in front of his feet. The angel would like to stay, awaken the dead, and make whole what has been smashed. But a storm is blowing in from Paradise; it has got caught in his wings with such a violence that the angel can no longer close them. This storm irresistibly propels him into the future to which his back is turned, while the pile of debris before him grows skyward. This storm is what we call progress.

I was hoping the weeklies might reason away the angel and provide some more reassuring portrait of events. *Time* magazine had had a special edition out very early. Like everyone in the business, *Time*'s editors and writers had to try and fit all that had happened into boxes where it didn't fit very well. "If you want to humble an empire," the lead writer, Nancy Gibbs, began,

it makes sense to maim its cathedrals. . . . The Twin Towers of the World Trade Center, planted at the base of Manhattan island with the Statue of Liberty as their sentry, and the Pentagon, a squat, concrete fort on the banks of the Po-tomac, are the sanctuaries of money and power that our enemies may imagine define us. But that assumes our faith rests on what we can buy and build, and that has never been America's true God.

Gibbs, prudently, did not go on to say what our "true God" is. Clearly she thought the terrorists believed we are an empire and they had destroyed our symbols. Gibbs did not think those were truly our symbols, but she did seem to accept that we are an empire and we may not be so powerful or safe now.

Newsweek had a cartoon of a girl and her father sitting on a big chair before the TV. Over an arm of the chair was a magazine with the headline "Act of War." The girl asks her father, "Will we hate back?" *Newsweek* gave a page over to a picture of a man flying down the side of one tower. *Time* had shown several people flying. *Newsweek*, however, was alone in noting that an eyewitness had seen "that a pink mist of gore rose from the sidewalk as they hit."

All these darknesses. All these sounds of slapping and smashing. As I write I can hear them.

The conservative *Weekly Standard* searched for a mission. It seemed . . . happy. Ours should not be a small war, "a campaign of missiles and lawyers." That kind of war would not only "aggravate . . . the evil it is meant to eliminate, but it will fritter away, perhaps forever, the potential of Americans to join in common purpose—the potential that is the definition of a nation." Now, how could a nation possibly fritter away, seemingly in the dark of one night, "perhaps forever," the potential that is its very definition? A certain cast of political mind worked like this, ever on the cusp of either exaltation or apocalyptic disappointment.

Ours was apparently a moment for exaltation. "We fret a great deal these days," the *Standard's* opinion editor, David Tell, wrote, "that the nation isn't indivisible any more, that our 'mosaic' is badly frayed, that we no longer know who we are. It turns out that is nonsense. At the moment, America fairly vibrates with an almost tribal sense of identity, a fraternal concern that can barely be contained. We know exactly who we are. And we love ourselves as we should and must." Tell was living a dream of political ecstasy. We loved ourselves so much that we each, freely, as individuals, had the same thoughts about the great issues of the day—and these were identical to the thoughts of David Tell: "Not because debate was suppressed or obscured by the emotion of the moment. But because debate was unnecessary.

We are all thinking the same things, and reaching the same conclusions, and all by ourselves, individually, at lightning speed."

The *Standard*'s executive editor, Fred Barnes, expressed his faith in the president. "My guess is he will stand firm," Barnes wrote. "As a war president, he has something he didn't have before. It's a purpose for his presidency."

The New Yorker struggled to hit the right tone. The pieces about fear were the sharpest. Denis Johnson, a novelist, wrote,

> For nearly a century, war has rolled lopsidedly over the world, crushing the innocent in their homes. For half that century, the United States has been seen, by some people, as keeping the destruction rolling without getting too much in the way of it—has been seen, by some people, to lurk behind it. And those people hate us. . . . They hate us as people hate a bad God, and they'll kill themselves to hurt us.

The piece that stayed with me, though, was the one that helped me. It was by Roger Angell. He mentioned with light mockery the "goo about our generation" that he had been reading and hearing, that his generation was the Greatest Generation. Angell had been at *The New Yorker* since the dawn of time and probably was the only one left there who still had the jive going in his head that would make him snap up the word "goo."

"Bad news is unimaginable," Angell wrote,

> but it keeps on coming and keeps on ending, as the distantly awful or immediately scary wears down into Then and, in time, to Back Then. Pearl Harbor came in the middle of a Sunday-afternoon bridge game at college. A first friend went down piloting a Navy bomber in Louisiana, in training, and there were more. . . . We woke up to Hiroshima, Dallas came at lunchtime, and My Lai by slow degrees. Young people have been looking at us and saying, "I don't see how you could have done that, gone through so much. It's beyond my imagination," and we think, Kid, there's nothing to it. Just wait and see.
>
> Now that's over. Now we're all the same age together. None of us is young this week. . . .

The issue ended with a poem. It was a perfect poem. I read it over and over. It told me to praise the mutilated world. It didn't say how. But it did put into words what I wanted to do and felt I had to find a way to do. "Praise the mutilated world": it was written by Adam Zagajewski, who split his time between Houston, Texas, and Paris, and it was translated from the Polish by Clare Cavanagh.

> Try to praise the mutilated world.
> Remember June's long days,
> and wild strawberries, drops of wine, the dew.
> The nettles that methodically overgrow
> the abandoned homesteads of exiles.
> You must praise the mutilated world.
> You watched the stylish yachts and ships;
> one of them had a long trip ahead of it,
> while salty oblivion awaited others.
>
> You've seen the refugees heading nowhere,
> you've heard the executioners sing joyfully.
> You should praise the mutilated world.
> Remember the moments when we were together
> in a white room and the curtain fluttered.
> Return in thought to the concert where music flared.
> You gathered acorns in the park in autumn
> and leaves eddied over the earth's scars.
> Praise the mutilated world
> and the gray feather a thrush lost,
> and the gentle light that strays and vanishes
> and returns.

At home that night I read to Hannah. We were reading E. B. White's *Charlotte's Web*, which is about a clever spider (Charlotte) that comes up with various schemes to ensure that her friend, the pig Wilbur, is not killed and eaten. I was enjoying the story so much that we kept on reading until the end. I had not read the story for thirty years. I had forgotten how it ends. Charlotte dies. It took a minute for this to settle in, then Hannah was at the limit of human distress. "Charlotte dies?!" Hannah cried.

"I don't know what to tell you, sweetheart," I said. "Charlotte's dead. It's just a story. Charlotte's not real."

"Yes, she is!" Hannah shouted. "Charlotte is real! I don't want her to be not real!"

It was no good: either way, I was destroying Charlotte. It took forever to get Hannah to sleep.

I went across to the fire station to say hello. Tommy was there, Tommy the survivor, his eye now fixed up. "This is a special time for us," he said.

We were sitting on folding chairs at the mouth of the station, with the candles all around, the flowers, the prayers. People kept coming up to say hello. A couple brought some food.

Tommy figured the other four guys probably knew they weren't going to get out. "You're just fighting the fire," he said.

"I just hope they didn't get scared," he said. I nodded. It was a nice night out. "I just hope they didn't get scared," Tommy said.

"I just hope they didn't get scared," Tommy said again.

He gazed out into our street. "That would add insult to injury," he said.

We were joined by other firemen, all of whom seemed to be spending a lot of time at the site. They said the burning-body smell was getting overwhelming. It was like a barbecue, one of the guys said.

Someone asked how my family was. I said I had finished reading *Charlotte's Web* to Hannah, and it had made her a complete weeping wreck. I said I had forgotten how it ends and then it was too late.

"Charlotte didn't make it," the fireman on my left said. I nodded and smiled faintly.

The minute-by-minute destructiveness of living can be strangely mesmerizing. Tick, tick, tick.

9/20

Sometimes the distinct smell of the burning site would gust into the train when the doors opened at Broadway/Nassau Street. Sometimes it wouldn't. Depended which way the wind was blowing. Coming and going, I would wait for it.

This morning—my birthday—I got off the train early, at Broadway/Nassau, next to ground zero, hoping my resulting lateness would not be noted at work. Dust covered almost every surface, despite some rain. There was still plenty of smoke coming from the wreckage. All the shifting about of things, the trucks and so on, would have created more grime as well. On Maiden Lane in the dust on a brown window someone had written with a finger, "They Can Take Our Lives but they can not Take our Freedom." Broadway was jammed with visitors like me, people going to work; National Guard members in camouflage; and "emergency workers" of all descriptions. The term had become elastic; it included anyone in the ironworkers' union, for example, because there was a lot of iron and steel to cut and move. It included all the firefighters who could come as well as retired firefighters and firefighters from other states. In midtown I often came across knots of men in identical T-shirts marking them as members of a fire department somewhere in Texas or Michigan. There was plenty to do at the site. Though vast, it was being picked apart very gently because everyone—the number of people who had worked on the site was by now reaching into the thousands—wanted to preserve the scraps of people they were finding. Whole bodies were rare, but parts were being found: arms and legs and fingers, portions of torso flesh. Also nonhuman parts—wallets, photos—were precious, anything that might help decide the question of one person's death, decide whether it had occurred yet or not.

This was the story that was never told in photographs or on TV and rarely even in print, perhaps because it was too primitive. There was no preexisting form for the ground zero story; the closest fit was the weary worker-hero Just Doing His Job (crinkly face, calloused hands, laconic asides). Not such a good fit, really. This activity was at a depth where heroism has nothing to do or say. Nor was this anyone's job. This activity at the site was somewhere else in the human world, an unplaceable fact: hundreds of people pawing at the ground to tenderly remove the bits of men and women so one day they could get a proper burial.

Underneath all this were the presumed open spaces, the "pockets" of underground garage, subcellars. You guessed there must have been people whose last moments of living had come in such caverns. Or were about to. Workers had spoken of hearing "pings" on the steel beams. But it was so hot. The fires were all underground, huge smoldering fires. We had a lot of smoke. This was the week when people were complaining about the smell simply because for some reason this was when many corpses were burning.

"Move it along," the cop said at the corner of Broadway and Maiden Lane. "Keep moving. We got a bottleneck here." Down Broadway between Maiden and Liberty Street the Westinghouse Building was already gleaming glass and brass. The World of Golf was still a shattered wreck. A man was shining up the McDonald's nearby. In front of Grace Deli a man showed photos joyfully to several people gathered around him, photos of his newborn baby. "This is the first one!" he said, hopping with excitement. Looking down Dey Street past the fence, the guards, the guns, the trucks, and through the smoke I saw the twisting arc of metal that remained of the Trade Center, which opened almost like a cone to the sky, and beyond that I could see what remained of the great glass atrium of the Winter Garden where we used to play.

At work I tried to get some hold on the problem of Iraq. This was the point of cleavage within the Bush administration: whether to try to force Saddam Hussein from power. About the Taliban there appeared to be little question. Patrick Tyler and Elaine Sciolino had a page 1 story about the Iraq question, "Bush Advisers Split on Scope of Retaliation," next to a picture of the *Theodore Roosevelt* leaving Virginia for Afghanistan. The personalities and issues involved went back to the administration of Gerald Ford and in some ways back to Vietnam and the lessons taken from that war by, for example, the young soldier Colin Powell and the young congressman Donald Rumsfeld. Rumsfeld had served as an aviator in the navy during a quiet period in the mid-1950s, but most of the senior Bush officials lacked military experience. The president himself had been safely parked in Texas's National Guard while he was of draft age. Dick Cheney had been in college, then graduate school, as the war in Vietnam escalated. (University students were exempt from the draft.) In 1969, at the age of twenty-eight, Cheney became an aide to Donald Rumsfeld and continued with him as Rumsfeld moved from post to post in the Nixon administration. Paul Wolfowitz, now deputy secretary of defense—Rumsfeld's number two—was also a student from America's earliest involvement in Vietnam to 1972, when President Nixon was pushing hard for peace. Among Wolfowitz's students (in political science) at Yale in 1973 was Lewis Libby, now Dick Cheney's chief of staff and national security adviser. Just as Rumsfeld and Cheney did a few years earlier, Wolfowitz and Libby became close friends.

Three of these four men served in the Ford administration, Rumsfeld as White House chief of staff and then as secretary of defense. Cheney served as Rumsfeld's senior aide and then succeeded him as chief of staff. They were and remained Washington insiders. Yet all of them shared a radical cast of mind that was unusual for government career men: they believed the United States could, and probably should, use its power aggressively to make the world a better place.

The containment and détente policies of the Nixon and Ford administrations set the tone for an indefinite future of coexistence with communism. This was reasonable, mainstream policy because the Soviet Union and its system of satellite states showed no signs of going away. But the radicals thought there must be a way to destroy communism, and in 1974 Wolfowitz joined some of his elders in drawing up a report that advocated an arms race of such magnitude that the Soviets would, in trying to keep up, spend themselves into disaster.

This became policy in the Reagan administration (during which Libby and Wolfowitz worked closely together in the State Department). Whether it destroyed the Soviets is hard to say, but the Communist system certainly did begin its collapse in the late eighties, to the amazement of nearly everyone but the always serene President Reagan. The radicals took this as proof of their rightness in opposing the caution of the foreign policy establishment. The establishment they had particularly in mind was, of course, the one with which they competed, and would continue to compete, for employment and influence—namely, the conservative realists: Brent Scowcroft and Henry Kissinger (the top foreign policymakers under Ford), James Baker III, even Zbigniew Brzezinski. The agencies that the radicals opposed were the Central Intelligence Agency—because it had erred on the side of caution and failed in its main mission, namely, to understand and undermine the Communists—and, for much the same reasons, the State Department.

Where the radical vision faced its greatest test was in the administration of George H. W. Bush, which saw both the final Soviet collapse and America's first substantial post-Vietnam war (against Saddam Hussein). Cheney was secretary of defense, Wolfowitz his undersecretary for policy, and Libby was back again as a subordinate to Wolfowitz. On the other side, so to speak, were Colin Powell as head of the Joint Chiefs of Staff, James Baker running the State Department, and Brent Scowcroft as national security adviser, helped—beginning in 1989, just as the Berlin Wall was being chipped apart—by a young scholar from Stanford, Condoleezza Rice. Above them all was President Bush, an odd character who had gone from strength to strength in his Washington career but always seemed a little lost and too easily surprised. He had run the CIA when it was failing to assess correctly the Soviets' predicament. His disposition was toward caution.

Caution was not what the radicals wanted. They wanted to dump Mikhail Gorbachev, raise up the idealist firebrand Boris Yeltsin, and bury communism once and for all. Their opponents, including Scowcroft and Rice, sought to preserve stability by preserving Gorbachev and his efforts to retool the Soviet system through perestroika (restructuring) and glasnost (openness). President Bush went to Kiev in the summer of 1991 and demonstrated his support for "the Soviet government of President Gorbachev" in a speech that William Safire labeled "Chicken Kiev." ("Do not doubt our real commitment" to reform, Bush had said. "But do not think we can presume to solve your problems for you.") The Soviet government fell apart anyway.

The sharper contest was in the Persian Gulf—a much smaller field of battle, but therefore more in American control and more revealing of the nature of American power in a new era. Would the Bush administration deal with Saddam Hussein's invasion of Kuwait in a radical way? A war to oust his forces from Kuwait did not have solid popular support and was vigorously contested by Democrats (mostly) in Congress. Yet Iraq's occupation of Kuwait, with one sovereign country annexing another, was almost a laboratory specimen of unacceptable behavior under international norms. The Bush administration did not have to pursue the conflict radically and didn't. It sought allies; it went to the UN Security Council for approval; it led a coalition force and restored the sovereignty of Kuwait. The Persian Gulf War was done by the rules and constituted a promising victory for existing multilateral norms.

It was the endgame that presented problems. The radicals' urge was to keep going to Baghdad—in essence, to take the fight beyond defense of international order and into the transformative realm of idealism. Change the world. Depose the dictator. End one-party rule. Bring democracy to Baghdad.

Gen. Henry Shelton had led a force that chased Iraqi soldiers up the western side of Iraq. It might have destroyed them but didn't; Shelton's force turned back. He later told Richard Butler, the Australian diplomat who had headed weapons inspection efforts in Iraq from 1997 through their demise the following year, that "the army of a democracy doesn't shoot teenaged soldiers in the back. If they'd stood and fought, even for ten minutes, we would have engaged them. But we weren't going to mow them down as they ran away." Now, in 2001, with the *Roosevelt* steaming to Afghanistan, Shelton was head of the military's Joint Chiefs of Staff.

Part of the settlement of the Gulf War was a set of UN Security Council resolutions; there never was a peace treaty. Resolution 687 specified that Iraq's weapons of mass destruction (nuclear, chemical, and biological weapons and any missiles with a range of over 150 kilometers) be "destroyed, removed, or rendered harmless." To that end, the council created a United Nations Special Commission, or Unscom, a new bureaucratic creature. The expectation was that inspections and the securing of compliance from Iraq would take a year. Until compliance was complete, the economic sanctions imposed in 1990 after Iraq invaded Kuwait, and elaborated over the six months that Iraq continued its looting occupation, would stay in place.

Two obstacles stood in the way of this relatively happy resolution. The first was that inspections showed that Iraq's capabilities were considerable, particularly with chemical and biological weapons and in missile stocks. Hussein had shown his willingness to use missiles already: in the course of the brief Persian Gulf War he had hit Israel with thirty-nine, Saudi Arabia with four or five, Bahrain with a few. These Scud missiles did not do much damage, but they did demonstrate Hussein's ability to project force. He had already used chemical weapons in the long war with Iran and in northern Iraq against domestic enemies. These were not quite decisive battlefield weapons, as the Scuds were not themselves fearsome missiles. Rather, his strategy seemed to be of the mad-dog variety: *Look, I really will do anything.* So when inspections revealed how extensive Saddam's research and development program had been, it was terrifying.

The second major obstacle to a peaceful resolution was the extreme reluctance on the part of Iraq's authorities to go along with inspections, destruction of weapons, and the institutionalization of compliance. The war, it was becoming clear, had not ended. It hadn't even really begun in 1991. The war, if that was the right word, was really the regime of Saddam Hussein. He was a war president. He had no other talents or use and few enough other interests. He had become president in 1979. The socialist state he took over had given Iraqis an excellent standard of living. Childhood education was mandatory and women could attend night school for free. Literacy was reaching 80 percent. The government spent more on social programs than any of its Arab peers did.

All that ended under Hussein. Taking advantage of military weakness in Iran following Ayatollah Ruhollah Khomeini's Islamist revolution, Saddam attempted to grab ninety square miles of the Shatt al-Arab waterway. The Iranian revolutionaries had been stirring Iraq's Shiites; Hussein (a secular Sunni) opted for a show of force and, with luck, an easy, intimidating victory. Eight years later, more than a million Iranians and Iraqis were dead. And within two years of that war's ending, Hussein had begun another by invading Kuwait.

For Hussein to be zealously pursuing weapons of mass destruction was hideous beyond imagining. Everyone knew what he was capable of. He had been our ally, after a fashion, in his eight years of war with Iran. (The United States had helped supply his army; in 1987, we even flew some limited sorties against Iranian vessels. Donald Rumsfeld had visited Hussein in 1983 to show President Reagan's support. We supplied him with intelligence and pointedly looked the other way when he used chemical weapons.) He was habitually nervous about his power, not least because his base was among Sunni Muslims while the Iraqi majority was Shiite, and the northern border with Turkey was dominated by Kurds who had a long tradition of rebellion against government from Baghdad. And by now Saddam Hussein was, objectively, facing a world filled with his enemies.

He took politics very personally. Whether he was psychotic was hard to determine. Whether, for example, he delighted in killing opponents. But he did go out of his way to do so, even when those opponents were tired and through with the game. He had a fantastic vanity, a palace-building, twenty-four-carat gold bathroom fixtures vanity. He reminded me of Nicolae Ceausescu, the Romanian Communist dictator, another of our former allies. Hussein's absolute power made him compelling to his people; wielding it was all he ever did for them. He gave them war upon war. Now his peace was like war. You couldn't help wondering if that was what he wanted; it kept Iraqi society in the form that best perpetuated him.

In any case, the Americans who had run the 1991 war against Hussein were stuck with the grotesque worry that if he did destroy some great number of people with, say, nerve gas, they would have been responsible—not directly, of course, but close enough. Because some of them had once (in the spirit of realism) coddled the man. Because once they decided to fight him, they hadn't Finished the Job. The radicals told themselves they would have done it differently (although they hadn't really tried, at the time). They would have broken the rules, made new and better ones. Eliminated Hussein, destroyed his weapons, freed his people. They would have overcome the fearfulness of George H. W. Bush—Chicken Kiev, indeed!— and Brent Scowcroft and James Baker and Colin Powell and young Rice and made the world new.

They were soon out of power. The Clinton administration continued the elder Bush's containment policies, more or less. A covert coup attempt in 1996 failed horribly. The decision by Clinton and Congress in 1998 to make "regime change" declared policy (in the Iraq Liberation Act) was a curious dysfunction: its grandeur only drew attention to its hollowness. Meanwhile, the diplomatic ground at the Security Council was frozen: France and Russia opposed the sanctions but could not end them, so they opposed American efforts to make the sanctions more humanitarian and more effective. That Iraq's "friends" would oppose making improvements in Iraqis' lives was in keeping with the Iraqi government's willingness to do the same in the name of protecting weapons programs.

Former Bush and Reagan officials, however, kept alive the battle to destroy Hussein. The leader of this group was Richard Perle, who had earned a hard-liner's reputation in the Reagan administration, sometimes reveling, as a plucky young man might, in being labeled "the Prince of Darkness." As the years of sanctions, patrols over no-fly zones, bombings, and brinksmanship over weapons inspections dragged on, Perle and others kept the pots bubbling with Iraqi opposition groups and American foreign policy hawks. In 1998, as relations between UN inspectors and Hussein's government headed toward collapse, a letter circulated around Washington for signatures. It urged President Clinton to "remove Saddam Hussein and his regime from power." Signers included Donald Rumsfeld, Richard Armitage, Paul Wolfowitz, John Bolton, Paula Dobriansky, Elliott Abrams, Zalmay Khalilzad, and Richard Perle. Richard Butler gave his last Unscom report, finding Iraq not in compliance, and Clinton launched the little-remembered Operation Desert Fox, a four-day air war undertaken with Britain.

This, too, had no effect. Saddam Hussein was unmoved. Under the UN sanctions, he had plenty of resources to live in luxury along with his cronies. At the same time, the United States lost a little more each month in the public relations battle. Along with Washington's ingrained reluctance to argue publicly for the wisdom of its policies, the politics of the grinding conflict were sordid enough that no one would want to bring much attention to them. American companies were, after all, doing business with Iraq and finding more ways to evade sanctions. Iraq was America's second-largest source of Persian Gulf oil, after Saudi Arabia. For convenience's sake, Turkey was being allowed (informally) to trade with Iraq in oil. There was a similar business with Jordan and Syria. In a crooked and slow fashion, Iraq and the world were normalizing. The problem remained, however: Saddam Hussein was a strange, dangerous man with a taste for weapons of mass destruction, and he would not let international inspectors see if he had them.

Meanwhile, his enemies in American foreign policy circles were pursuing a new line: that Iraq was a sponsor of terrorism, and specifically that Saddam Hussein had ordered the first attack on the World Trade Center. This was the thrust of a book by the journalist Laurie Mylroie called *Study of Revenge: Saddam Hussein's Unfinished War Against America*, published in 2000. Few people believed her argument, but among them were James Woolsey, who was director of central intelligence (DCI) from 1993 to 1995, and Richard Perle—or so one would assume from their endorsements of her book. And even if they didn't believe all of it, they wanted to and wanted others to do so.

Now, a week after the 9/11 attacks, a report had begun to circulate that Mohammed Atta had met an Iraqi intelligence officer in Prague, either once or twice, and a letter was going around Washington once again in search of signatures. The letter quoted Secretary Powell's characterization of Saddam Hussein as "one of the leading terrorists on the face of the Earth." The letter argued that "even if evidence does not link Iraq directly" to the September 11 attacks, "any strategy aimed at the eradication of terrorism and its sponsors must include a determined effort to remove Saddam Hussein from power in Iraq. Failure to undertake such an effort will constitute an early and perhaps decisive surrender in the war on international terrorism."

Those last words—"an early and perhaps decisive surrender in the war on international terrorism"—were the critical ones. We didn't even have a war yet, and here there was already a warning against premature surrender, a surrender that somehow might be "decisive." The sentence, indeed, made very little sense when you broke it down. But it was intended to push the administration at a sensitive point; it was directed straight at the emotions. Many of the signatories on the similar letter of 1998—Rumsfeld, Dobriansky, Bolton, Khalilzad, Wolfowitz, Armitage—were in the current administration. They were at the Departments of State and Defense and the National Security Council; in fact, they covered many of the second and some of the first tier of policymakers. Perle was at the Pentagon, chairing a group recently retooled (by him) and known as the Defense Policy Board. Perle was no longer called the Prince of Darkness, just as Dick Cheney was no longer a chain-smoking, young blade from Wyoming. Perle spent summers and a bit more in the French countryside, hardly the recreation of a fevered America Firster, and Cheney had to remind himself to take it easy. But they had been worrying together about Saddam Hussein since the Gulf War. Perle was admired in Washington for never having let go of this particular obsession.

Would it become the nation's obsession? Would we take this war to Baghdad? President Bush had declared early on that ours was a war on terror against al Qaeda, against the Taliban if they didn't unconditionally and very promptly hand over bin Laden and his men, against other terrorist groups, and against their sponsors, including their state sponsors. Who these all might be beyond the Afghan case was hard to say, but Saddam Hussein was one person who sprang to mind. The strange policy phrase for people like him was "bad actors."

The critical point about Saddam Hussein, it seemed to me, was that he had not changed between September 10 and September 12. What had changed in that period was our president, who had once spoken of "humility" and seemed to think (as did a few others in his administration) of foreign policy as a place to trim American commitments and expenditures. Forty-eight hours later he was speaking of a global fight of good against evil, with him leading the way. The deep anti–Saddam Hussein current in his administration was waiting there for this changed president; an old bit of policy business would help give shape to his new, unexpectedly threatening world. This was what made Saddam Hussein different even though he had not changed in any way, even though he did not seem to be supporting much terrorism these days except his own contemptible rule of Iraq's citizens, even though his army was considerably weaker now than during the George H. W. Bush administration.

But this could not then properly be called a war on terrorism. It was a war on our terrors and, in particular, a war on the terrors of George W. Bush and the men and women near him.

This evening President Bush came before Congress to tell us where we were going. We were going to war. That didn't mean the strange formalities of addressing Congress had to be changed. The president first needed to have everyone clap in recognizing a civilian standing in the balcony to his upper left. I don't know who started this ritual. Gerald Ford? It had always struck me as democratic kitsch—a human applause line. This time the human was a young woman who, just nine days ago, heard that her husband had not reached his flight's destination. No, he had got up from his seat on the plane and tried to interfere with a group of terrorists. The plane smashed into a field in Pennsylvania. Her husband's body was ground into dirt. It seemed indecent to me that she was here now as some sort of inspirational warm-blooded greeting card. It showed such a tenacious devotion to form, in this case the formal device of a president asking for everybody to give a hand to someone standing in that spot up to his left, stoically representing an idea or group—here, the group of the very recently murdered. The display seemed obscene, but why should the White House be any different? We were all clinging to our ritual forms: the Op-Ed, the breaking-news report, the affronted letter of protest, the expert commentary, the uplifting obituary, the feature story ("Tuesday was a day like any other for Mr. and Mrs. Smith . . ."), the retired general explaining at his map. The forms outlast everything. With reality so hard to believe, the forms were that much stronger.

"And would you please help me welcome his wife, Lisa Beamer, here tonight?" the president said. *Welcome, welcome, Lisa Beamer.*

The president proceeded to recognize the resolve of the American people and the many countries that had lost citizens nine days ago. "Americans have many questions tonight," the president said. "Americans are asking, 'Who attacked our country?' The evidence we have gathered all points to a collection of loosely affiliated terrorist organizations known as al Qaeda." There were, he said, "thousands of these terrorists in more than 60 countries." They are trained "in places like Afghanistan" and "sent back to their homes or sent to hide in countries around the world to plot evil and destruction." Afghanistan under the Taliban, the president said, illustrated the life that these terrorists thought everyone should lead: "Women are not allowed to attend school. You can be jailed for owning a television. Religion can be practiced only as their leaders dictate. A man can be jailed in Afghanistan if his beard is not long enough."

The president noted that we had no fight with Afghans or Afghanistan as such—"after all, we are currently its largest source of humanitarian aid"—but "we condemn the Taliban regime." He also demanded that it do everything we wanted:

> hand over every terrorist and every person and their support structure to appropriate authorities. Give the United States full access to terrorist training camps, so we can make sure they are no longer operating. These demands are not open to negotiation or discussion. The Taliban must act and act immediately. They will hand over the terrorists, or they will share in their fate.

The president emphasized his belief that Islam was a "good and peaceful" faith. He also emphasized that this was going to be a long war, and more than a little difficult to define, because, it seemed, our enemy was difficult to define.

"Americans are asking, 'Why do they hate us?'" How odd it was to hear him ask this. Some men in Pakistan had held up an angry banner days before, written in English, saying, "America ask yourself, Why are you so hated?" It ought to have been (I imagined the Pakistani men assuming) a startling question for Americans. Yet here was the American president asking it himself.

He answered: "They hate our freedoms: our freedom of religion, our freedom of speech, our freedom to vote and assemble and disagree with each other. They want to overthrow existing governments in many Muslim countries such as Egypt, Saudi Arabia and Jordan."

Maybe the Pakistani men were right that it was a startling question, since asking it seemed to have driven the president's speechwriters off the rails. What could they have been thinking, juxtaposing our precious, precious freedoms with the "existing governments" of Egypt, Saudi Arabia, and Jordan, governments that, to different degrees, denied those freedoms to their citizens?

The pressure of this question, why do they hate us? seemed to be pushing the speech into random phrasemaking and ideological free association:

These terrorists kill not merely to end lives, but to disrupt and end a way of life. With every atrocity, they hope that America grows fearful, retreating from the world and forsaking our friends. They stand against us because we stand in their way. We're not deceived by their pretenses to piety. We have seen their kind before. They're the heirs of all the murderous ideologies of the 20th century. By sacrificing human life to serve their radical visions, by abandoning every value except the will to power, they follow in the path of fascism, Nazism and totalitarianism. And they will follow that path all the way to where it ends in history's unmarked grave of discarded lies.

Here was the Cold War style returned, the mix-and-match approach to all our American terror of the outside world—the dark territory to which our special providence sometimes leads. Oh, we were grand, so grand that we held the patent on freedom. Democracy was our special possession, too. This was why they came to attack us: because we were particularly good, stand-out good. We had to be this exceptional, this historically huge to deserve such enemies as had killed us the other day. We had to be big enough to defeat such enemies and big enough to deserve them. Because we were so big, we had to make our enemy enormous so that he would deserve our big retribution. Thousands in more than sixty countries! Heirs to the Nazis and, for safe measure, "all the murderous ideologies of the 20th century," which was not a skimpy century when it came to murderous ideologies. A worthy enemy.

In Bush's strange words was the ancient wish to erase your enemy's name (even if he had once been your ally or your friend), to make him go silent, to take him out of the story entirely and put him in an unmarked grave. The story that would last needed to be a story about us and, to some decisive extent, only about us.

So our enemy was a global menace *and* less than a footnote to history, a mere unmarked dead lie. Our own shape-shifting mirrored his: the United States as a last born of nations, distant, vulnerable, and misunderstood, a fragile experiment; and the United States as the culminating event of world history, the nation in which all people find their purest, simplest, truest expression. As when the president said this evening, "America is successful because of the hard work and creativity and enterprise of our people"—as if our incredible wealth is merely a reflection of our fine character. As when the president said, "This is civilization's fight." Or when he said:

> Freedom and fear are at war. The advance of human freedom, the great achievement of our time and the great hope of every time, now depends on us. Our nation, this generation, will lift the dark threat of violence from our people and our future. We will rally the world to this cause by our efforts, by our courage. We will not tire, we will not falter, and we will not fail. . . . Freedom and fear, justice and cruelty, have always been at war, and we know that God is not neutral between them. . . . In all that lies before us, may God grant us wisdom, and may He watch over the United States of America.

The president went off the screen. The holy men in the courtyard returned. They had been a jumpy video apparition for hours, the clerical council to whom Mullah Omar had given the task of deciding whether to give up Osama bin Laden. The clip was very short, but it was enough to remind me of afternoons ten years ago in Uzbekistan, where I had traveled. I watched the clip of the Afghan council; I thought maybe I knew how the sour milk, drunk from a bowl, had tasted that morning, and the sugared tea. I felt the grains of rice swollen with mutton fat, rolled into a ball with the fingers of the right hand, the unclean left hand curled; I knew the distinct look of men walking, pensive, in robes in the heat and in the shade of trees with teasing light green leaves, an unusual sight for a California boy like me except when I remembered my father in his own preacher's black robe on certain Sundays. I had sat in Uzbek courtyards and talked religion with men like these in the jumpy video. They did not know what was coming. None of us did.

The clerics recommended that the Taliban persuade bin Laden to leave Afghanistan "in the proper time and of his own free will." The Bush administration appeared to feel this meant nothing at all; the clerics had also announced that if Afghanistan was attacked it was the responsibility of all Muslims to rally to its defense and combat the infidel. I wasn't through saying good-bye yet to Brian and Dave and the others on my street. But say good-bye in advance to these men walking in the courtyard. They won't all be seeing the end of the year because we are going to war.

9/21

The paper now had an entire section, called A Nation Challenged, devoted to news of the attacks, the war, the investigations, the Justice Department's rather bold suspension of the civil liberties of thousands of Americans and American residents, the long lines at the airports and the expressionless people going through everyone's luggage, the military surplus stores running out of gas masks, the gun stores selling more guns, the pharmacies running out of an antibiotic called Cipro that was supposed to be effective against anthrax, Mayor Giuliani thinking of spending a few extra months as mayor, young women wearing scarves in Tehran and lighting candles in the streets for our dead, looters stealing watches from stores in the World Trade Center's ruins. In today's A Nation Challenged, Kate Zernike and Evelyn Nieves wrote about campus protests: yesterday alone, there had been 146 demonstrations on campuses in 36 states. One phrase stuck out as especially popular: "An eye for an eye leaves the whole world blind." I was surprised that students would be toying with a phrase from the Bible.

The Pentagon was rethinking its name for the military operation known as Infinite Justice. It was mentioned to reporters on Wednesday. Yesterday a journalist told Secretary Rumsfeld that Muslim scholars had said that justice on that scale—the infinite scale—was something only God could render. Rumsfeld said he would consider the matter.

A Nation Challenged also had brief descriptions of the missing, whose number the mayor raised today to 6,333. They were not quite obituaries; the running heads were Portraits of Grief and The Missing. But, yes, you knew that really they were obituaries. They were based on interviews, usually by phone, with relatives and friends of the missing. They were always positive: "Keeping Life Fresh," "Balancing Work and Play," "Mr. Fix-It," "The Kiss Monster." The missing always loved their jobs and put family first. Almost all of them were happy almost all of the time.

Some of the reporters liked doing these "portraits of grief"; others hated it. Calling on the relatives of the murder victim is a task as old as popular journalism, and the reporter's mixed feelings are as old as the form. Like a lot of what we do, it is vampiric, yet it feels necessary. If we didn't tell these stories, no one would. The thousands of dead would disappear even more quickly than they were, which was quick enough. The pinging was getting fainter. "Do not analogize," I wrote last night in my notes, overcome again by one of those sudden cascades of grief. "Do not compare. Do not metaphorize do not look for similarities do not try to find the right words." The pinging was getting fainter all right. I read the portraits of grief knowing they were only a little true, but they were a connection. Soon there would be plenty of time for forgetting.

People read those portraits not just because they knew how easy it is to forget. They read them because they could see how quickly the events of ten days ago were either veering off into abstraction or being superseded by new, horrific events, like the killing that a majority of us thought was necessary to prevent yet more attacks on us. They read them also—at least, we did this as New Yorkers—to see what was said about people we knew and because we still knew, and felt, that it was happenstance that had made them die and not us, so reading these obituaries was a bit like reading our own obituaries in advance. It was ghoulish. It was weak, it was necessary.

There would be another attack. It seemed beyond doubt that there would be another attack. We had to make them stop.

Zacarias Moussaoui's mother was located in Narbonne, France. She was a retired telephone company employee. She said: "How could he be involved in such a thing? I cannot eat. I cannot sleep. I keep saying to myself, could this be? All my children, they each had their own rooms. They had pocket money. They went on vacations. I could understand if they had grown up unhappy or poor. But they had everything."

Yesterday before it rained the Parks Department had people clear away from Union Square Park the poems, candles, bouquets, notices of rallies, and posters identifying the missing. They put a fence up around the equestrian statue of George Washington, which had "Love" and "Give Peace a Chance" scrawled all over it, a peace sign on the horse's flank and "My Friends we will be fine" written on its belly, an American flag as the bit between its teeth.

"Huddling under a tree as crews threw away candles," Andrew Jacobs wrote in A Nation Challenged today,

> Nathaniel Hammel, 20, bemoaned the changing atmosphere. He said that he and a group of friends had sparked the public display of emotion by spreading out sheets of butcher paper and supplying markers.
>
> For nine days, he added, they kept the votives lighted and comforted strangers. "It was an incredible time," he said, looking bedraggled as he stood in a puddle. "There was such a feeling of community. Now it seems like New York is getting back to its old self."

9/22

We took the kids and walked across the Brooklyn Bridge today. We had a little flag on Ben's stroller. On the bridge I said, This is where I climbed back up, this is where I saw a wheezing man carrying a lawyer's folder stuffed with paper, this is where I was when the north tower dropped. In Manhattan Becky halted us at a table where a woman was selling photos of the World Trade Center before it was destroyed. We bought one to put on the mantle. We stopped in Chinatown and bought a larger flag to hang at home. We stopped in Tribeca at a deserted restaurant and had some soup. We wandered through streets we knew very well, and everything looked about normal. Then we came out onto Greenwich Street, and there it was, I guess fifty feet high, smoking, steaming. What the hell was I thinking coming down here? Suddenly I was so scared. I pushed Ben quickly along in his stroller down the street, heading east so we wouldn't see, and the stroller's wheels rattled on the cobblestones.

9/24

Before work, I went by Union Square again. There were cleanup trucks here and there. Two generations of memorials had already come and gone. After the big cleanup last Thursday, people simply came back, in large numbers, with yet more candles and posters. The mourners and the cleaners were now clearly at odds. Islands of hardened multicolored wax held out, the wide flagstone walkways surrounding them swept clean right up to the waxen peripheries. On the islands were more candles. On the steps, at the Fourteenth Street end, in front of the fenced-off George Washington, were three little pairs of World Trade Center towers. One was made of wire mesh (quarter-inch squares) and stood four feet tall. Each tower had a slot in the top. There was a note saying that you should feel free to put messages or photos in the towers, each of which had a pad of paper and a pen on top and was about a quarter full. A second pair of World Trade Center towers was made of those little vanity license plates you buy in souvenir shops, maybe 2 ½ by 4 inches, with first names on them. There was TONY, there was KAREN. These towers were protected with silver corrosion-resistant paint. A third pair of towers, made of paper, had fallen over. They were lying collapsed near the steps.

The park had been filled with people and TV crews over the weekend. It was as close as we came to a peace park, though the pro-peace materials were mostly gone now. What you saw was mourning, mainly—there were still missing posters up—and some fliers announcing a "brotherhood" that would be recruiting "only the brave" to fight against the "infidel," which appeared to mean bin Laden.

At work, I noticed that the State Department had announced it would be presenting its proof of bin Laden's guilt, soon, in two versions, one public and one classified. *Could I have the classified one, please? Because either you're right or you're not, and if we're not sure who the enemy really is, I would like to know that.*

The unsolicited manuscripts at Op-Ed continued running strongly against a war. They often suggested that the United States spend its stupendous military sums on highway construction and medicine in Afghanistan. If it didn't work, at least we wouldn't have done any harm.

9/25

Mullah Omar gave his harshest judgment yet. "The American people must know that the sad events that took place recently were the result of their government's wrong policies," he said. "Your government is perpetrating all sorts of atrocities in Muslim countries. Instead of supporting your government's policies you should urge your government to reconsider these wrong and cruel policies. The recent sad event in America was the result of these cruel policies and was meant to avenge this cruelty."

Osama bin Laden also had a new statement: "Wherever there are Americans and Jews, they will be targeted. We can defend ourselves. The holy warriors are fully prepared. Wherever there are Muslims, they should prepare for jihad and by the grace of God, the victory will be Islam's."

———

Secretary Rumsfeld: "Good afternoon. The answer to the first question—"
Reporter: "We haven't asked it yet. What's the name?"
Secretary Rumsfeld: "Is 'Enduring Freedom.'"
A jocular mood prevailed in the Pentagon briefing room, as it often did. The Defense Department had come up with a name to replace Operation Infinite Justice.

Rumsfeld chose this briefing to explain the type of war in which we would be engaged.

We do not intend to simply go after one or two people or one or two net-works. We do intend to have the entire United States government engaged in this over a sustained period of time. . . . Needless to say, there's not going to be a D-Day as such, and I'm sure there will not be a signing ceremony on the Missouri as such. This is not something that begins with a significant event or ends with a significant event. It is something that will involve a sustained effort over a good period of time.

This war sounded as if it might never end, or if it did end we couldn't know. Rumsfeld continued,

And it's a little like a billiard table, trying to figure out exactly how it might happen. The balls career around for a while, you don't know what'll do it, but the end result, we would hope, would be a situation where the al Qaeda is heaved out and the people in Taliban who think that it's good for them and good for the world to harbor terrorists and to foment and encourage and facilitate that kind of activity, lose, and lose seriously.

Rumsfeld had an odd way of expressing himself. Like Cheney, he wore his power with obvious comfort and pleasure. Neither man lacked credibility or self-assurance, which is one reason why they were useful (though also threatening) to have close by a president like Bush. But Cheney always looked as if something might send his blood pressure soaring, just as Powell appeared to be worried much of the time, whereas Rumsfeld seemed quizzical and abstracted. He was a man who regularly had ideas and fragments of ideas and would write them down. They would appear from time to time on a staffer's desk and were known as "snowflakes."

He had a sense of humor. The day before we were attacked he had given a speech at the Pentagon:

> The topic today is an adversary that poses a threat, a serious threat, to the security of the United States of America. This adversary is one of the world's last bastions of central planning. It governs by dictating five-year plans. From a single capital, it attempts to impose its demands across time zones, continents, oceans and beyond. With brutal consistency it stifles free thought and crushes new ideas. It disrupts the defense of the United States and places the lives of men and women in uniform at risk. . . .
>
> Perhaps this adversary sounds like the former Soviet Union, but that enemy is gone: our foes are more subtle and implacable today. . . .
>
> The adversary's closer to home. It's the Pentagon bureaucracy.

Rumsfeld could go from this revolutionary stance to, the next day, helping evacuate bureaucrats from a burning Pentagon, and in a week and a half to joshing with reporters about Enduring Freedom versus Infinite Justice and whether he was planning to have a psychological operations office dedicated to strategically misinforming journalists (he said he wasn't). Through it all he remained "Uncle Donald," with his cardigans, his squint, and his snowflakes.

I couldn't decide, for myself, whether this serenity was reassuring or a sign of some enviable but problematic mental ailment. I did push to have a version of his remarks printed on our page, not just as a policy statement, though that was important, but as a political-literary artifact. To me, it was worth it just to get his amazing phrase "floating coalitions of countries" into the historical record. On Forty-third Street, Terry and I had laughed anxiously over how Rumsfeld, in the text he sent in, put words in quotation marks, as if to hold their apparent meanings in suspension: "Forget about 'exit strategies' and other 'rules' of the use of military force. The public may see some dramatic military engagements that produce no apparent 'victory.'" We laughed because this was altogether too reminiscent of the postmodern "strategies" we had learned at university and later. Such postmodernism aimed at draining power from official language and official histories by showing that the terms used by the powerful to justify (or explain) their power—terms such as "progress," "the West," "objectivity," "modern," "profit," "justice"—were not stable. Rather, they were provisional and could be contested by the less powerful but very clever (that is, university students and professors). Putting words in quote marks was a way of saying that the official version was just one version among many possibilities. But now here was Rumsfeld, seemingly as remote from literary theory of the 1980s as a person could be, putting important words in quotation marks.

We laughed, but it was deeply unnerving. I did not want official anything to be unstable right now. Instability looked like a plane with a lunatic at the controls flying into my city to kill us. Terry and I laughed about "snowflakes." Through her window I saw the sky above the Hudson, not a plane in it for a week and a half. I did not want our secretary of defense putting victory in quotation marks as if this suspended state we were in would go on forever.

9/26

The NATO allies began to rebel today. The administration, despite Powell's promises, wasn't coming across with its evidence. It did, however, state for the first time that al Qaeda was involved somehow in the Chechen rebellion against Russian rule. There was no pretense that this statement was anything but a thank you to Vladimir Putin for his help since September 11 and his declaration of broad support for antiterror operations in Afghanistan, a statement he made two days ago. There was likewise no pretense about the reason for the International Monetary Fund (IMF) deciding today to lend Pakistan $135 million.

Italy's prime minister, Silvio Berlusconi, told reporters that the West is "bound to occidentalize and conquer new people": "It has done it with the Communist world and part of the Islamic world, but unfortunately, a part of the Islamic world is 1,400 years behind. From this point of view, we must be conscious of the strength and force of our civilization."

Yesterday, Mayor Giuliani issued an order commanding that no one (except journalists) be allowed to take pictures or videos of ground zero, because, he had suddenly decided, it was "a crime scene." This was more like our old familiar Giuliani; he plain enjoyed telling people how to behave. He'd got it in his head that all the visitors gazing at the workers picking across the ruins was disrespectful; he wanted us to Move It Along. I thought he was wrong. I thought everyone should go down, take a picture, see exactly what it was like at ground zero. It might as easily have been each one of them scattered across the rubble, and it might yet be; their turn just hadn't come. So they should take a good long look at it.

9/27

We published Rumsfeld's piece this morning—"A New Kind of War: Fewer beach-heads and no exit strategies"—and the last standing sections of the World Trade Center were pulled down. Giuliani took a group of relatives of the missing to ground zero to help them begin to accept that their loved ones were really dead. Today was Yom Kippur, the Day of Atonement. I took the subway to Fourteenth Street to see Union Square Park again. Everything was gone. Parks workers were spread out across the lawns and paths. Even the missing posters were gone, all of them. The twin towers made of nameplates, the towers made of wire mesh, and the towers made of paper were all gone.

A worker told me everything had been taken away for "a museum." A tall, thin man with a long-handled tool that had a metal edge scraped at the few remaining bits of candle wax. George Washington and his horse had been cleaned. I found a doorman who told me the cleanup had been going on over the past few days. At night, he said, people come back and light more candles, but by 9:30 in the morning it is all gone again, the mourners, the candles, the wax. I guessed that the faces of all the people we had lost would begin to blur sometime around now, although on a bench in the park with my eyes closed I could still see them and taste their ashes.

9/28

At a press conference John Ashcroft, who as head of the Justice Department had held voluntary Christian prayer services every morning before work for whoever among his top people wanted to come, urged respect for Islam. Earlier, he had recorded a thirty-second public service radio spot urging tolerance of Muslims. It was bracing to see a Christian fundamentalist (for that is what Ashcroft was) coming out on behalf of Muslims and of Islam.

9/29

We had some errands to do and so drove into the city. The streets were nearly empty. There had been plenty of speculation, by now, as to how retailers would survive, because people were not shopping so much. The stores were just hoping to hold on until the holiday season and see how things went then. Business was way down for taxi drivers as well; it was easy to get a cab. One tended to give bigger tips. I had seen the city empty before, when there were hurricane warnings or when the second Rodney King verdict came down in Los Angeles and people expected rioting so they cleared out of town.

We were rattling through Midtown when Becky pointed and said, "Look at that building." I looked and said, "It's like it has a big Kick-Me sign on it." I was trying to be funny, but it didn't come out funny. She said, "I meant, look how pretty it is."

As we raced down the West Side Highway—traffic was no longer a problem—Hannah asked from the backseat about all the flags. Ben was interested in them, too. He had just learned how to say "American flag," so he was saying it quite a bit, calling out when we passed one. We passed a lot of them. "Some bad guys, who are bullies, are trying to scare us," I said, watching my daughter's face as she stared out her window. "The flags are there to show them we're not scared." It was the best I could do.

———

That night Becky and I sat on the couch, after the kids were in bed. We talked about the World Trade Center and the past two weeks. She had been avoiding reading the newspaper, she said, because she found that when she picked it up she started crying and couldn't function—or else her mind would travel down such dark paths of imagination that the effect was the same. I hadn't known this was what it had been like for her, we'd talked so little about it. (Her old office was still uninhabitable, choked with dust from the disaster.) I didn't talk much about it at home, either. Work was all about the towers, the war; we had not had a single Op-Ed that was unconnected to September 11. When I was home it mattered much more to play games with the kids, read them books, have dinner, and clean the dishes. But here we were on the couch, cool autumn air coming in through the windows.

I said I thought about jumping. I did not know why. I imagined being at a window, knowing I was doomed, and deciding to jump. There were pictures of people in this very situation. Becky started sobbing. I shouldn't have said anything, though it was a relief to have spoken it out loud. I wanted to cry too. I had wanted to every day for two weeks, but somehow the right moment never quite came, and now it felt as if it was too late. So I just held Becky. I shook as I thought about her and her neighbors downtown falling.

9/30

Adam Shatz had a piece in the paper this morning about dreams. Adam wrote that it had become "impossible to resume dreaming as usual. Our nightmares now seem like premonitions, and the necessary, fragile border between the lived city and the phantasmagoric city has disintegrated as surely as the towers themselves." Adam spoke to a Dr. Gail Saltz.

> "What I'm hearing from my patients is that the event itself was surreal," Dr. Saltz said. "If you think about it, what's so freaky is that a plane literally disappeared into a building. It's the kind of thing we expect to encounter in a dream, not in waking life.
>
> "You could say the same thing of the aftermath: who could have dreamed of Yankee Stadium packed with mourners?"
>
> "I saw the event with my own eyes, like I'm talking to you, and I still can't believe it," said William Morse, a retired Harlem resident, at the Lenox Lounge a few days ago. Has he had any dreams?
>
> With a shrug, he said he hadn't. "How can you dream about a dream?" he asked.

10/4

In the morning I saw Al across the street. He was a gentle fireman, with a friendly little smile and thinning hair. Lacking the swagger the younger guys usually had, he smoked and was a bit wide in the midsection. He'd been with Engine 226 for a while. He told me that Tommy, the survivor, had said they were "hooting and hollering" when they crossed over the Brooklyn Bridge the morning of September 11. As a Brooklyn house, they didn't often get into the city. Now they had a big fire to work on, these brave and joyful firemen. They parked near Chambers Street and west of Broadway, en route to the plaza that ran between the towers. Tommy stayed with the truck. Brian, Stan, Dave, and Lieutenant Bob probably crossed over to the south tower. Tommy, at least, remembered being downtown already when the second plane hit the south tower.

After the south tower went down, Al said, there were still cell phone and radio calls coming from it. When the north tower fell, the calls ceased. The theory, Al said, was that some portion of the south tower had been still standing and the impact of the north tower's falling had caused that southern portion to collapse.

"We were all over that area, looking for our guys," Al said.

Even now there was no sign of them, not a trace. Al pointed to a list on the wall next to the door that led into a communications cubbyhole where you took the radio calls. A black marker hung from a thick white string. He was keeping a tally on the wall of the names of the confirmed dead firefighters. I had heard these announcements many times already. They came over the firehouse system and were distinctive in their tone. I could hear them from my living room, almost daily, announcing the identification of the newly confirmed dead. "There's sixty so far," Al said with his little smile. "Three hundred more to go."

10/5

Sifting through the papers I came across yesterday's *Washington Post* and turned to the Home section. These "lifestyle" sections had had it tough for the last couple of weeks. They were inherently, intentionally trivial. But ours were not trivial times. Some writers had already declared an end to irony, relativism, even sarcasm, and a return of patriotism and selflessness and seriousness of purpose. We fought, too, the grotesque knowledge that many among the dead had led trivial lives, thinking only of themselves and maybe a few family members. Some had been unpatriotic, fond of irony, sometimes sarcastic, and without any sense of serious purpose at all. Statistically, it had to be so. In the *Times's* Portraits of Grief section, it often seemed that most of the dead had spent their days working sickeningly long hours—loved every minute of it!—then breaking out at the weekend into marathons of barbecuing. When the girlfriend of one dead man revealed in a portrait that he had hated his job and longed to quit, I laughed with relief. And then there was the woman who, asked what she missed about her husband, simply said she missed his body.

The *Post's* Home section featured an article that went like this:

"I've been terribly depressed," said Marni Lebovici, a teacher in McLean, expressing a near-universal reaction to the Sept. 11 terrorist attacks. Seized by the need to set things right—at least in her own surroundings—she drove to Dale City last week to buy bookshelves, frames and baskets for her new apartment. "I thought about getting a puppy. I thought, 'Why wait? Don't put it off.' In the meantime, I'm putting up some new pictures."

Derek White and Naketa Conley had reacted to September 11 by spending "untold hours" watching television: "Said White, 'We are trying to keep on with our everyday lives. We are trying to keep going.' So it was that the couple went to Ikea last week and bought two black-cushioned beechwood chairs for their very lived-in TV room."

10/7

I woke early and looked out the window and there was Al cleaning around the candles in front of the firehouse. They had these new plastic wraparounds on them, which were also American flags; they glowed prettily in the dawn light. There was a notice up for a memorial service for Stan, whose last name was Smegala. I wondered if he or part of him had been found.

That day, a Sunday, we planned to go to the Brooklyn Zoo in Prospect Park. We called Becky's sister to see if she wanted to go to the zoo with us, and she said the war had started. It was about 1:10 p.m. She gave me the details. I phoned Terry and left her a message at home, saying that the war had begun and that I would come into work later.

I could hardly say this was unexpected. I thought the war could go on for some time, taking me away from Hannah and Ben. So I decided to go to the zoo anyway. We would still be attacking Afghanistan in much the same way in an hour as we were now.

The sea lion feeding was scheduled for two o'clock. Brooklyn does not have much of a zoo. The sea lion feeding is not just the main event at the Brooklyn Zoo. It is the only event. Apart from the two sea lions there's just the odd goose, some wallabies (not even kangaroos), a sort of guinea fowl that looks like a bloated rat, monkeys, a clutch of prairie dogs, and, beneath a bridge, two wavering cranes, in an exquisite gray washed over with pale blue. I got Hannah up on my shoulders. The sea lion feeders were taking their time. We fell into conversation with a woman next to us. The railing around the sea lion pool was crowded with families. We introduced ourselves: Rebecca, Hannah, Benjamin. I tried to keep my name out of it, because the crowd at the sea lion pool was about 80 percent Orthodox Jewish, and my name was the only nonbiblical one in the family. Not that we looked Jewish exactly—at least not Orthodox, not with the black coats and the hair curls and the wigs. We were redheaded and blonde headed, and I was wearing a festive Hawaiian shirt. Yet we wanted to fit in on this Sunday, which was the first day of a new war and was also the day when Brooklyn's Orthodox Jews went to the zoo in Prospect Park. It all seemed to fit with what our lives had become, in just three weeks and change—a chaos of Christian-Muslim-Jewish, of heartbreaking violence, inexplicable collisions, peculiar attempts at civility, and gestures of unexpected generosity. Everything really had changed, after all.

III

WITH THAT GUN IN YOUR HAND

A t the Op-Ed page, as the war in Afghanistan began, we had to find something soon for the next morning. We had scheduled a piece by Stanley Fish, a controversy-loving scholar whose specialty was the work of the English poet John Milton. Fish was arguing that the attack on the United States could not be blamed on postmodernism or the cultural relativism attributed to it (and sometimes to him). He had written a good article—he always did—but it was answering a question that not too many of our readers would think to ask. It was also not an entirely serious article—his never were—and we had just begun an extensive killing campaign against people just like us. A semi-serious discussion of cultural relativism did not seem appropriate.

We only had a few hours. I phoned Holbrooke, among others who were level-headed and quick writers (not a long list, frankly); but he said it wasn't the moment for him to "bloviate" and that we should find a Muslim writer with some notion of what the reaction to the new war might be. I thought of Fawaz Gerges, a young scholar who had been telling me about his recent travels in the Middle East. He was fast and not yet prominent enough to be sniffy about mere journalism and last-minute phone calls and the little editorial torments we ritually applied to our contributors.

In his piece, Gerges described at length how much the United States was disliked among mainstream, educated Arabs. He had just returned from a well-attended conference in Beirut on the war on terrorism. Most of the participants, Gerges wrote, were suspicious of American intentions and believed the United

States had "an overarching strategy which includes control of the oil and gas resources in Central Asia, encroachment on Chinese and Russian spheres of influence, destruction of the Iraqi regime, and consolidation of America's grip on the oil-producing Persian Gulf regimes." Many of the people Gerges met offered alternative theories of who really had come and killed us—most often, it was the Jews—while those who had accepted that al Qaeda was responsible thought, as Gerges put it, that "America has reaped what it sowed." Pretty much everyone at the Beirut conference advised their own governments to stay out of the war or face the wrath of their populations.

Gerges emphasized that the United States had to undertake "the painful and frustrating, but critical, work of building bridges to Muslim peoples and societies. This task requires cultural sensitivity, understanding and full political and economic engagement with the Muslim world."

Next to Gerges's piece on the page for Monday was William Safire's column, which advocated taking the war onward to Iraq. "It's the same fight," he wrote, "against the same mortal enemy."

Both Gerges and Safire mentioned the communiqués released over the weekend by Osama bin Laden, Sulaiman Abu Ghaith (identified as an al Qaeda spokesman), and Ayman al-Zawahiri, a leader of Egyptian Jihad, which had merged earlier with al Qaeda. I was intensely glad to have these documents—they'd come over the Agence France-Presse wire from Dubai earlier in the day—because the Bush administration continued to be evidence-shy, at best. The British had published a white paper last week (vetted by the United States) that made great claims of decisiveness but delivered almost nothing new. The president, vice president, and defense secretary were notably unsure of themselves when justifying their policies; they could turn aggressive or petulant in the face of small challenges. And the challenges they were getting from the press corps were, to be frank, not big. Yet the fact was that we were starting a war with an enemy who had denied being behind the September 11 attacks, and the evidence so far offered for our alleged enemy's guilt was thin. So I was glad to hear from the three Muslim men who were certainly, as of some hours ago, on the run.

The sun had set by the time I was able to sit down and be mesmerized by their texts. "America has been hit by God at its most vulnerable point, destroying, thank

God, its most prestigious buildings," Osama bin Laden began. "America has been filled with fear from north to south and east to west, thank God.

> What America is suffering today does not constitute even a negligible part of what we have suffered for decades. Our nation has undergone more than 80 years of this humiliation, its sons are killed, its blood flows, its holy places are attacked without reason—but no one hears or answers. . . . God guided the path of a group of vanguard Muslims who destroyed America and we implore Allah to raise them up and admit them to paradise.

Bin Laden went on to emphasize the disproportion between the pinpricks America had suffered—although these pinpricks somehow also "destroyed America" and filled it with fear—and eighty years of unbroken misery among Muslims, manifested most recently (bin Laden said) in the deaths of Iraqi children due to sanctions and of Palestinians due to Israeli attacks. So our recent suffering was just the start of a balancing of accounts.

"These events have divided the world into two parts: a part that espouses faith and is devoid of hypocrisy, and an infidel part, may God protect us from it," Osama bin Laden concluded.

> Every Muslim must rise to defend his religion. The winds of faith, the winds of change have blown to sweep away evil from Muhammad's Peninsula. To America, I have only a few words to say: I swear by God that America and those who live in America won't dream of having security before we have it in Palestine and all infidel armies depart from the land of Muhammad.

Sulaiman Abu Ghaith was less literary and sounded depressingly close, at first, to Fawaz Gerges's conference goers and other critics of the United States.

> We say that what happened to America on Tuesday, September 11 is natural, it is the result of the foolish policy followed by America, characterized by hostility to Islam and to Muslims and by direct interference in the politics of Arab and Islamic countries. The American people must know that what happened

to it is the result of this foolish policy and that if it continues with this policy Muslims will never, but never stop their revenge for the injustice they suffer.

He continued that he, bin Laden, their fighters, and the people of Afghanistan would press on to victory "even if the Arabs" opposed them. He appealed to all Muslims to do what he thought their faith required them to do. "The confrontation has begun. It is the decisive war between faith and atheism. You have to choose your side. There are only two sides and no third. Either you choose the side of faith or that of atheism. Why are you not fighting for God, for the oppressed among men and women?"

Ayman al-Zawahiri, an older man, seemed to be the historian of the three. He said,

Have you asked yourselves why there is so much hostility to America and to Israel, and why the Muslims' hearts are filled with such hatred for America? The answer is clear and simple: America has committed crimes against the Islamic nation that no person, let alone a Muslim mujahid, can bear. America is the chief of criminals. . . . Remember that your government was defeated in Vietnam, fled in panic from Lebanon and Somalia, and received a blow in Aden. Your government is leading you into a new war it is certain to lose and in which you will lose your children and your money. You American people and the whole world should know that we will not tolerate a recurrence of the Andalusia tragedy.

To Muslims he said, "The epic is recurring, so rush to the honor of jihad."

It hit me that bin Laden, Abu Ghaith, and Zawahiri weren't taking responsibility. They were presenting themselves as leaders of a global jihad and guardians of the realm of the faithful—as the next rulers of the world, God willing—but they couldn't openly take responsibility for even one act. They were coy and smug. They frightened me, but that was nothing new. What was new to me, now that I'd seen their words, was that they were so petty and manipulative. Of course, it was possible that they truly weren't responsible, in which case they were just getting whatever political-spiritual juju they could from attacks undertaken by others. That did not make them any less weak. I felt the first, very faint empathy for the nineteen men who had killed themselves to kill so many of us; they would have been played with like warm-blooded toys by these romantic little sheikhs.

Also for the first time, I found myself staring out the window, wondering whether there wasn't some way I could get over to Afghanistan and kill these men myself. I was simply amazed that their communiqués hinted at making an appeal to the American people to direct their government away from its poor policies. It was as if they had no understanding of their own cruelty. The American people were certainly ready for another look at foreign policy. A poll last week showed 75 percent thought the media should broadcast the arguments of those who believed the United States was "to blame for the terrorist attacks." This struck me as a heroically calm reaction to being killed on a massive scale one morning and even more so because 73 percent of those polled strongly suspected there would be another attack soon. But the calm could not extend to sitting down for a debate with Sulaiman Abu Ghaith about the future of Jerusalem, and I was astounded that he appeared to think it could.

Americans were willing to entertain the notion that they or their elected representatives were somehow responsible for the attack, even though they didn't commit it, whereas the three men who rousingly endorsed the attack and may well have ordered it lacked the strength even to describe their own role. Their pettiness and weakness they extended to all Muslims—all 1 billion of them—who apparently had been helpless spectators of their own lives for over eighty years, the exception to the pattern being their bad Muslim rulers who, either because they were bad or because they were tools of America and the Jews, did not really count as Muslims. I could see that this emphasis on the subjection and passivity of all Muslims was necessary to inflate the grandeur of their saviors bin Laden, Abu Ghaith, and Zawahiri. But it was still an insult, as if every one of our world's Muslims, like these three men, couldn't bear responsibility at all. No wonder Abu Ghaith, at least, entertained the idea that he and his band of brothers might have to struggle on in the name of Islam without many Muslims, per se, to follow them. The radicals' view of Islam might well be too pure to include many actually existing Muslims.

Their struggle also required a dangerous inflation of the importance of the United States and of Israel. Both countries, it seemed to me, already had an inflated enough sense of their own importance without being elevated to the transcendent status of "chief of criminals" (Zawahiri) or "henchmen of the devil" (Abu Ghaith) or "leader of global infidelity and injustice" (bin Laden). It could not do Muslims or anyone else any good to further puff up Israel or the United States.

Yet these three men also spoke as though the United States was a naked emperor who could be driven from the field by a few stout-hearted mujahideen. Everything was changing shape so rapidly. Some students from Hamburg with gleams in their eyes manage to knock the World Trade Center down by flying planes into it. The United States is Satan; it is a cowardly mouse. Muslims are favored by God; Muslims are the most miserable of history's victims.

The final battle between faith and atheism had been joined, except that the real culprit was "the policy followed by the American government"—which surely was something smaller than the Last Days—and the only tangible problems were the existence of "the Jewish entity," American troops in Saudi Arabia, UN sanctions against Iraq, and perhaps the poor quality of Arab governments. These were not insignificant difficulties, but they were not altogether huge, either. They were not Armageddon huge. Funny to say it, but I could feel myself trying to extract some hope from that.

I had never known a political vertigo quite like the one I felt on this night. It was gravely worsened by Osama bin Laden's mention of "more than 80 years." I could have been wrong, but I assumed he must have been referring to the end of the caliphate—that is, the line of succession of the supreme leader and spiritual guide of the Muslim community that begins with Muhammad. In the Gregorian calendar commonly used, the caliphate ended in 1924, but years in the Muslim lunar calendar are shorter; the caliphate ended 1342 years after Muhammad emigrated to Medina, and today, October 7, 2001, was past the middle of the year 1422. In breaking with Turkey's past as the heart of the Ottoman Empire, secular Turkey had abolished the caliphate, which the Ottomans, with incomplete but real success for several centuries, had claimed was theirs in descent from the Prophet.

This seemed to be what bin Laden was aiming at, especially when you took into account Zawahiri's line about "the Andalusia tragedy." Zawahiri was alluding to the end of Muslim Spain in AD 1492, when Ferdinand and Isabella took Granada, the last major outpost of the Muslim government in Spain. Muslim Spain is known in Spanish as Andalusia, from the Arabic *al-Andalus*.

Zawahiri's lost Andalusia was not the only version of the story, however. The Granadan sultanate had laid a claim, however vestigial, to the prestige of the

Umayyad caliphate, which had been based in nearby Cordoba and lasted roughly from AD 756 to AD 1031. The Umayyad caliphate had a certain magic, because it included a period of fruitful coexistence among Muslims, Christians, and Jews—Spain's "golden age." Modern Europeans and Americans and perhaps some others—if they have the temperament to look for Lost Ages—have normally been drawn to the Enlightenment or the Renaissance, or beyond them to classical Rome and Greece. But none of those (with some exception for Rome) have the distinct appeal of religious coexistence that characterized Umayyad Andalusia. It was really the only consequential period in Mediterranean or European history when the spiritual, political, intellectual, and artistic hit a sustained, powerful rhythm together across religious lines. And it had long been a particular obsession of mine, this period of what the Spanish called *convivencia*, of the sharing of life among Muslim, Christian, and Jewish peoples. In this period Jewish poets learned to make Arabic meters their own, notably in imitation of Arabic poems celebrating wine-drinking parties.

My Andalusia fantasy was quite real and it helped me make real connections—it was a fantasy of connections, after all. Once I read Edmond Jabès's book *A Foreigner, Carrying in the Crook of His Arm a Little Book*. The foreigner was a Jew, the tiny book was the Torah; he carried it in the crook of his arm as he went about being something like a Christian in a Spanish Christian world. Jabès connected me to Ammiel Alcalay, a poet in Brooklyn, who became my friend and had known Jabès (now deceased)—Jabès was among the Jews who were sent out of Egypt by the nationalist president Gamal Abdul Nasser—which, in turn, led to a very hot night on a friend's balcony in Brooklyn, drinking warm whisky with Paul Auster. A novelist who made a specialty of odd connections in his work, Paul knew Ammiel and, as it happened, had been close to Jabès. Talking to Paul, I mentioned Semezdin Mehmedinovic, whom I had met through Ammiel (a true Andalusian) and whose book *Sarajevo Blues* Paul had praised and I adored. I brought it with me when Sem took me to Sarajevo, his town, so Andalusian a place for so long but now, after the war, so broken up and dispirited.

The Andalusia I carried with me to Sarajevo and everywhere, my Andalusia, brought these friends, books, and places together and always promised to bring more, not least because Andalusia was also a long-standing fantasy of the past few generations of liberal-minded but not especially secularist Arab writers. Their Andalusia was a form that hope took.

But it was also potentially a word for revenge, along the lines of one more place the beset Arabs were expelled from as the evildoers cruelly deprived them of their Rightful Place in History. God, I am sick from this narcissism of defeat! And this tasteless vanity apparently formed a big part of the daily meal somewhere in Afghanistan, where bin Laden and his comrades, gathered by their caves, talked of the splendid caliphate they had under way, fortified by the big success in Manhattan.

Little did they know they had in fact attacked Andalusia, which was temporarily resident (in my opinion) in New York City. They had attacked it in Sarajevo, too; I had seen what the Wahhabis were doing there, reconstructing mosques the Serbs had shelled, but doing it Wahhabi-style, smooth and featureless, without the decorations, with very little allowed to survive of the Ottoman beauty—in short, with the Andalusia removed. These al Qaeda men and their Saudi friends were actually destroying al-Andalus a second time. They had ruined for me the lines of Abd Allah ibn al-Simak of Granada: "These are splendors of such perfection / they call to mind / the beauty of absolute certainty, / the radiance of faith." I saw no beauty left in absolute certainty.

It was agonizing to think it was precisely these same poems that had inspired Federico Garcia Lorca to write a book of verse that was not published until after he was shot to death in 1936 by Fascists. (He was shot in Andalusia, where he had thought he would be safe.) "The rose / was not looking for the rose. / Through the sky, immobile, / it looked for something else." His book before that had been *Poet in New York*. He wrote, "Agony, agony, dream, ferment, and dream. / This is the world, my friend, agony, agony. / Bodies decompose beneath the city clocks, / war passes by in tears, followed by a million gray rats."

The Afghan war began in green: blotches and vibrating lines form, perhaps, a hill, which waits, in green and black, until it is shaken by a streaking blast that comes too fast. It's always too fast! The reporters were using a new kind of camera (the videophone) that conveyed images that look like details from some vast, anxious surgery.

In the paper we had many speculations about whether the United States could possibly win. The war plans reportedly extended over almost a year, into next summer. The Afghan warriors had the reputation of never giving up. Those too-fast blasts jolted me; the effect they must be having, the tearing and pain. Fears of death, then death. In the middle of the week, President Bush gave the Taliban another chance to give up bin Laden without preconditions; then that passed. We read about Afghanistan as the "graveyard of empires" and how the Pathans once cut up the British. The ancient feuds of mountain people, little boys raised with the code of the warrior. Honor and shame, the things that drive people to extraordinary lengths, of every kind. Weird tales of grandeur and submission.

The Pentagon was controlling access, so we saw either these sudden green concussions or life far behind the lines, with men in green high valleys and then in treeless empty places, gazing down on some unwatered village that didn't look worth a fight.

Such was the moment when we got the first lengthy argument for an American imperialism. The *Weekly Standard*'s cover story, "The Case for American Empire," was by Max Boot. "The September 11 attack," he said, "was a result of *insufficient* American involvement and ambition; the solution is to be more expansive in our goals and more assertive in their implementation." The problem with our Afghan policy, he wrote, was that we left Afghanistan after 1989. We abandoned people too much. We should not have abandoned the South Vietnamese in 1975. President Reagan should not have withdrawn from Lebanon in 1983, and President Clinton should not have withdrawn from Somalia.

Boot believed we should have stayed, and that the challenges of being an imperialist were smaller than was commonly thought. Yes, the British were driven from Kabul in 1842: "This British failure has been much mentioned in recent weeks to support the proposition that the Afghans are invincible fighters." But the British went back in, several times, and fought well. "Afghanistan," Boot wrote, "and other troubled lands cry out for the sort of enlightened foreign administration once provided by self-confident Englishmen in jodhpurs and pith helmets." Boot felt we should start with Afghanistan, then go on to "impose an American-led, international regency in Baghdad." This would restore "American seriousness and credibility" and bring democracy to the Arab world.

Although Boot was a student of history, he seemed almost to think that British imperialism was motivated by a longing to spread the benefits of sound civil administration. The darker delights of wielding great power, for example, did not appear in his analysis. Neither did greed. His was in some ways a very American view, and he had fun pointing out that his vision of an activist America was widely held on the American Left. The failure of the United States to act, in a prompt manner, in the Balkans and in Rwanda had led many on the American Left to accept the use of American military power. It might, they believed, have prevented genocide. Some of America's bitterest leftist critics soon developed the habit of ending their perorations with a call for increased American involvement, whether aid or arms. Yes, a left intervention would be humanitarian and animated by guilt, while a right intervention might be imperial. Boot sensibly wondered how much difference there was. As long as the imperialism was not brutal or venal—and Boot did not think it would be—what could be wrong with it?

Perhaps the language of imperialism was not the right one to use when speaking of humanitarian interventions and efforts to spread democracy. The imperial vocabulary was blood soaked for many millions of people. To many, the assertion that a renovated imperialism could be selfless would sound only like the first note in some vast new symphony of hypocrisy.

Perhaps Boot's use of "imperialism" just meant that Americans could not seriously contemplate imperialism because we didn't understand what imperialism was. A far-flung imperialism, to me, seemed contrary to the basic nature of Americanism. Leaving aside ideas about differing racial qualities—an enormous thing to leave aside, in the American case, but still—Americans have tended to believe that all peoples are equally able and decent. They should not be, and do not need to be, told how to live. What made people live poorly were constraints imposed on them by tyrants, evildoers, sick people, and enemies of liberty. How *those* evildoing people come into being, given basic human goodness—well, Americans, uniquely among prosperous Western peoples, have preserved a premodern intensity of religious feeling, and perhaps that is one reason why American modernism has managed to stay optimistic. Evil is understood to come from outside it.

Our American idea of human nature was that all people are naturally free. This idea of liberty had to be negative: freedom from this or that, from all the constraints that are, on the American view, unnatural. Similarly, the American idea of rights is that you have the right to be free of various constraints—not the right to have one thing or another. Positive rights don't quite make sense to Americans. Positive rights would need to be enforced; the enforcing would lead to a loss of liberty. Enforcing positive rights would involve someone telling you how to live, even forcing you to live in a certain manner, and that would harm American liberty in the most visceral way.

American imperialism likewise doesn't make sense because it would seem to mean telling people how to live. However, one could imagine an aggressive foreign policy aimed exclusively at removing constraints on the liberty of others or protecting them from the imposition of such constraints (for example, from a genocidal attack by their neighbors or by their own government). Even when heavily institutionalized, such a foreign policy would always—to preserve intact its root concept of human freedom—envision an ideal future when it would become unnecessary and Americans could return home. A characteristically American foreign policy would conspire at its own demise. The sincere motivation was to Do Good. This ideal Boot and the Left had in common, and it was a lot.

The news did not suggest a world ready to accept the American imperial hand. All this week there were anti-American protests around the world. At least a hundred people died in Nigeria in the attendant rioting. Sulaiman Bu Ghaith—the wire services hadn't yet settled on how to spell the al Qaeda spokesman's name—asked on a video, "Is it logical that America and its allies carry out all this killing and bloodshed and looting over these long years and it is not called terrorism and when the victim rises to even the score he is considered a terrorist?" He added, "Terrorism against oppressors is a belief in our religion and our teachings. . . . Americans should know the storm of planes will not stop, God willing." UK prime minister Tony Blair, meanwhile, insisted that Islam was "a peaceful, tolerant religion."

Condoleezza Rice had called the networks to ask them not to air al Qaeda videos so much, and Bu Ghaith's remarks were difficult to find. One reason she gave was that the tapes might contain hidden messages. This was patently silly: anyone with $22.99 (per month) could subscribe to Al Jazeera, the Qatar-based TV station, and get those messages right at home in Michigan. (Al Jazeera was part of the seven-channel Arabic Enhanced Pack from the Dish Network, and about 150,000 people in America subscribed to it.)

But the hidden-messages idea—coming from our imperturbable national security adviser!—caught the spirit of the week. At the paper we wanted war news and couldn't get it. On Thursday the Justice Department said terrorist attacks were probably imminent, maybe as soon as this weekend. Then on Friday, in the newsroom, Judy Miller opened an envelope (postmarked St. Petersburg, Florida) that sprayed white powder all over her.

A week earlier, Robert Stevens, a photo editor at the scandal sheet *Sun*, in Boca Raton, Florida, had died of anthrax. He was an Englishman who'd become an American citizen. He'd retired not long ago—he was sixty-three years old—but got bored and came back. His infection had been announced just the day before. That Sunday another employee of the *Sun*'s parent company—American Media, Inc.—tested positive for anthrax. Spores were located on Stevens's keyboard. On Wednesday, a third employee tested positive. And today, Friday, October 12, someone at NBC who had handled a suspect letter had tested positive.

Hidden messages: could anyone have shown me a pattern, please? Sudden green concussions and a nasal swab for anthrax testing. What the hell is the matter with Palm Beach County, Florida? This was where George W. Bush became, butterfly ballot by butterfly ballot, our forty-third president. This was where (reportedly) the wife of the *Sun*'s editor rented apartments to two of the September 11 hijackers. Among American Media's titles, the *Weekly World News* had called bin Laden "a lily-livered piece of crap," the *National Enquirer* had marketed bin Laden toilet paper, and the *Globe* had said bin Laden was a "mentally ill, drug-addicted fanatic" with "underdeveloped sexual organs." Was Robert Stevens dead because of tabloid insults? Or was someone so mad at the American media and so ill informed that he or she simply mailed off some deadly poison c/o The American Media? Was Judy covered in white powder because she had cowritten (with *Times* colleagues William Broad and Stephen Engelberg) a book called *Germs: Biological Weapons and America's Secret War?*

Of course, Judy's colleagues ran over to help her get the powder off and got it on themselves. Soon the hazardous materials team came to seal off the area. The building's exits were closed, then the whole building locked down. The lobby was jammed with *Times* people who couldn't go anywhere. One of our Op-Ed team, Nora, was stuck outside. The rest of us were in our little corner room on the tenth floor when the announcement came over our public address system that we should stay at our desks and there was no reason to evacuate the building. Someone cried out (was it me?), "That's what they said in the south tower!"

And then we stayed at our desks to get out the weekend pages. The *Times* was getting used to this sort of thing—whatever This Sort of Thing was—and by early evening we received a memo saying an emergency information number had been established. We were asked to put our personal information onto the company intranet, including where each of us would be this weekend, just in case. (Soon we were told to inform our supervisors what floors we had been on that day.) Mail service was suspended indefinitely. We were told not to open any already delivered mail that (point 1) seemed "suspicious" or (point 2) "is postmarked from Florida."

I got home very late. Becky insisted I take my clothes off in the foyer and put them in a plastic bag. This could have been sensible, or hysterical. I had no idea. I did learn that undressing like that offered one more new experience of humiliation.

Was hysteria the sensible reaction? On October 9, David Rees, a young writer in Brooklyn, had begun posting a comic strip online. It featured clip art, static images of people at work. Each panel was usually a single person with a phone to his or her ear and a speech bubble above. Rees hit the hysteria note perfectly. He had a whole new series of panels this Sunday, October 14.

Panel 1—guy in his office says: "You know, us bombing Afghanistan isn't going to do shit—*except for somehow releasing anthrax throughout America!* Can we just fucking surrender or something? Fuck *Operation: Enduring Freedom*, I want some *Operation: My Ass Enduring Without Anthrax!*"

Panel 2—woman sitting at her desk says: "For real! So Osama bin Laden becomes our president—so what? All of a sudden I'm not allowed to read or go to work and men can throw acid at me if they can see my face? Shit, that's better than *anthrax*!"

Guy replies: "I want to take out a full-page ad in the newspaper: Dear Whoever Is Mailing All the Anthrax All Over the Place—You can be my ruler! Now can I please just forswear alcohol and denounce Israel or whatever so I can fucking open my credit card offers without thinking my organs are gonna turn inside-out?"

That same day a New York Police Department (NYPD) detective and two Health Department technicians who had been at NBC tested positive for skin exposure. Weren't they wearing gloves?

It got worse on Monday as our rudderless boat drifted into a zone Terry called Anthraxistan. A piece of mail (postmarked Trenton, New Jersey) arrived laced with anthrax at the office of Senate majority leader Tom Daschle. By evening we heard the seven-month-old son of an ABC producer had tested positive for skin anthrax after visiting the station with his mother for a birthday party last month. The thirty-two *Times* people who were tested after Friday's powder event had come up negative. I was, however, still glad I had stripped when I got home. Someone was trying to poison the major media, and I was part of the major media.

Is there a saturation point that you can reach, fear-wise? One of our reporters had managed to get through the Pentagon's veil and saw the kind of damage the Coalition's bombs were doing. It was easy enough to imagine the sudden trembling, crashing, the terror of it; it was hardly a month ago that I'd seen and felt the towers fall. A debate had begun in the government over how much killing should be undertaken in Afghanistan and at what pace—about whether the bombing should be directed at people or "positions." The distinction may seem overly fine. Yet we do distinguish, like grammarians, among the forms of killing. I remembered visiting a refugee camp in the Sahara Desert on the Algerian side of the border with what had been Spanish Western Sahara. This was in 1984. I was a guest of the Polisario Front, which for years already had been fighting Morocco for control of the old Spanish colony. Some of the Polisario men took me to a field where they had lined up all the different weapons that were being used against them. These included American-made cluster bombs, a common antipersonnel weapon; it was a kind of super-grenade that burst into fragments, each of which could cut deeply into your body. They were ancestors of the "daisy cutters" being used in Afghanistan. Touching these weapons out in the desert accompanied by the people at whom the bombs had been aimed made life seem temporary indeed. And the way all the munitions had been arranged there, in the corner of a brown walled-in yard, in neat rows: it was like a pre-cemetery.

Back then, in Tunisia, Morocco, and Algeria in the mid-eighties, I had no sense of jihad-style militancy—although I wasn't looking for it, either. The dominant note in the streets of the overcrowded cities was the dull pathos of coming to modernity late—dull because one felt that the social emotions of modernization had already been had elsewhere, in the West. Even alienation was a hand-me-down. It seemed to me that the only new, original, or wholly owned social emotion that a young man or woman in this environment could cling to, while embarking on adulthood, was resentment that the future had already been worn out by their Western predecessors. I imagined this ambient anger would simmer along forever as secular, anticolonial bitterness in a postcolonial world. But various people in North Africa and elsewhere were plotting to claim their future for themselves by shaping it into the culmination of another, different past—an Islamic past of purity, self-determination, authenticity, and glory. Andalusia. Their imaginary past occurred long enough before their parents' time that they could use it against them. That past could give today's youngish people—if only they had the will to believe strongly enough—all the psychic goods they were being deprived of in their present.

So now we had a new generation. Strange news came from Rome over the Reuters wire:

> In one conversation, the Tunisian, Essid Sami Ben Khemais, told his Libyan friend Ben Heni Lased that there was a plan to "try out" a drum of a "liquid" in France, according to a 50-page police transcript of the phone calls given to Reuters on Monday. "This liquid is more efficient because as soon as it opens, people are suffocated," Khemais said. He did not identify the liquid but said that it could be transported in tins of tomatoes.
>
> Lased is quoted as saying on March 9 that he wanted one or two 10 litre cans of unspecified poison for a planned attack. "Tell the sheikh . . . that I don't need an army, just two people who have got brains, training . . . and nothing to lose or to gain," he said.

"I'm sorry that if someone wants to become a martyr they must ask for authorisation from Sheikh Ali Abdullah," he [Lased] added. Italian police noted that Ali Abdullah was one of bin Laden's aliases.

In that same conversation, late on the evening of March 9, 2001, Lased told his Tunisian friend, "God loves us, because while it was once our wish to arrive in Europe and then return home with money, God loves us because now Europe is in our hands, because God showed us the way and we understood."

I couldn't help thinking this young Libyan man's sense of triumph had as much to do with money—overcoming the old, humiliating guest-worker remittance relationship—as with God's love. What a way to slough off economic subservience: "We have to be like serpents," he said that evening to his friend, "we have to strike, and then hide."

This week flowed on into the next in a lurid rush of anxieties. More bombing, more anthrax, more real or alleged jihadists hustled off into the twilight, and every day or so another body or fragment downtown brought out of the hot rubble. The firemen, police, and others—the "rescue workers" who had no one to rescue—would assemble in two lines and salute as remains covered in a flag were carried slowly by. Someone had the idea to plant a million daffodil bulbs across the city; in one day volunteers planted the first 250,000.

On TV we saw, over and over and over, Osama bin Laden walking tranquilly along surrounded by very fearful-looking bodyguards in his own camp. We saw that and what I thought of as the "ninja video." It featured jihadists wrapped in black emerging from the ground, then running around in slow motion, and leaping over obstacles. The scenes were part of a Come Visit Camp Jihad tape that was used, so it was reported, to attract recruits. I supposed it was shown to funders, too.

One thing that impressed me about this second video was that the networks were allowed to show it. Evidently, from the Bush administration's perspective, we should not be exposed to our enemies' explanations for their actions, but it was fine to be reminded ceaselessly that weird Muslim ninjas were coming to get us. Maybe this reflected the administration's own state of mind. There had been more than six hundred arrests already made around the world of people allegedly associated with al Qaeda. How many other tapes were there of men gabbing about how to turn a can of tomatoes or a pressure cooker into a weapon of mass destruction?

Man! I like a good stiff *Operation Enduring Freedom* as much as the next guy, but I've reached my limits of understanding! All of a sudden my fucking mailman is a Hero on the Front Lines in the War Against Terror? My daughter wants to sell cookies to help the people my nephew's been sent to fucking *bomb?* I'm supposed to help the FBI find clues and solve crimes? I'M A CLAIMS ADJUSTER, NOT FUCK-ING ENCYCLOPEDIA BROWN! Who's in charge of this shit?

Agreed! This is totally Loony Toons— I love that the fate of the world hangs in the balance! Bush is talking about conquering evildoers, yet the CIA *can't fucking translate the evildoers' Arabic voodoo-spells!* The "Office of Homeland Security" makes the DMV look like fucking Delta Force! And, look, I understand why *bin Laden* sounds crazy— he's an eleven-foot tall motherfucker who lives in a cave! But why does Bush sound like he's addressing a fucking Dungeons & Dragons convention? At least I can tear my hair out full-time now that I've been laid off!

November 8, 2001

A strip from David Rees's *Get Your War On*, November 8, 2001
© David Rees. Used with permission.

And what was it like to sit in the White House or CIA headquarters thinking that you had already screwed up by missing the first "storm of planes" and you might, right this minute, be screwing up again? It wasn't World War II but it had to be pretty white-knuckle governing all the same. Who could know which way it would go? Would a billion Muslims rise up, as bin Laden was urging them to do? Would Islam Karimov of Uzbekistan, probably the worst of our new allies, fall apart? Would the Hindu nationalists in India lose their nerve and start lobbing missiles at Pakistan? Would Pervez Musharraf of Pakistan lose his own grip? Would Pakistani militants get ahold of the fabled Islamic bomb? What if Megawati's new government in Indonesia collapsed, or if Vladimir Putin decided he just couldn't bear Eduard Shevardnadze another minute and sent Russia's troops on from Chechnya into Georgia? None of these were idle speculations. And the extent of American control over events was not at all clear.

I couldn't blame the administration for being rattled—an impression confirmed by a number of our editorial board guests and by the grudging appearance of administration officials on Al Jazeera—but I was still not prepared for the downpour of policy initiatives of Thursday, October 25, all coming over the Reuters wire. I did not like this Anthraxistan. First, on homeland security:

The Bush administration on Thursday warned that anthrax sent to the U.S. Congress was a particularly dangerous strain sent by "shadow soldiers," as

New York City officials confirmed that a second NBC News employee is infected with the skin form of the disease. In yet another sign of the spreading reach of the anthrax attacks, a worker at a State Department mail facility outside Washington has tested positive for exposure to the bacteria, spokesman Richard Boucher said. . . . Homeland Security Director Tom Ridge put the health system on alert nationwide . . . "Clearly we are up against a shadow enemy, shadow soldiers, people who have no regard for human life. They are determined to murder innocent people," Ridge said. . . . The new NBC case brings to 13 the total number of people who have been confirmed with an anthrax infection. Three people—a Florida photo editor and two Washington postal workers—have died.

Second, the administration launched an adopt-a-Muslim-school program:

"We're here talking about how we can best conduct a war against evil, and you can play a part," Bush told students at Thurgood Marshall Elementary in Northeast Washington. "You can be an integral part of that by establishing friendship."

Announcing a "Friendship Through Education" program to help bridge American and Muslim cultures, Bush said: "It is very important for us to combat evil with understanding. It's very important for us to reinforce our message in all ways possible to the people in the Islamic world, that we don't hold you accountable for what took place."

Finally, and most unnerving of all, was "Pentagon Fishes for Good Ideas to Thwart Terror":

The Pentagon cast a wide net Thursday for bright ideas on thwarting terrorism, seeking to pick the brains of just about everyone from tinkerers in their garages to big corporations worldwide. The Defense Department said it was seeking help in "defeating difficult targets, conducting protracted operations in remote areas and developing countermeasures to weapons of mass destruction."

"We're open to ideas from just about everybody," added Glenn Flood, a Pentagon spokesman.

I was spending a lot of time in the *Times*'s smoking room. The open cama-
raderie of self-destructive people had a nice, calming effect, given that the world
itself seemed bent on self-destruction. It was a bit as though we were getting a jump
on our enemies by harming ourselves first. I was always glad to see Lloyd Stevens
there; he was a painter whose day job was as a layout artist. Bronx-born, Lloyd was
a veteran (Korea) and had a terrific sense of humor. I told him about the article and
that we had to come up with some good ideas to help the Pentagon thwart terrorism. Lloyd said he'd seen a program once on television that showed an experimental
tank that had TVs on its sides and little cameras. That way, instead of seeing the
tank, you'd see a projection of what was on the other side of it. Why not do that
with big buildings?

If we'd done that with the twin towers Mohammed Atta would have just seen
Staten Island and probably would have landed the plane and gone back to Hamburg, frustrated and confused, to do something constructive with his urban-plan-
ning degree.

Lloyd and I also thought about hinged buildings that could be folded down
when the terrorist threat was judged to be high. If you had a spare set of office
furniture nailed to the wall, you wouldn't even have to disturb the workday when
terrorists came flying. We discussed rubbery buildings that planes would bounce off
of and wide but very thin buildings that could turn, in an evasive maneuver, when
notified of incoming planes. Lloyd suggested making cities of long, low buildings—
knocked down in advance, so to speak.

I called my wife to share these ideas with her. (She was in temporary quarters
in Brooklyn, as her old building downtown remained unusable.) She worriedly
acknowledged the humor in our ideas, then pointed out—after reminding me that
I had promised to buy more life insurance—that what bin Laden really wanted was
submission. That made sense to me. He didn't want to govern. He didn't have a
plan or anything. He just wanted to win.

Becky and I decided we should have a day or an hour when all Americans
could lie down and pretend to be dead. Al Qaeda could fly over and walk around
chuckling, pat themselves on the back for having humbled the only superpower,
and return to Kandahar. Once they were gone we could all get back up and do what
we do. It would be like paying annual tribute to a conquering power—a symbolic

submission. Al Qaeda's politics were themselves symbolic at heart. Maybe if we were to lie down for a day they'd lose interest in killing us.

I sent all this around in a memo to my immediate colleagues. The response was cool. Barbara Ireland, in particular—an unerringly sensible, upstate New York native—had a concerned look in her eyes when I asked her what she thought of our ideas for helping the Pentagon. But I felt slightly happy for the first time in weeks. I was glad to have my sense of humor back, even in the form of hysteria.

On October 29 we learned of possibly more threats. The next morning's front page had this lead paragraph:

> The government warned tonight that new terrorist attacks were planned against the United States in the next week, but it offered no specifics about the nature of the attacks or what the targets might be. "The administration views this information as credible," Attorney General John Ashcroft said. "But unfortunately, it does not contain specific information as to the type of attack or specific targets."

That day David Rees brought out a new strip. First guy on phone says: "Are the bombs we've been dropping in Afghanistan for the past four weeks fucking *hollow*? The Taliban are still rocking like a hurricane!"

Guy on the other end of the line says: "Two words, my friend: *Fucking invincible.*"

First guy replies: "You know, I wouldn't have even noticed, but then Ashcroft said everyone had to go into a 'Heightened Awareness' and in my 'Heightened Awareness' I became 'Highly Aware' that our bombs aren't cutting the mustard! Let's declare war on some foes *who aren't immortal*, for fuck's sake! If the Taliban had our defense budget, they'd have conquered Earth by now! Those motherfuckers would be waging *jihad* on Mars!"

I was walking down our street in the evening, to go to the deli, when I smelled the smell again. I hadn't smelled it in weeks. Other people noticed it, too: it smelled like September 11 again. The smell stayed all night and well into the next morning.

By the beginning of November several things that were said to have been changed by the attacks on September 11 no longer looked so changed. Irony and relativism were meant to end; they didn't. Patriotism was said to have returned; I did not think it had ever gone away. Perhaps what was really meant (and also often expressed) was that Americans had recovered a sense of purpose in the world and of respect for the importance of our government. This seemed much truer. Polls showed that trust in government had soared, as had approval ratings for Congress and the president. In June, four in ten Americans polled had believed the country was heading in the right direction; the ratio now was six in ten.

But here again, there was confusion. A majority of Americans expected another terrorist attack soon, and confidence in the government's ability to prevent such an attack had plummeted. So had confidence in the government's ability to capture bin Laden and maintain the military coalition in Afghanstan. Half of Americans believed the government was not telling us everything we needed to know about the anthrax attacks. The Afghanistan war was being conducted in secret, and that, too, did not sit at all well with the idea of national purpose.

Osama bin Laden himself was paying close attention to the polls. He cited one showing that "80 percent of Westerners . . . have been saddened by the strikes that hit the United States. The polls showed that the vast majority of the sons of the Islamic world were happy about these strikes because they believed that the strikes were in reaction to the huge criminality practiced by Israel and the United States in Palestine and other Muslim countries." Now, he said, the positions were reversed in the case of strikes on Afghanistan: "The entire West, with the exception of a few countries, supports this unfair, barbaric campaign, although there is no evidence of the involvement of the people of Afghanistan in what happened in America." Muslims everywhere, he said, opposed the strikes on Afghanistan. "This clearly indicates the nature of this war," he said. "This war is fundamentally religious. The people of the East are Muslims. They sympathized with Muslims against the people of the West, who are crusaders."

Bin Laden cited Palestine, Iraq, Sudan, Lebanon, Somalia, Bosnia, Kashmir, and the loss by Indonesia of East Timor as instances of Western violence against Islam. "These battles cannot be viewed in any case whatsoever as isolated battles," he said, "but rather, as part of a chain of the long, fierce, and ugly crusader war." It was amazing: bin Laden was watching the polls and adjusting his message.

He must have seen, particularly after September 11, that his usual big issue—removing infidel troops from the land of the two holy places, Mecca and Medina—was not a big enough issue to many Muslims. He added a strong emphasis on Palestine. ("He just remembered Palestine two days ago," replied Palestinian Authority planning minister Nabil Shaath.) Now he was scanning the globe to gather instances of crusader onslaught. East Timor, indeed! He also stressed that the United Nations was part of the crusade. ("Under no circumstances should any Muslim or sane person resort to the United Nations. The United Nations is nothing but a tool of crime.") This was why I wanted real evidence tying bin Laden to September 11: because it was obvious that he would happily take credit for the killings of that day or the invention of electricity or anything else that might pile a little more tribute before his sleepless, unappeasable ego. I doubted he even knew what was true.

But then, who did? On November 5, Jonathan Alter wondered in his *Newsweek* column whether it was time to consider permitting torture. ("Nobody said this was going to be pretty.") Now where were we going? How do you know when an entire people is losing its grip? John Ashcroft decided that his Justice Department could listen in on any conversation a lawyer might have with a client in federal custody, regardless of whether the detained person had been charged. Ashcroft's feeling that he was the best judge of what rights Americans have had never been clearer; the decision itself only gradually became public.

As President Bush prepared to give a major speech at the Centers for Disease Control and Prevention in Atlanta aimed at reassuring the public, bin Laden gave an interview to Hamid Mir, the editor of the Pakistani daily *Ausaf*. Bin Laden was still not taking responsibility for the September 11 attacks. "America does not have solid proof against us," he said. "It just has some surmises. It is unjust to start bombing on the basis of those surmises." This is often the way guilty people avoid answering the question of their responsibility: they question the evidence. Bin Laden, in this interview, was at least refining his legal argument that attacking

Americans was "defensive jihad," preemptive in nature. As to our dead, he said, "The September 11 attacks were not targeted at women and children. The real targets were America's icons of military and economic power."

Icons. God help us. *Well, then, just kill the icons next time.*

Bin Laden reiterated that the problem was not the American people but American policy, notably in Palestine. It was as though he now wanted to be not just a holy warrior and terrorist mastermind but a center-left politician as well. "I ask the American people to force their government to give up anti-Muslim policies," he said. "The American people had risen against their government's war in Vietnam. They must do the same today. The American people should stop the massacre of Muslims by their government." He emphasized that his "mission is to spread the word of God" (also noting that "only Afghanistan is an Islamic country"). Finally, he announced, "I wish to declare that if America used chemical or nuclear weapons against us, then we may retort with chemical and nuclear weapons. We have the weapons as a deterrent."

This statement, and the interview as a whole, had very little impact that I could see. That surprised and disturbed me, because Osama bin Laden was trying to speak the Western language and play the Western game. American economic power, Palestine, Vietnam, weapons of mass destruction—this was our talk. And if al Qaeda did have weapons of mass destruction, it was a very serious matter. The possibility had always lurked in the back of the mind, particularly when anthrax started appearing in the mail. So why did this announcement get so little attention?

It might have been that the White House and other capitals knew that bin Laden did not have weapons of mass destruction. But that was not likely. Intelligence on bin Laden had been pretty poor. It is pleasant, in a way, to think that a major nation's intelligence is good and that major political leaders, while they may be untruthful or hypocritical, are nonetheless well informed. However, decision makers in politics actually live in a rushed world of extremely imperfect information. They are much better informed than the average person. That does not mean they know what they're doing or that they have the information they need to make sensible decisions. Wielding power is more art than science, and most art is not very good art.

This was true also among American intelligence people, who had been deeply divided since the 1970s on what was, in essence, a question of political art: what were the appropriate uses of intelligence? The Pentagon people—with their characteristic conviction that what they do is more concrete and even scientific than what diplomats, politicians, and CIA officers do—had been gradually aggrandizing their own apparatuses to the point where their share of intelligence resources now greatly outweighed that of the CIA. The military men thought they knew better about what to do with intelligence because they were not political. This was a delusion. War really is politics by other means, and politics is not rational or scientific. The political artist spoke: "The real targets were America's icons."

My feeling was that bin Laden's remarks were ignored because our decision makers had already settled their minds. They, too, were political artists, and often an artist just chooses his palette, medium, and motifs—that is, pursues a certain style—then sees what happens. Because he does not know in advance what will happen, he has to stay the course.

Or maybe the situation we were in was so chaotic, so fundamentally terrifying that there was no room left for new information? All was calm, in a paralytic way. Bin Laden's announcement that he had weapons of mass destruction was ignored, as was (to a different degree) President Bush's own big speech in Atlanta. It was the most extraordinary thing. The White House had not specifically requested that the networks clear time for his speech. Probably the White House had not thought it needed to. (Probably bin Laden had thought his first interview since September 11 would get some attention, too!) But two of the networks had hit shows on Thursday nights at 8:00 p.m.—*Friends* on NBC (also hugely popular in Arab countries) and *Survivor* on CBS—and decided not to broadcast the president's speech. Fox's head, Roger Ailes, waited until he had seen a synopsis of the speech, then decided to air *Family Guy*, a cartoon, instead; and Fox was determinedly pro-Bush. Only ABC, which had a terrible program scheduled (a comedy improv show, *Whose Line Is It Anyway?*), broadcast President Bush's speech.

Irony was certainly not dead! For the main goal of this speech, which had been preempted by *Family Guy*, was . . . to affirm that a certain national aimlessness, pre-9/11, had definitively ended. The president urged Americans to get involved in the fight against terror. "None of us would ever wish the evil that has been done to our country," President Bush said, "but we have learned that out of evil can come great good. During the last two months, we have shown the world America is a great nation." He also said,

Too many have the wrong idea of Americans as shallow, materialist consumers. . . . But this isn't the America I know. Ours is a wonderful nation full of kind and loving people, people of faith who want freedom and opportunity for people everywhere. One way to defeat terrorism is to show the world the true values of America through the gathering momentum of a million acts of responsibility and decency and service.

He emphasized that "Afghanistan is only the beginning of our efforts in the world."

The speech did not hold together well. In a way, with all the faint praise about how we Really Aren't That Bad, it was insulting. "Many ask, 'What can I do to help in our fight?' The answer is simple. All of us can become a September the 11th volunteer by making a commitment to service in our communities. So you can serve your country by tutoring or mentoring a child, comforting the afflicted, housing those in need of sheltering and a home." Did it really take mass murder to spur us to tutor children? The link, of course, was that, for President Bush, America was goodness and goodness was American, so any good act advanced the nation and was therefore a blow against its enemies, who were evil. Every American was thus a hero-in-waiting ready to combat evil. This was a childish worldview. It was, in fact, the one I was taught as a child in school and in the Boy Scouts. It has many virtues, but it was not at all appropriate in speaking to adults.

Besides—this was a terrible thought, but I had it anyway—I imagined Mohammed Atta had conceived of his own heroism in these boyish terms, or in this fundamentally narcissistic, childish way. You didn't see too many gray-haired suicide bombers, did you? As an adult you know how real death is and how murky goodness can be. The child-hero is vain and doesn't know. Speaking in Atlanta, President Bush did not seem to know either.

Heroism did not come up at the Engine 226 beer bash to raise money for Dave DeRubbio's widow and children. It was at a venerable Italian place in Bay Ridge, Brooklyn, with a long wooden bar in front, mirrors behind it; farther into the building were booths and tables. There was Tommy; and wonderful, solid Jack, who hadn't gone in that day; and pensive Al, who tallied the dead on the firehouse wall with the black marker that hung on a string. There were T-shirts and baseball caps for sale, with the names on them of Engine 226's four dead men. The social world they came from—all the people in the bar that night, smoking and drinking as if there was no tomorrow—had a very complicated and deep-running relationship to physical bravery, to kindness, to public service. It wasn't pure or always pretty. I don't know that I ever heard firemen talk about heroes. They were more than that, or just different; the word wasn't right.

So all the news articles and broadcasts about how ineffective the Afghans' Northern Alliance was, how sturdy the Taliban was, and how unimaginative the American commander, Tommy Franks, was—they may have been correct, but Kabul was falling anyway, regardless of whether bin Laden had nuclear weapons and regardless of whether Americans are materialists who would rather watch *Survivor* than hear their president address them in wartime. The United States had insisted, urged on by Pakistan, that the Northern Alliance not enter Kabul. The alliance was going to enter anyway.

A Northern Alliance force under Gen. Abdul Rashid Dostum took the northern city of Mazar-i-Sharif last Friday. Other alliance forces captured Taliqan on Sunday. Taliban troops retreated from both cities to a town that lay between them, Kunduz. The alliance forces took uneasy control of Herat, Afghanistan's major western city, near the border with Iran.

On the morning of November 12 an American Airlines flight took off from John F. Kennedy International Airport, then ripped into Belle Harbor, in the Rockaways in Queens, a little neighborhood that, having a high proportion of firemen and police officers, was already mourning the loss of dozens in the World Trade Center. I called a friend who was an adviser to the United Nations secretary-general, thinking as I did and he did that perhaps the plane had been heading for him—to make good bin Laden's anger by hitting the UN, a tall building that sits fully exposed alongside the East River and can be felt to sway when the winds are high.

That same Monday the Northern Alliance entered Kabul's outskirts and the Taliban began to flee. In the next morning's paper, across the top of A Nation Challenged, was a triptych I won't forget. The most distinctive change in the paper's approach to news since Howell took over as editor was in the selection and

"Near an abandoned Taliban bunker," David Rohde wrote in the *New York Times* (November 13, 2001), "Northern Alliance soldiers dragged a wounded Taliban soldier out of a ditch today." *Tyler Hicks/New York Times*

placement of photos. Almost overnight, the paper became much more visually expressive. Here were three photos by Tyler Hicks, next to the report by David Rohde, which read:

> Near an abandoned Taliban bunker, Northern Alliance soldiers dragged a wounded Taliban soldier out of a ditch today. As the terrified man begged for his life, the alliance soldiers pulled him to his feet.
>
> They searched him and emptied his pockets. Then, one soldier fired two bursts from his rifle into the man's chest. A second soldier beat the lifeless body with his rifle butt. A third repeatedly smashed a rocket-propelled-grenade launcher into the man's head.

In this triptych of Hicks's photos, the upper-left-hand picture showed the man being dragged onto a narrow dirt road. One of our allies is pulling the man by the hand; a second Northern Alliance soldier pulls him by the foot. I wondered what his name was. Rohde probably hadn't had enough time to find out. In the second picture, the upper-right-hand corner of the triptych, you saw his face. Blood showed on his lower abdomen. He was sitting up on the ground. One man, seen on the left in the first picture, was now holding his shirt as though to pull him up. The wounded man's eyes were a gray blue. His dark hair was thinning on top and lightly streaked with gray as was his thick beard. In this picture he is not speaking, he is just looking up with his deep gray blue eyes at the men who might kill him.

The third picture was across the bottom and twice the width of the others: a panorama. Down the center is the road that crosses a level plain. In the far distance, a hazy mountain ridge. In the middle distance to the right, a crowded tank; to the left, the low mud walls of a suburban settlement. In the foreground center lies the man, in the middle of the road, so far to the fore that his right foot and buttocks are outside the frame. He is on his back. His knees are up and his hands are off the ground. A man on the right is firing into him, a man at center is firing into him, a man at the left is firing into him and smiling.

Why were the Taliban soldier's hands still in the air? Was he still alive? Or was the force of the bullets keeping his body in motion? The man in the purple trousers who had dragged him by the hand is already walking on. The description Rohde gave appeared to have left something out; at least, it was not explained. Because between the second picture and this final one the man's trousers had been pulled down. They were now around his ankles. His muscular legs are bare and there are streaks of blood running down them.

Nora and Barbara looked at the page with me, and we were both struck by the sequence. This man's family members were not *Times* readers and we showed his death. We had not showed the bodies of the dead downtown or at the Pentagon or in the Pennsylvania field. We never would. We showed them alive and happy. Today in Portraits of Grief it was Mary Rubina Sperando, thirty-nine, "known to almost everyone as Mitzi"; and Vishnoo Ramsaroop, originally of Trinidad ("when he visited the twin towers, he fell in love with their size and majesty"); and smiling Ervin Gailliard of the South Bronx, who could beat computers at chess and worked as a security guard at the Trade Center. And here was a nameless man dying in the road, in three pictures in color. We wondered—Nora, Barbara, and I—about the propriety of it. Barbara said: No, this is right. Just show it.

These kinds of horrors were still new to us; it had been thirty years since we had had to reckon with such things. The hope was that the war would be quick, and we could get on to what was fundamentally a positive agenda, as President Bush constantly reminded us. Although the United States had spurned offers of military assistance in Afghanistan, the State Department did want allies in the war's aftermath, and it wanted the help of the United Nations, which for Afghan matters was represented by the veteran Algerian diplomat Lakhdar Brahimi. "As things are moving very fast," Kofi Annan said, "we need to bring the political aspects in line with the military developments on the ground." Colin Powell emphasized that the war on terrorism should not be limited to military and police action but must include "increased support for democracy programs, judicial reform, conflict resolution, poverty alleviation, economic reform and health and education programs."

The two-month anniversary of the attacks wouldn't have meant anything to me if I hadn't got the paper that Sunday and seen a short piece by an old friend and colleague, Colson Whitehead, in the magazine section. "No matter how long you have been here, you are a New Yorker the first time you say, 'That used to be

Munsey's' or 'That used to be the Tic Toc Lounge,'" Colson wrote. "That before the Internet cafe plugged itself in, you got your shoes resoled in the mom-and-pop operation that used to be there. You are a New Yorker when what was there before is more real and solid than what is here now."

This was odd to read because the truth of it jumped out in a startling way, and because Colson himself was part of my New York. So was the building we used to work in, our cubicles pushed up against the wall, and so (for example) was the Temple Bar, where I took him for martinis when he got a column (to write about TV). Temple Bar was done up as a cramped bordello and served vast martinis. Colson's piece was about how you make New York your private city out of memories only you can have; because the city is so changeable, your private New York, in no time at all, contains a large helping of missing places, and along with its distinct vitality it has a sharper atmosphere of loss than is common elsewhere.

Colson wrote:

We can never make proper goodbyes. It was your last ride in a Checker cab, and you had no warning. It was the last time you were going to have Lake Tung Ting shrimp in that entirely suspect Chinese restaurant, and you had no idea. If you had known, perhaps you would have stepped behind the counter and shaken everyone's hand, pulled out the disposable camera and issued posing instructions. But you had no idea. . . .

I never got a chance to say goodbye to the twin towers. And they never got a chance to say goodbye to me. I think they would have liked to; I refuse to believe in their indifference. You say you know these streets pretty well? The city knows you better than any living person because it has seen you when you are alone. It saw you steeling yourself for the job interview, slowly walking home after the late date. . . . It saw you half-running up the street after you got the keys to your first apartment. It saw all that. Remembers too.

———

In Afghanistan, with the fall of Kabul, the war seemed to be winding down. Military attention shifted to Kunduz and south to Kandahar, where Mullah Omar had his headquarters and said he would make his stand. The retreat from the northern cities, he told the BBC by phone, was part of a strategy to destroy the United States. "If God's help is with us," he said, "this will happen within a short period of time. Keep in mind this prediction. The real matter is the extinction of America, and God willing, it will fall to the ground." Nonetheless, by Saturday, November 24, one large group of Taliban had surrendered and left Kunduz, supposedly with guarantees that they would be freed. Instead, they were imprisoned in a vast fortress called Qala Jangi on a fertile plain a few miles outside Mazar-i-Sharif. On Sunday morning they revolted; by that evening their old comrades in Kunduz, the last Taliban stronghold in northern Afghanistan, gave way to the alliance. There was joy in Kunduz, and a famous picture was soon taken of happy men riding in a cart. Freedom was being delivered by American arms! Max Boot's imperial vision appeared to be vindicated.

What really happened at Qala Jangi became clear only by degrees. One report had it that the prisoners had revolted in the course of being interviewed by a Western journalist. Another report said a CIA officer had been killed. The ensuing slaughter, at least, was abundantly clear. It was the worst incident yet in this odd war. Journalists were there for much of it, including Carlotta Gall of the *Times*, mainly because the nineteenth-century fortress also housed the headquarters of General Dostum, the lord of this part of Afghanistan, and, along one of the fortress's huge walls, there was a military airport where American and British special forces were stationed. For a time, at Qala Jangi, war reporting became much more intimate, more real than shaky green pantomimes and earnest stand-ups.

By midweek we learned that CIA officer Johnny Micheal "Mike" Spann, thirty-two years old, had been killed as the uprising began. Director of Central Intelligence George Tenet called Spann "an American hero." On TV we met his wife, saw the town he was from. His dad, in Winfield, Alabama, told reporters,

> When he decided to leave the military service to work for the C.I.A., he told me he did so because he felt that he would be able to make the world a better place for us to live. We recall him saying, "Someone has got to do the things no one else wants to do." That's exactly what he was doing in Afghanistan.

Dexter Filkins interviewed survivors of the uprising while James Hill took portraits of them. "The holy war of Fahad Nasir ends here," Filkins wrote from Mazar-i-Sharif, "in a filthy corner of a lonely room with a bullet in his arm. . . .

When the prison where he was taken exploded in riot, Mr. Nasir leaped its walls and raced through the streets of this city's main bazaar.

"Home," he said to himself as he weaved through the stalls in a panic. "I want to go home."

But his smooth Arab skin betrayed him. A gunshot pierced his right arm.

Today, Mr. Nasir lies on the floor of an abandoned home, wrapped in a dirty blanket, with an infection gnawing his limb and Northern Alliance guards debating his future. He has come a long way from his working-class home in Riyadh, and the pep talk from Osama bin Laden a few months before offers little succor now.

"Can I ask anything of you?" Mr. Nasir inquires of a visitor. "Before they kill me, will you please contact my parents?"

Filkins described the young men he met as seeming "less diabolical than deluded, ignorant men on a fool's journey that has landed them in a cell. Many of the men say they heeded the call of aged mullahs who told them to wage a holy war, and the men set off with little sense of where they were going or what their war was about."

Only in the next week did we learn how the uprising at Qala Jangi really began. Spann, it turned out, had been interrogating an American among the ex-defenders of Kunduz. It was almost, at this point, unsurprising. Why not have Americans on both sides? These sorts of doublings were becoming more and more common, as the special forces guys grew their beards and looked increasingly like vaguely mercenary thugs—or like Northern Alliance gunmen. Now into the story walked John Walker Lindh, the young idealist from Marin County, California, who wanted to find something to believe in. He was known as Abdul Hamid among his fellow Taliban (though back in Marin he'd asked people to call him Suleiman). Between Spann and Walker and Fahad Nasir and, I suppose, hundreds of others, there had been quite a concentration of idealists killing each other in the Qala Jangi fortress.

Newsweek got the story first. It had the videotape of Spann interrogating Walker. It had been, the *Newsweek* text read, "a bright Sunday morning."

Dozens of prisoners have been taken out of the prison and placed outside, near the center of the compound. Waiting for them are the Americans, Johnny "Mike" Spann, and another CIA agent known only as Dave. . . . Walker had

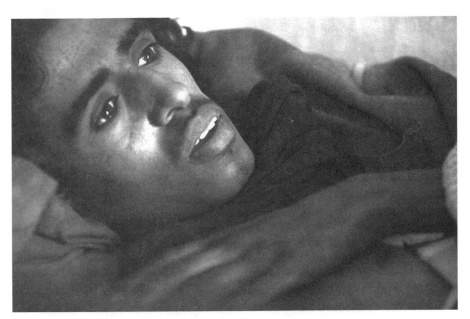

"The holy war of Fahad Nasir ends here," Dexter Filkins wrote in the *New York Times* (December 2, 2001), "in a filthy corner of a lonely room with a bullet in his arm." *James Hill*

apparently been pointed out to Spann as a Westerner, or someone who spoke English.

Spann squats down on the edge of the blanket, facing Walker.

Spann: Where are you from? You believe in what you're doing here that much, you're willing to be killed here? How were you recruited to come here? Who brought you here? Hey! [*Spann snaps his fingers in front of Walker's face. Walker is unresponsive.*]

Spann: Who brought you here? Wake up! Who brought you here to Afghanistan?

Long pause as Spann looks at Walker.

Spann: What, are you puzzled?

Spann kneels on the blanket and takes aim with a digital camera.

Spann: Put your head up. Don't make me have to get them to hold your head up. Push your hair back. Push your hair back so I can see your face.

An Afghan soldier pulls Walker's hair back, and holds his head up for the picture.

Spann: You got to talk to me. All I want to do is talk to you and find out what your story is. I know you speak English.

The other CIA agent, known only as Dave, walks up .

Dave: Mike!

Spann [to Dave]: Yeah, he won't talk to me.

Dave: OK, all right. We explained what the deal is to him.

Spann: I was explaining to the guy we just want to talk to him, find out what his story is. . . .

Spann and Dave speak, inaudible. . . .

Dave [to Spann]: The problem is, he needs to decide if he wants to live or die, and die here. We're just going to leave him, and he's going to fucking sit in prison the rest of his fucking short life. It's his decision, man. We can only help the guys who want to talk to us. We can only get the Red Cross to help so many guys. . . .

Spann [to Walker]: Do you know the people here you're working with are terrorists and killed other Muslims? There were several hundred Muslims killed in the bombing in New York City. Is that what the Quran teaches? I don't think so. Are you going to talk to us?

Walker does not respond.

Dave [to Spann]: That's all right man. Gotta give him a chance, he got his chance.

Walker was helped to his feet and returned to a group of prisoners. Shortly thereafter, some prisoners rushed the guards, throwing grenades and grabbing the guards' rifles. According to *Newsweek*, Spann was beaten and shot until he was dead. Dave got away and, with a German television crew, holed up in the fort's headquarters. *Newsweek* online had a photo of Dave, taken from German TV footage; he is holding a rifle and staring out a window. (In the original footage, you could see Dave, in conversation with the German reporter, trying over and over again to put his pistol back in its holster, and continually failing.) Dave called the American Embassy in Tashkent, Uzbekistan, to ask for assistance. Soon American planes bombarded the prison.

Back at the Op-Ed page I was having quite a week. I brought in a piece by Vince Cannistraro, a high-spirited Italian American from New England, former head of counterterrorism at the CIA, and former director of intelligence programs at the National Security Council for much of the Reagan administration. Vince assessed how the administration was doing against al Qaeda and urged the White House not to get distracted into a fight with Saddam Hussein, which Vince thought would be a disaster. The president, Rice, and Powell had begun making more noises about Hussein being their next target, and it was good to have a Reagan-era, senior ex-CIA man opposing them.

But my favorite piece was by Saad Mehio, a regular contributor to the *Daily Star* in Beirut. "So what comes after the Taliban and Osama bin Laden are finished?" he asked at the start. "Probably more Talibans and new Osama bin Ladens. That is the sad and shocking reality that we must confront."

> Basically, this phenomenon involves the immoral, unscrupulous and irreligious exploitation of Islam as a political weapon—by everyone. The West, the United States, Arab and other Muslim tyrannies have all used the weapon of Islam. And all are paying their different prices for it. . . .
>
> The policy of using political Islam as an anti-Communist tool was a crucial reason why so much of the Muslim world came to be dominated by stagnant, undemocratic but stable (so it seemed) and adequately pro-Western governments, on one hand, and the traditional forces of political Islam, reconfigured for the latter half of the 20th century, on the other. . . . State power may have been, in most cases, secular, but political hope and political mobility were left in the hands of God's representatives.
>
> After the cold war ended in 1989, and while the rest of the world was gearing up to join the march of globalization and making great strides toward democracy, liberty and human rights, the Middle East looked like a bombed-out city. More political oppression, more intellectual and cultural stagnation, more economic and social despair—and an ideological void that only the fundamentalists were able or were permitted to fill, under the demagogic banner of protecting identity and character.

Mehio hoped, in his article, for some new attitude in which these disastrous uses of Islam would end. Many Muslims had the same hope, of course, and many more still after they saw what was done in the name of their faith on September 11.

On December 9 a tape surfaced of Osama bin Laden chatting with a cleric visiting from Saudi Arabia. We watched it on the wall-mounted TV in Terry's office. Bin Laden is seated against a wall, with pillows around. His visitor arrives stage right. The soft gestures and body language, the ritual mumbled humility, and the half smile that leaves you guessing as to how much steel is behind it: the martial art of clerics.

Someone at the *Times* wrote the perfect head: "Dreams of Holy War Over a Quiet Evening." Sarah Boxer wrote the piece:

> Mr. bin Laden uses gentle hand motions to narrate. "We calculated in advance the number of casualties from the enemy," he says, raising his fingers, as if he were calculating people at a party.
>
> "We calculated that the floors that would be hit would be three or four floors," he adds, lightly hitting his upright hand, representing the tower, with the tips of the fingers of his other hand, representing the plane.

Ayman al-Zawahiri and Sulaiman Abu Ghaith are there on the tape with bin Laden.

> Bin Laden: " . . . Due to my experience in the field, I was thinking that the fire from the gas in the plane would melt the iron structure of the building and collapse the area where the plane hit and all the floors above it only. . . . This is all that we had hoped for."
>
> Sheikh: "Allah be praised."
>
> Bin Laden: "We were at (inaudible) when the event took place. We had notification since the previous Thursday that the event would take place that day. We had finished our work that day and had the radio on. It was 5:30 p.m. our time. I was sitting with Dr. Ahmad Abu-al (Khair). Immediately, we heard the news that a plane had hit the World Trade Center. We turned the radio station to the news from Washington. The news continued and (there was) no mention of the attack until the end. . . .

Earlier Abu Ghaith told how he had gone to another room to watch TV, then when he saw the attack he came back to tell bin Laden, but bin Laden "made a gesture with his hands, meaning: 'I know, I know.'"

> Bin Laden: "He [meaning Abu Ghaith] did not know about the operation. Not everybody knew (inaudible). Mohammed (Atta), from the Egyptian family (meaning the Egyptian al Qaeda group), was in charge of the group."
>
> Sheikh: "A plane crashing into a tall building was out of anyone's imagination. This was a great job. He was one of the pious men in the organization. He became a martyr. Allah bless his soul. . . ."
>
> Bin Laden: "The brothers, who conducted the operation, all they knew was that they have a martyrdom operation, and we asked each of them to go to America but they didn't know anything about the operation, not even one letter. But they were trained and we did not reveal the operation to them until they are there and just before they boarded the planes. . . ."

Then bin Laden, smiling at the tale, told of the dream of Abu Daud:

> We were at a camp of one of the brother's guards in Kandahar. This brother belonged to the majority of the group. He came close and he told me that he saw, in a dream, a tall building in America. . . . At that point, I was worried that maybe the secret would be revealed if everyone starts seeing it in a dream. So I closed the subject. I told him if he sees another dream, not to tell anybody, because people will be upset with him.

These dreams of holy war on a quiet evening: they talked about soccer games and dreams of pilots, happy dreaming men. I'd promised Becky I would call once I'd seen the tape, so I left Terry's office and phoned. She asked, "So is it proof?" I said, "It's close enough."

What stuck with me was the phrase "due to my experience in this field." What a little egotist he was, this Yemeni-Saudi plutocrat having his desert-ascetic fantasy. Mesmerizing the young men before sending them to die smiling.

The pile downtown was smaller but still burning. The three-month anniversary passed. The war itself became, to me, less interesting than the politics emerging in Washington and other capitals, including Kabul. The Afghan fight would be won but what about the peace? How serious was the administration about Iraq? How badly did the Bush administration want grandeur?

It was my job to think about this type of thing, and I was particularly focused on postwar Afghanistan's prospects when I met a journalist recently back from Mazar-i-Sharif. He talked about the special forces people there and mentioned one who was an adviser to Dostum. Something he said jogged my memory. The next morning I made several calls, then sat at my desk staring at the picture of Dave as he was under siege in Qala Jangi, his partner dead. I knew Dave. So that's who you are now, "Dave."

I had not recognized him before because it had been ten years since we were together in Uzbekistan. Now I noticed the gray in his beard. I had always liked Dave. He had introduced me to the people who made my stay in Uzbekistan possible. My visit was mostly in violation of Uzbek law; so I had to travel under the radar—no hotels, no paperwork, no contact with police, all cash. I was dependent on others for everything. Many of those people I would not have met without Dave.

He was not in the CIA at the time, in 1991. He was a student in love with Central Asia. He was bright as hell, gentle, and a hard worker. He was idealistic; we were idealistic together. It was a very different time. The Soviet Union had just recently collapsed. Optimism was in the air: for people like us, optimism about democracy and human rights, a shrinking of the nuclear threat, an end to the stagnation of the 1970s. This was before "globalization" became a term for what might be a rising tide lifting all boats, and of course it was before antiglobalization. It was before President Clinton and Fleetwood Mac singing "Don't Stop (Thinking About Tomorrow)" at the inaugural ball. It was much more Vaclav Havel, really, or middle-period Havel and late Lech Walesa. For me, it was meeting Ana Blandiana, the Romanian poet, in Bucharest before her brief political career ended. It was transiting through the Belgrade airport when Yugoslavia still existed. In the former Soviet bloc, it was a small moment in time. This was supposed to be—wanted to be—the bright beginning.

Yet it looked, already, dark in Yugoslavia and where we were, Dave and I, in Uzbekistan circa 1991. It seemed darker to me than it did to him; he teased me about that, my inability to fully share his optimism. I thought the old Communists were going to crush the opposition and spur radicalism among those young Muslim preachers who were inclined that way and generally make a hash of this whole incomparable, beautiful opportunity; and I was right, damn it. I was right about these morons and the incredible precious chance they were about to piss away. When I sent Dave my manuscript about it all and he read it, he was still resisting. Later he accepted that our moment had quickly gone. I told him I hadn't wanted things to go that way—this stupid oppression—but that was just the way it looked to me.

Our optimism had not been altogether foolish. I guess, looking back on it, that we had expected that the peoples of the world, freed from the false promises, lies, and half-truths of communism, would reach their natural state (as one thought) of reasonable coexistence with a gradual extension of health, material comfort, and mutual appreciation. But this did not occur; and it was not easy, given the intellectual tools at our disposal and given our wish to hope, to say why.

Everything I had feared for the lovely country of Uzbekistan happened, and worse still. It left Dave at loose ends. He was a true expert, but who cared about Uzbekistan anyway? It was just one of what policy people had come to call the Stans. Dave drifted into the suburbs of CIA-land, then into the real deal.

Now here we were: me at my desk, nearing the end of 2001, hoping my colleagues didn't notice how preoccupied I was staring at this photo; and Dave with an automatic rifle in his hands, looking out the window at a massacre people said he and his colleague Spann had caused. Watching it, determined to survive. "The problem is, he needs to decide if he wants to live or die, and die here." Was that really you, Dave, saying that? Little did you know. Were you determined to survive with your hopes intact for a better world?

How strange to meet you again, in this place! How did we get here, Dave? How did we get here—and how can we get out?

IV

THE LAST AMERICAN ERA

wish I could paint the picture of a new and better era. *The New Yorker*'s cover for the New Year showed an almost sad-eyed baby, representing 2002, drawing sketch after sketch of what could be built where the twin towers had been. Pictures were rising around the city. A group of artists painted a block-long mural in Sunnyside, Queens, showing the flag, firefighters, whirling smoke, the curving fragment of the Trade Center, an eagle. A similar set of painted images overlooked the elementary school playground where my kids soon would learn to ride bikes. Ceramic works began to cover a fence and wall along Seventh Avenue in the Village. A starry nightscape—with the twin towers textured like the surface of a bright moon—looked over Cooper Square, the stars drawn rather like a thick snow so that they all seemed to be slowly falling. In SoHo, the gallery Exit Art had selected twenty-five hundred pieces, each the size of a sheet of paper, by as many artists, from famous to unknown, in a show called Reactions. The organizers promised every piece would get its chance to be seen. The same was going on with the "here is new york" project, which showed photographs in a one-story building on Sixth Avenue that would soon be torn down. There were murals and shows all over town; one I found entirely by chance, with poems and images, in the lobby of a German bank.

The snaps of our dead neighbors, the Portraits of Grief, ceased being a daily feature of the *Times* while ground zero became less ours and more of a picture or tableau: a viewing platform had been built of wood. On the cold December morning the platform opened, the bells at St. Paul's rang "The First Noel"—we had just made it, straggling, through Christmas—and people waited in a line six blocks long for their chance to tramp up the long ramp of boards and look over the site, a dozen at a time.

The childish pictures, sent by school classes, that had decorated the *Times's* cafeteria were taken down. Similar pictures were disappearing from the city's walls. Moira Smith was still smiling at my subway stop, though; no trace of her yet.

The fires hadn't gone out. In my mind I had a set of images I wanted to paint: black rectangles and red emerging around them. Not very imaginative, but then I wasn't a painter, just as the hundreds of people who sent us poetry were not poets. You wanted to put what you were feeling into some form. Maybe it was better done without great refinement. A painter friend, Bob Baker, told me to sketch the pictures in my mind right away or they'd go. He said he hadn't been able to find any way of painting what he was feeling. I did not take his advice—who had the time?—but I also found that the images were not going away. Sometimes they were all I could think about, black rectangles and red, in the shades Paul Klee used at the end of his life. My friend Lloyd Stevens had been unable to paint since September 11, but lately he had begun making pictures, on big canvases, of empty chairs. They were in colors similar to those of Henri Matisse if Matisse had been from the Caribbean. Soon Lloyd was painting empty chairs on beaches, then sometimes an empty chair appearing to float away: images of a lonely prettiness that gently shredded the heart. Lloyd said these were all he could think to paint and that painting them made him feel better. He lived a few blocks from ground zero.

Really it was extraordinary all the things people sent in to us at the Op-Ed page, not just poems but many, many pictures and photos. I kept one. It showed three smiling young women at a corner table at Windows on the World, at the top of the Trade Center. They had big shoulders—perhaps they were on the swim team—and rosy glows, a camera on the table, a glass of white wine, and two red drinks that might have been vodka-cranberries or Bloody Marys, just the sort of drinks such young women would have had on a trip to the big city. It was bright out behind them. On the back of the photo was: "Took picture of group of girls at another Table at the Windows of the World Rest on the 107th floor of the World Trade Center on Sept 8, 2001."

This picture was like a hole in time. There was something about it that defied expression. The photo became significant because of what happened in that room three days later. Now the red chairs with their worn upholstery, the wine glasses, plates, cutlery, walls, and windows were gone, fallen down. The girls, almost certainly, by chance had been spirited away out of their chairs and were now alive. What was inexpressible, to me, was the sense that their being alive could feel unusual, that death had, rather stealthily, become the rule and life the exception. To me this view of death as the norm was a point I did not want to reach, and it just played havoc with time. It made both remembering and forgetting lose their coherence so that I could not always know which one I was doing. These three girls in their pre-death state, faces flushed: to really remember that moment would seem to require forgetting what was about to happen in the room; but to remember what happened on September 11 seemed to consume and destroy one's memory of what it could have been like three days before on their visit to the big city. There wasn't enough space left in time for all the possibilities.

As the past fragmented, then compulsively rearranged itself, then fragmented again, the Bush administration sought to impose a plotline on the future. The plotline had a gentle part (development aid, democracy promotion), a brutal part (war, torture, and assassination), and a combination of the two in a diplomatic effort that demanded strict obedience to American leadership in the name of common values. Feeling it had triumphed in Afghanistan, the White House, too, wanted to picture a new era. It believed other countries would follow it into that new era.

President Bush and some in his administration had such strong optimistic streaks. Their idealism had not found a focus in the beginning months of their power. The turning point for President Bush—the point at which, as Fred Barnes had said, his administration found a purpose—was the attack of September 11. This basic reality underlay the president's State of the Union address to Congress at the end of January and determined the logic of its distinctive fears and idealism.

"None of us would ever wish the evil that was done on September 11," President Bush said, "yet after America was attacked, it was as if our entire country looked into a mirror, and saw our better selves . . . This time of adversity offers a unique moment of opportunity, a moment we must seize to change our culture. . . ."

He had two ideas of national mobilization. One of them—"My call tonight is for every American to commit at least two years . . . to the service of your neighbors and your nation"—was based on everyone snapping to attention and marching forth to Do Good. It was an echo of his speech in Atlanta on November 8, 2001, the one that was preempted by *Family Guy* and *Survivor* and had urged us onward to "a million acts of responsibility and decency and service." (As he had said then and implied again now, "Afghanistan is only the beginning of our efforts in the world.")

This repeated call to service: wasn't it bound to bring disappointment to the president and anyone else who took it seriously? And wasn't there something authoritarian about calling on every American to serve the nation for at least two years? Of course, we were allowed the option, and most would take it, of ignoring the president's call, just as most of us had ignored it two months earlier. That did not remove the fact that he was trying to tell every American what to do.

The president's second idea for national mobilization was a long war, fought by us and paid for by us. ("It costs a lot to fight this war. We have spent more than a billion dollars a month, over $30 million a day, and we must be prepared for future operations.") He did not ask for our support in this war, he just assumed it.

And he made it clear that anything less than complete ongoing support would threaten the nation, for the speech was soaked in an intense fear. Time, the president said, "is not on our side. I will not wait on events while dangers gather. I will not stand by as peril draws closer and closer."

The source of this fear was perhaps obvious: our enemies, who had killed us and wanted to kill more of us. They had to be found and stopped. But I thought the fear had a second source, impossible to eliminate—namely, the knowledge that Americans were not all going to volunteer their two years; that they were, like all people, in fact materialistic and selfish and fearful and weak. Their better selves were not their whole selves.

The fear of this fact—that Americans are not all that special—is a powerful one, for it constantly threatens the legitimacy of the exercise of American power, particularly for conservatives. Liberals will speak of American institutions and explicit principles as sources of American greatness; conservatives are more personal, looking to an idea of the American character. When the American people let them down—as will always happen, at some point—conservatives fall hard. The way Bush's remarks were worded anticipated this: "We've been offered a unique opportunity, and we must not let this moment pass. . . . This time of adversity offers a unique moment of opportunity, a moment we must seize to change our culture." But why, if we are so special, did we need so desperately to change our culture? And why the jittery worry that the moment for this transformation was so delicate we might lose it?

Finally—this was the worst of it—were we really such a ghastly people, we Americans, that the experience of being slaughtered followed by flying off to slaughter our enemies had to be "a unique moment of opportunity"? The whole notion seemed so intellectually and emotionally severed. The calm of it, so weirdly expressed (you call that an *opportunity*?), had to be deceptive. I wondered if there wasn't some permanent fury behind it. Our enemies alone were not big enough to justify this.

Certainly, the administration's emotional state could not have been put in starker terms. The speech had three basic points: evil exists, God is with us, freedom is powerful. States such as Iraq, Iran, and North Korea, the president said,

> constitute an axis of evil, arming to threaten the peace of the world. . . . Our enemies believed America was weak and materialistic, that we would splinter in fear and selfishness. They were as wrong as they are evil. . . . Those of us who have lived through these challenging times have been changed by them. We've come to know truths that we will never question: Evil is real, and it must be opposed. . . . And many have discovered again that even in tragedy, especially in tragedy, God is near. . . . We have known freedom's price. We have shown freedom's power. And in this great conflict, my fellow Americans, we will see freedom's victory. Thank you all and may God bless.

I hoped we wouldn't go over the line into believing that evil is "other people," God prefers us, and freedom is power. We were, after all, a democracy of imperfect people, not a tribe and not a cult. Bush seemed not to realize that if we were, indeed, a people chosen by God (or at least by nature or history), then our virtues could not be easily shared. They would not be so universal or accessible. As a candidate, Bush had been criticized (as his father had been) for lacking a vision. Now he had one, and I wished he hadn't.

———

The "axis of evil" speech, as it was immediately known, got some support, but it also sparked alarm and ridicule. This was partly owing to its religiosity, which could have the shocking effect of making Bush sound faintly like bin Laden, who was thought to be still out there somewhere bingeing on God in a cave. It was one thing for our nation to be under God, quite another to be *for* God. And Bush's religiosity was itself a puzzle. It made an interesting contrast with that of his predecessor. Bill Clinton's faith was down-home Southern, working- and middle-class Protestantism: love the sinner, hate the sin. Bush's belief seemed more to be: hate sinners, hate sin, save your love for the good people. This was not so much religion as an instrumental creed. (You didn't really need religion to help you in the easy work of loving what is good.) Such a creed implied that Bush would tend to pick hard means over soft, when it came down to a choice; that's the direction in which hatred for sinners always leads.

Bill Clinton was, in the Christian sense, a worldly man. He might have thought he was smarter than you, but he never gave you the sense he thought he was any better. His imperfections were crucial to his democratic credentials and appeal. Clinton's political warmth seemed to thrive on mundane human fallibility. Bush's did not: his modesty and warmth could go cold so quickly; his sympathy was for (some) victims, not sinners. I supposed this might have been a result of his northeastern, Anglo-Saxon, well-to-do roots.

I also imagined it had to do with his addiction. There is a distinctly American insatiability, which Clinton embodied in every way: passionate, sloppy, changeable, nimbly defensive, repentant, helpless. Bush was not that different, perhaps. But he had had to overcome. He actually had been an addict—at least, he genuinely believed he had been—so he knew what that meant and he knew how much it took to keep it under control. You have to will yourself into accepting that your will is not enough. Often, and seemingly in his case, you have to believe fervently in God in order to be saved from yourself. It requires a clean break with your addiction. Allowing yourself to perceive shades of gray may seem perilously close to Just

One Little Drink. I had sometimes thought the early Bush administration's ferocious anti-Clintonism was in part owing to the sense of a real, dangerous psychic closeness between the two presidents along precisely these lines—the passion they brought to managing their desires.

The relevance of a president's personality is hard to assess. In the case of Bush, his individual character seemed to me of unusual importance. His administration was divided, which heightened the effects of his preferences and moods. His party was weak, fragmented, and adrift, and so was the opposition party; this increased his personal power. The leading issue of the day was war. Congress had apparently decided, at last, that war was an entirely executive branch affair; so Bush's personal wishes had an outsize weight. The vice president, moreover, and others had a theory of enlarged presidential power (the "unitary executive" theory) that they were working to advance where possible, while some of the president's lawyers were quietly parsing the laws of war with an eye toward maximizing the reach of presidential power.

Finally, the ideological camps—particularly regarding foreign policy—of American life had become indistinct. Some sincere people (right, left, and center) were growing more interventionist and much less respectful of the sovereignty and cultural distinctness of other nations, a trend the Bush administration was taking over from its predecessor. Others were becoming more rigidly, even mystically pacifist. Many others were simply unable to develop a lasting opinion. Potentially, all this left President Bush in command of the field. In the axis of evil speech, he was attempting to take American power after September 11 and shape it into a form he understood, liked, and thought he could control.

To me the axis of evil speech was an apex; one could only descend. It seemed like a spasm of furious, contradictory self-love as we tried to deal with the terror of our vulnerability and the terror of our own power. This had become a very American experience and a lonely one, for no other people were in a position to feel this way or even come close: America really is exceptional. From such strange heights we had to descend, as any people would, to surer ground.

I was hoping for a soft, smart landing into something Eisenhowerian. The Bush administration could take its victory in Afghanistan and run with it, pursuing fresher enemies and the unmatched thrills of benign omnipotence; or, as Eisenhower's administration did, it could calm down, and deliberate, and build. I had no great love for Dwight Eisenhower but President Bush said that he did, and he could have done worse. Eisenhower may have been our last president who was as much wise as smart. He had known war and he had known peace, as in his phrase "that yet more hopeful spring of 1945, bright with the promise of victory and freedom." Eisenhower was speaking in 1953, at the beginning of his presidency, and looking back. "The hope of all just men in that moment too was a just and lasting peace. The eight years that have passed have seen that hope waver, grow dim, and almost die."

We, too, had just had a war, in Afghanistan. Now we had peace there. I thought we ought to try and keep it from dying.

In 1953, Eisenhower told his listeners that the way chosen by the United States

was plainly marked by a few clear precepts. . . . First: No people on earth can be held, as a people, to be an enemy, for all humanity shares the common hunger for peace and fellowship and justice.

Second: No nation's security and well-being can be lastingly achieved in isolation but only in effective cooperation with fellow-nations.

Third: Every nation's right to a form of government and an economic system of its own choosing is inalienable.

Fourth: Any nation's attempt to dictate to other nations their form of government is indefensible. . . .

This way was faithful to the spirit that inspired the United Nations: to prohibit strife, to relieve tensions, to banish fears.

It certainly was a different time, 1953! Eisenhower had a special hatred for the waste of military spending. ". . . [E]very rocket fired signifies, in the final sense, a theft from those who hunger and are not fed. . . ," he said.

Was this the Greatest Generation? Since September 11, I had sifted through countless Op-Ed submissions arguing that the United States uniquely had the strength and moral fiber to defeat terrorism. Ritual reference was made to the Greatest Generation pushing back the monster of fascism—and to the risks of appeasement and letting dangers gather. The sudden profusion of references to Neville Chamberlain and the League of Nations at least implied some recognition of what a mixed bag the Greatest Generation really was: the generation that embraced fascism, as well as the generation that destroyed it. As Winston Churchill said to Parliament, on the third of four days of debate about Britain's 1938 agreement with Adolf Hitler, signed by Prime Minister Chamberlain in Munich, "[T]he terrible words have for the time being been pronounced against the Western democracies: 'Thou art weighed in the balance and found wanting.'"

Churchill was, with Eisenhower, a particular hero to President Bush, and the inflamed language of their war had many echoes in the aftermath of September 11. But what stood out for me, in looking back on that period, was not just the resolve of such men but, as in the cases of Churchill and Eisenhower, their awareness of their own complicity in the making of their enemies. Indeed, some of the braver arguments for war against Nazism came from Neville Chamberlain himself, who had brought the Munich agreement home to cheering crowds (that part is sometimes forgotten). By mid-March 1939, as Czechoslovakia fell to the Nazis, Chamberlain had realized his mistake. "Every man and woman in this country who remembers the fate of the Jews and the political prisoners in Austria must be filled today with distress and foreboding," he said in Birmingham. He mentioned, to loud cheers, "the liberty that we have enjoyed for hundreds of years, and which we will never surrender. That I, of all men, should feel called upon to make such a declaration—that is the measure of the extent to which these events have shattered the confidence which was just beginning to show its head"—namely, his own confidence that peace could be achieved without war. Chamberlain declared war on Germany that September.

These sorts of complications—the mature, public admission of error, for example, and even the recognition of one's involvement in the rise of one's enemy—were altogether missing from President Bush's rhetoric and indeed from most commentary on the war, whether for or against. The years 1938, 1941, 1953 were not simpler times, and the men and women who distinguished themselves in those years were not simpler people. The whole Greatest Generation obsession amounted to a pretty spectacular form of denial, a denial of the realities of the war years and the Cold War that was shaped by them, and maybe a denial of the simple realities of war itself.

All the generation talk failed to mention rebellion: the rebellious jazz and poetry and rock 'n' roll of the fifties, the careening rebellions of the sixties. Yet this was where so much of our "soft power" (Joseph Nye's phrase) came from. This power was in the freedom to oppose power; to scream and rant; to mock and expose the protean complacency of power. Americans, we should remember, exported anti-Americanism. This was when so many abroad really fell in love with us and our freedom.

There had been a grandeur to the defeat of the Taliban, if you closed your eyes to the horrors and focused on women being able to go to school again and children to fly kites. You could concentrate on the giddiness of liberation from tyranny and identify a bright future. Victory would create its own momentum. More tyrannies would fall. This would happen both at the point of a gun and as a result of enlightened international encouragement.

For some, the question was whether this would amount to a revival of imperialism. Certainly a new, benevolent imperialism was in the air. Just days after the axis of evil speech came the Davos conference—the annual World Economic Forum—held in New York rather than Switzerland as a gesture of solidarity against terrorism. This year the Davos organizers had reached out to "civil society" and development people to join the usual lineup of big-business leaders and politicians. The idea was that these days we were all on the same side—a disarming sort of solidarity, when you saw it bring together (attempting to bring together) the pharmaceutical company heads, third world feminists, Saudi intelligence, American Express, and "people's bankers." Disarming, too, to know that this was partly an effect of those planes hitting the towers.

When Colin Powell and Treasury Secretary O'Neill spoke at Davos, each emphasized the United States' absolute autonomy in political and economic policy—and each also emphasized, as Powell put it, that "terrorism really flourishes in areas of poverty, despair and hopelessness, where people see no future. . . . We have to show people who might move in the direction of terrorism that there is a better way."

Michael Ignatieff came down for the Davos conference from Harvard, where he was teaching human rights—it had become a legitimate academic subject lately. He was not the usual type of Davos invitee. His invitation was part of the corporate reaching out. We had a cup of coffee in the *Times*'s cafeteria on the eleventh floor, overlooking the fading billboard for the musical *42nd Street*. We gabbed about human rights and our jobs and that sort of thing. Soon he had to leave for a Davos roundtable on something and, as the elevator door shut, said with a wry smile, "Pray for me."

I almost did; for we were at a turning point. If human rights, economic development, and peace were to advance, one felt one had to get near power. Yet who knew what the consequences of engaging with tangible power might be? Thus: "Pray for me."

I had just edited a piece by Ignatieff on human rights, and it included these lines: "Rome has been attacked, and Rome is fighting to re-establish its security and its hegemony. This may permanently demote human rights in the hierarchy of America's foreign policy priorities." The attribution of Romanness to the United States would have offended many a year earlier, but it didn't now, just as talk of benign imperialism had become possible. "Imperial" was no longer automatically a term of abuse, perhaps rather as "capitalist" had become acceptable around 1989. A few public figures were even willing to call themselves neo-imperialists. The *Times* was thinking about doing a series on empire, if it could find a way to talk about the subject.

A year before, the Italian Antonio Negri and the American Michael Hardt published a scholarly book called, simply, *Empire*. A scattershot and contradictory work of provocation, written as if by militant New Left librarians, it became a best seller. "Just as in the first century of the Christian era the Roman senators asked Augustus to assume imperial powers of the administration for the public good," Hardt and Negri wrote, "so too today the international organizations (the United Nations, the international monetary organizations, and even the humanitarian organizations) ask the United States to assume the central role in a new world order. . . . This is perhaps one of the central characteristics of Empire—that is, it resides in a world context that continually calls it into existence." In other words, our world requires empire. The book was written from the political Left, and made a best seller in great part by the antiglobalization movement.

From the Right came Max Boot with a book-length expansion of the pro-imperialist argument he had made so soon after September 11. In *The Savage Wars of Peace: Small Wars and the Rise of American Power*, Boot presented a quick tour of small twentieth-century wars undertaken by the United States to argue that they were mostly to the good, and decently motivated, and therefore Washington should not be shy about undertaking more such wars in the future.

It was, then, unsurprising when Sebastian Mallaby announced that "a new imperial moment has arrived" and that it was, on balance, a good thing. An eloquent, informed advocate—on the *Washington Post*'s opinion page—of increased foreign aid and development-oriented trade policies, Mallaby was able, without contradiction, to support an aggressive military policy for intervening in problematic states. It was the lack of contradiction that was new. There actually could be a consensus on building a humanitarian empire. "The logic of neoimperialism is too compelling for the Bush administration to resist," Mallaby wrote. "The chaos in the world is too threatening to ignore, and existing methods for dealing with that chaos have been tried and found wanting."

Would this be our role in the world? *Wall Street Journal* columnist Gerald F. Seib wrote, in the course of presenting an interview with Brent Scowcroft:

Forty years ago, the world's 20 richest nations had a per-capita gross domestic product 18 times higher than that in the world's 20 poorest countries. The most recent statistics indicate the rich countries' GDP now is 37 times higher. About 1.2 billion people around the world live on less than $1 a day. . . . This situation doesn't really explain the attacks of 9/11, of course, but it can breed the same kinds of resentments that spurred them. . . .

So what's the U.S. to do? In the Scowcroft view, it needs to do more than defend itself; it needs to become actively engaged, along with its allies, in helping the world develop in a more healthy way. . . . "The president personally has got the right feeling about it," says Mr. Scowcroft, adviser to four Republican presidents. "His party isn't there yet." But Republicans, and the rest of the country, have little choice.

It gave me a certain hope. The agile coordination of alliances and a frank recognition of global inequities and the need to correct them—and an understanding that, as Franklin Roosevelt had said in his Four Freedoms speech, "freedom means the supremacy of human rights everywhere"—might be the future. Why not? None of it was all that difficult, arcane, or expensive. Not $30-million-a-day expensive. Not accidentally bombing-the-family expensive, or Qala Jangi bullet-in-the-back expensive. Not the begging, soon-dead-man-on-the-road-to-Kabul expensive. Maybe Dave could put that gun down. Hadn't the president himself vowed, after September 11, to "defeat the terrorists by building an enduring prosperity that promises more opportunity and better lives for all the world's people"?

Maybe there could be an Eisenhower project of some kind, as a use of our power? The United Nations had a development summit coming up in March in Monterrey, Mexico, and I worked with Kofi Annan's communications chief, Edward Mortimer, on an Op-Ed for the secretary-general concerning the importance of development. I pressed Mortimer to have Annan acknowledge the administration's pro-development, pro-good-governance tendencies, and to frame his argument so as to draw out the administration's better angels. It wasn't much, but it was something: an alternative to all the war talk.

At Monterrey, the administration increased its foreign aid commitment by several billion dollars. Bush made it abundantly clear that money would not be paid out unless recipient governments would spend it wisely, which was reasonable enough. The proof would come in the practice.

Walking around Brooklyn and Manhattan I would be surprised by the white lights. Like the towers themselves, they could pierce the lowest layer of clouds and keep right on going. They were illuminated on March 11, huge lights where the Trade Center's towers had been. I know the neighbors complained, but those lights were perfect. They were unassuming when you came upon them like this, quietly at night, when you were alone, like they were.

In a neurotic city that rusts quickly, something had actually worked just right, no fuss. This intangible monument, soon gone, was like a curtain call for Colson Whitehead's buildings—the ones he said remember you—our towers back for one more performance.

Work at the Op-Ed page was back to something like normal. In fact, I noticed we were returning to issues (whither the deficit, Arctic oil drilling) that we had been treating at the same time last year. We were treading lightly around the Iraq story until a *Times* consensus emerged: the editorial board was temporizing, waiting for more evidence; the newsroom's investigative capacity, meanwhile, was not being fully exploited, in large part because both the White House and the Iraqis were, for their different reasons, unwilling to grant access to the *Times*. And the *Times*'s journalistic practice depended on access. Geopolitically, as an institution, we were waiting.

This immobility on a key question of the day was frustrating, and in office conversations I tried to find the reasons for it. There were many personnel factors involved, of course, but there was also a larger story that was basically political and economic. The *Times*'s very high social status, painstakingly built up since the 1960s, had, in the past few years, become endangered. The paper had always easily withstood criticisms from the political Left, which had no important constituencies among either voters or readers. Criticisms from the Right were a different matter. The country's center of political gravity had been shifting rightward since the election of Ronald Reagan in 1980. The *Times*'s reaction to this was not to shift right (or left) but to insist on a certain centrist rectitude. The paper's constant emphasis on objectivity and balance reinforced its claim to be the setter of standards and the pole around which others must revolve. The growth of the paper in breadth of coverage and geographical reach—the company bought production facilities across the continent in a bid to become the national paper of record—reflected business ambitions and no small will to power. It also reflected the deep belief of the Sulzberger family, which owned the *Times*, in the social mission of their company, a belief that I, just as most *Times* employees in my experience, respected and shared, however critical we might sometimes be.

This positioning of the *Times* as a national media power and a national arbiter did, however, make it the target of choice for the conservative movement. That movement—its politicians, activists, and media adherents, particularly in talk radio and later on cable TV and the Internet—developed a durable hatred for the *Times* and aimed its jabs at the company's core claims of objectivity and balance.

The conservative offensive might not have affected the paper all that much except that the *Times* continued to be, politically, somewhat peripheral. The alienation of the *Times* from Washington continued even under the Clinton administration, with which leading personalities at the *Times* had an extremely contentious and complicated relationship.

But the real threat to the *Times* was economic rather than political. They were related: what began politically, with the talk radio of Rush Limbaugh, ended economically and technologically with the growth of the Web. What began as a threat to the authority of the *Times* ended as a very real threat to its viability as a business. In 2002, it was already becoming clear to Arthur Sulzberger, Jr., the publisher, and to Howell Raines, the editor, that the paper was going to have to shift its revenue model toward exploitation of the Web. The nature of our journalistic enterprise would also have to change. The Web was where the future competition would take place, and it was quite unsuited to the kind of resource-intensive information gathering, rigor, and authority that were central to the paper's brand and its sense of itself. The Web appeared to be best suited to something like talk radio—endless commentary (left as well as right) aimed at undermining the media establishment. And the *Times* was, of course, very much part of the media establishment, even as that establishment's "mind share" (a Web term of the day) shrank.

In short, the political and economic trends were running against the paper at the very moment when it was trying to develop a position on the possible invasion of Iraq. The paper's influence and income were starting to decline and were constantly under attack. The Bush White House did not much care what the *Times* thought. Neither did the president's many supporters; quite the contrary. And there were risks to opposing the push toward war with Iraq, whether editorially or by putting more resources into investigating the administration's pro-war claims. Opposition would have invited yet more charges of nonobjectivity. Worse still, perhaps, it would have meant initiating a break with the executive branch of government and accepting a period of being out in the cold when things were already getting pretty chilly, both in business and in politics.

This all created a pervasive atmosphere of indecision and a certain vacuum of authority. Into this vacuum happily stepped the extraordinary figure of Judy Miller. Hard working and extremely competitive, she was, unlike most *Times* reporters, well regarded within the White House. She had an expertise in weapons of mass destruction and in Iraqi matters; she had coauthored *Saddam Hussein and the Crisis in the Gulf*, which had been a best seller. Her coauthor was the same Laurie Mylroie who had dedicated herself in recent years to pushing the theory that Saddam Hussein was behind the first bombing of the World Trade Center in 1993 as well as other acts of terror. This somewhat nutty argument, in the relatively lighthearted days before September 11, had of course played a real role among the small group of people who obsessed about Iraq. Miller was likewise accepted by this same group: Lewis Libby, John Bolton, and, most important, the handful of Iraqi exiles who were the main conduits for the intelligence describing Hussein's weapons programs.

Given the lack of information coming out of Iraq, these exiles assumed an outsized importance. Most intelligence professionals were very skeptical about them (as they tend to be about all exiles, who are, by their nature, political salesmen). But the Iraqi exiles had steadfast friends within the Pentagon and the White House; and this was the milieu that fed Miller her information. Editors at the *Times*, with little else to report on this crucial topic—and unwilling to do daily battle with one of their few reporters who had access to fresh information—gave Miller's undersourced reports great prominence. Fear of what Donald Rumsfeld called unknown unknowns was seeping into our journalistic system. It made self-assurance and decisiveness, which Miller had in abundance, more impressive than they were in normal times.

Indecision was not unique to the *Times*. In handling Op-Eds, attending board meetings, and so forth, I was able to discuss Iraq—usually off the record—with heads of state and foreign ministers, intelligence experts, senior administration officials, arms inspectors, and members of Congress, and the plain fact was that, across this group, the general unwillingness to be led by President Bush was overmatched by an unwillingness to be led by anyone else or to press decisively in any alternative direction. The seemingly intractable vagueness of the information about terrorism on the whole, and Iraq in particular, only intensified this pervasive indecisiveness. The rest of the major media were either gearing up for war on ideological grounds or sitting on the same fence as the *Times*. So, in its own way, was Congress (and, differently, the United Nations). All these big institutions were waiting for a push, which the Bush administration was all too willing to give. It was running the sole superpower. It was on a winning streak. It expected to go on winning. Who was to say it wouldn't?

As we made the turn into the spring of 2002 the last bits of the Trade Center were being sifted through at the edge of a landfill on Staten Island. The team on what was called the Hill had been through 1.6 million tons of material. Only 25,000 to go. Dan Barry reported that the sifters had found more than 4,100 body parts, helping identify more than 150 of the dead. Every bit of the Pile (as it was known) either went onto a conveyor belt or was spread across a field to be raked through. A couple of people, usually police officers, sat and watched the chunks go by on the conveyor belt. Whenever they saw something that might be significant, say, an earring, hair, or a photo, they would put it in a black bucket.

The guys at Engine 226 had got rid of the temporary memorials and built a sturdy one out of red metal and glass. It had photos of Dave, Stan, Lieutenant Bob, and Brian. There was a book, with a page describing each man, and room alongside for candles. The memorial was constructed to stand up to the weather. I wondered how long it would be there. Next they would make a memorial wall inside, something more permanent than Al's handwritten list.

At the end of May an elaborate ceremony occurred to mark the removal of the last girder of the Trade Center. It was a peculiar rite, overwrought, almost comically pompous, yet also utterly touching and right and so human—the holy relic, splinter of the cross, temple wall, tomb of Ali, remains of the saint—so primitive, pathetic, physical, naked.

Late May was also when the administration decided to scare the hell out of us. I started keeping a file labeled The Fear. On a Sunday, Vice President Cheney said, "The prospects of a future attack against the United States are almost certain." The next day, the FBI director said suicide attacks against us were "inevitable," and the day after that Defense Secretary Rumsfeld said terrorists would "inevitably" be obtaining weapons of mass destruction. As usual, some of the expected targets were right nearby: Brooklyn Bridge, Statue of Liberty. This was as irritating as it was scary. We had heard similar warnings before, delivered in solemn tones, and nothing had happened. Since there wasn't anything more, not one single thing, that we as individuals could do to make ourselves safer, these warnings seemed abusive at best, politically opportunistic at worst. They weren't doing the administration's credibility any good, either. The White House's apparent fears were becoming unbelievable; yet its residents appeared to have grown quite attached to them.

The administration's obsession with Iraq made all this significantly more worrying. It seemed like an obsession because there had been no convincing facts offered to support an aggressive strategy against Iraq, and because the administration had been so visibly, frantically trying to establish links between Iraq and terrorism—and failing. When the anthrax attacks came, the administration searched high and low for Iraqi ties and came up empty. The reports of a meeting between Mohammed Atta and an Iraqi agent in Prague looked extremely weak. Yes, there was a tiny group of militants holed up in a valley in northeastern Iraq, some of whom might have trained in al Qaeda camps, but the truth was they threatened no one except some nearby Kurds. Pentagon intelligence was working overtime to get evidence of an al Qaeda link to one thing or another. It, too, was failing. The CIA, meanwhile, clearly thought evidence churning was a bit beneath it and, in any case, didn't share the enthusiasm of Pentagon civilians for an Iraq war.

By this time it seemed to me that the administration was not really interested in the al Qaeda link as such. It just wanted the link to be true so it could use it to legitimate the goal of removing Saddam Hussein from power. This made the administration's vague assertions of a link hard to believe, just as its warnings of imminent terrorist attack were hard to believe.

Over the summer, the emphasis shifted heavily to arguing that Iraq still had programs to develop weapons of mass destruction. With this emphasis, the administration seemed to believe that it didn't have to worry any longer about proving its case for removing Saddam Hussein; instead, it was up to Iraq to disprove that case. For a closed tyranny to make itself entirely open to highly suspicious and demanding foreigners seemed unlikely. Therefore, Iraq, by doing nothing much, could be said to be inviting attack.

It seemed to me there were two ways to block the movement toward war. One was to influence the president; the other was to slow the process down with UN machinery and hope for the best. On August 15, a fax came through from Brent Scowcroft's office, with a thought-you-might-find-this-interesting note attached.

The piece was from that morning's *Wall Street Journal* and headlined "Don't Attack Saddam."

I was really getting to like Brent Scowcroft, even though he had sent his piece to the *Journal* rather than to us. (And fair enough: given the *Journal's* conservative bent, it would have more effect there.) The Op-Ed was strong in its central point that attacking Iraq would weaken the war on terrorism because it would alienate countries whose help we needed against terrorists. Scowcroft also advocated having the Security Council insist on a new weapons inspection regime.

I called James Baker's office and asked if he would care to write an article on the same topic. His assistant said no. I called again. I sent pleading e-mails. By the end of the week the piece was in. That day, Gen. Anthony Zinni, former head of U.S. Central Command and a Mideast adviser to the administration, urged caution on Iraq, as had Gen. Norman Schwarzkopf, who had run the Gulf War. "All the generals see this the same way," Zinni said, "and all those that never fired a shot in anger are really hell-bent to go to war." Baker's piece came out on Sunday, the twenty-fifth. He argued sturdily for building an alliance for war through the Security Council. He also, like Scowcroft, wrote in such a way that he neither advocated nor rejected war itself. Henry Kissinger had done much the same thing in a long *Washington Post* Op-Ed, to such a degree that he had convinced both sides that he supported them.

When Richard Perle, contacted at his home in France, described Scowcroft as "naive," I thought the game might be won. It was silly to describe Scowcroft as naive, and it was the kind of insult George H. W. Bush and his circle would not take lightly. The president's father had no public position, but it seemed he would have to be in accord with Baker and Scowcroft. That was a formidable lobby, made up of men whose opinions should have mattered to this president and who had all played key roles in the Gulf War. Rather a lot, too much, depended on the president's relations with his father.

Dick Cheney had been active in the Gulf War too, however, as secretary of defense, and he was now vice president, and he was not overly impressed by the lions of the elder Bush's administration. He counterattacked on Monday, August 26, with what he must have thought was his strongest argument. He flatly said Saddam Hussein "will acquire nuclear weapons fairly soon." He said, "There is no doubt that Saddam Hussein now has weapons of mass destruction. There is no doubt that he is amassing them to use against our friends, against our allies and against us." He mentioned in passing that "a return of inspectors would provide no assurance whatsoever of his compliance with U.N. resolutions."

Cheney was speaking in Nashville, Tennessee, to the 103rd National Conference of the Veterans of Foreign Wars. Some in the audience, he noted, had fought in World War II. He referred to "the Axis powers" and how the attack on Pearl Harbor had exacted a high price for America's failure to engage the gathering enemy: "Only then did we recognize the magnitude of the danger to our country." It was the axis of evil story again, this set of overlapping, mythical maps of our history and our destiny. Was everyone in the grip of some Oedipal struggle with the Greatest Generation? Appeasement–fascism–Pearl Harbor–war–victory–Marshall Plan. On top of that, somehow, were al Qaeda and September 11. We had appeased al Qaeda—"we" included the present administration, presumably—but we had rallied ourselves and fought back. Then the metaphorical mapping went awry. Iraq was meant to be a gathering danger, a potential Pearl Harbor or potential September 11, except that the vice president had offered no new evidence that this was so and presumably had none. Iraq had not perceptibly changed for several years. So what was new? What had changed?

What had changed were the perception of the threat and the ambition of projecting our power, an ambition encouraged by the evident ease of the victory in Afghanistan. Saddam Hussein was perceived as more threatening because terrorism was seen as more threatening—because the world was seen as more threatening. Cheney's Nashville speech had a fascinating passage: "If the United States could have preempted 9/11, we would have, no question. Should we be able to prevent another, much more devastating attack, we will, no question. This nation will not live at the mercy of terrorists or terror regimes." But what exactly kept the administration from preempting or preventing the attacks of September 11? The problem was not that they couldn't—the capacity was there—but that they hadn't. That was failure. Understandable, explicable, forgivable, but still failure. The administration seemed unable to acknowledge this.

I couldn't blame them for this inability, as such. Who would want to accept such responsibility? But I did worry very much that this willful deflection would lead the administration to seek to place the wayward blame for their failure where it didn't belong. On Saddam Hussein, for example. Iraq seemed to be understood as their chance to try again and get it right this time. If they could defeat Saddam Hussein they would gain a victory over a miserable tyrant and over their own fears—fears not so much of him as of their vulnerability to the murderous aggression and hatred that had surprised them on September 11. We might all partake of that victory if we, too, could feel less afraid. Less as if we were going to have to live the rest of our lives waiting for the other shoe to drop, and maybe even drop again.

What Scowcroft and others were arguing was that Iraq was not the right enemy at this time, and attacking it might well make America more vulnerable. This was where the ambition to project American power came in. Men such as Scowcroft and Baker were not, of course, shy about wielding power. But when they talked about working through the United Nations one felt that they meant it seriously. They were not imperialists, humanitarian or otherwise. One felt they had a great deal of respect for institutions, rules, and the acceptance of limits to power. One did not feel any of that with the Bush administration.

Amid all this, the personal prospect arose of my leaving the *Times* for the United Nations. Working on Op-Eds was, in its methods and goals, like politics by other means, and I had been thinking for a while that it might be interesting to do the real thing. Besides, I wanted to remove myself from this imperial moment. I wanted to get out of the war mentality. Part of me did not want to be in America if it was going to continue provoking other countries and peoples. The "with us or against us" notion resembled some trick charm that made your situation a little worse every time you used it. This America-centric world, enemies and allies alike, was under a devilish spell; I wanted out of its circle.

It was during lunch at one of the mezzanine restaurants overlooking Grand Central Station's main waiting room that Edward Mortimer, the former *Financial Times* writer who became chief of communications for Kofi Annan, mentioned there might be a job available. He waited until we had paid the check and were about to part before alluding to the matter at hand—namely, that a new high commissioner for human rights had been appointed and was looking for someone to handle communications. The new commissioner's name was Sergio Vieira de Mello. The job would be in Geneva. Was I interested?

I knew little about Vieira de Mello, but the notion of joining the United Nations had a strong counterintuitive, throw-caution-to-the-winds appeal, given that the institution appeared to be headed for a grand multilateral train wreck just as the United States was veering off on its unilateral quest to unseat Saddam Hussein. Not that there weren't countervailing, more optimistic signs as well. Kofi Annan was an exceptionally capable secretary-general with some solid achievements in peacekeeping and economic development. And for a moment, when President Bush addressed the General Assembly one day after the first anniversary of the September 11 attacks, it seemed that his administration might turn to the rules and work within a UN framework. "The Security Council resolutions will be enforced—the just demands of peace and security will be met—or action will be unavoidable. . . ," the president said. "We must stand up for our security, and for the permanent rights and hopes of mankind. By heritage and by choice, the United States of America will make that stand. Delegates to the United Nations, you have the power to make that stand as well."

Yet this invitation was really just another demand. The president had presented all his best reasons for attacking Iraq without the Security Council's approval or anything else besides the "heritage" and "choice" of the United States. In its way, it was more of a war speech than Cheney's had been the month before: Bush was making a preemptive strike on the old model of international structures, mutual respect, and law. A preemptive strike dressed up as an unexpected embrace.

The Security Council's Iraq negotiations began, and I was hopeful that all their noise might drown out the war drums. But when some comments that Rumsfeld had made in Poland came over the wires, I thought I was hearing the authentic voice of an Iraq war. Rumsfeld appeared to be particularly influential, I suppose because he thought the way Bush thought and he had, in Afghanistan, given the administration what appeared to be a solid victory. There hadn't been many others, not even small ones. War was the one thing the administration seemed to be pretty good at. That would be another reason, for them, to continue making it. Was it even possible they had come to like war? Sometimes it really appeared that way.

What Rumsfeld said in Poland was typical of him: rambling, self-justifying, strongly felt, with a certain sideways honesty. "We provided our allies with an intelligence briefing on the Iraqi threat that it poses to the world," he said at a press conference on September 25.

The deputy director of Central Intelligence presented a detailed discussion of Iraq's weapons of mass destruction programs and its support for terrorists. Everyone is on notice. All now have a clear understanding of the threats that are posed.

I noted how at this moment back in the United States the committees of the United States Congress are holding extensive hearings, analyzing what actually happened prior to September 11th and why it was that it wasn't possible to connect the dots and avoid the September 11th attack.

This was very much a hopeful White House view: that the congressional committees were working to find all the good reasons for the administration's failure, for why "it wasn't possible to . . . avoid" September 11. It seemed significant to me that administration leaders kept coming back to this 9/11 responsibility point, worrying over it, when strictly speaking it wasn't very relevant.

Rumsfeld continued,

Who knew what when are the questions, poring over tens of thousands of pieces of paper and documentation. Throughout our history we see that there have been many books written about threats that occurred and attacks that eventually resulted and why they were not anticipated and prevented. Books like "At Dawn We Slept—The Untold Story of Pearl Harbor," "From Munich to Pearl Harbor," "Why England Slept," are just three of the books. Already a couple of books have been written about September 11th and why it was that it could not have been anticipated.

The list of such books is endless. Indeed in the past year we've seen still more. Each is an attempt by the author to connect the dots after the fact—to determine what happened.

Our job today, however, those in positions of responsibility, of governments in the NATO alliance, is not to try to connect the dots after it happens, it's to try to connect the dots before it happens. . . .

That same day, President Bush finally went the whole hog and connected Iraq to al Qaeda. "The danger is, is that they work in concert," he said. "The danger is, is that al Qaeda becomes an extension of Saddam's madness and his hatred and his capacity to extend weapons of mass destruction around the world. . . . Clearly, al Qaeda is operating inside Iraq. In the shadowy world of terrorism, sometimes there is no precise way to have definitive information until it is too late." He added that "you can't distinguish between al Qaeda and Saddam when you talk about the war on terror."

The White House and the Pentagon had become impregnable to their own intelligence. They thought Iraq had weapons of mass destruction, or significant programs to manufacture them; therefore, it had to be true. Al Qaeda and Iraq were connected in their minds, and that was good enough. They could not be certain they were wrong about the connection between these dots, so they decided to assume they were right. There were rational arguments to be made for invading Iraq or overthrowing Saddam Hussein, but this was not one of them. It also seemed to be the decisive one.

Politically, meanwhile, we were somehow ceasing to think like a democracy. The biggest problem with the apparent decision to overthrow Saddam Hussein, apart from the deaths and injuries it would surely cause, was that it was a presidential obsession carrying all before it. Powered by fear and intoxicated by power, we were acting like an empire. And we were doing what the emperor wanted us to do. He was shaping reality to suit his apprehensions, and we were going to go along. All the major institutions were waiting for the push to take them out of indecision without leaving them exposed. This was the push.

I doubt you can have a democratic empire. On Capitol Hill, Senator Robert Byrd was railing against the undemocratic rush to war. On the Senate floor he quoted a letter from Abraham Lincoln to his law partner William Herndon:

The provision of the Constitution giving the war-making power to Congress was dictated, as I understand it, by the following reason. Kings had always been involving and impoverishing their people in wars, pretending generally, if not always, that the good of the people was the object. This, our Convention understood to be the most oppressive of all Kingly oppressions; and they resolved so to frame the Constitution that no one man should hold the power of bringing this oppression upon us. . . .

Byrd, the elderly bantam cock, a baroque, sometimes comic figure: how perfectly strange that it would be he standing alone on the parapet. The rest of Congress, however, was finally abdicating; it would give the king a promissory note of support should he decide on war at some point. The *Times* and the other big media were just now coming around to accepting the inevitability of conflict with Iraq; but coming around they were.

We weren't thinking like a democracy, we were thinking like an empire. When we have tended toward empire in the recent past, it has usually led to the short-circuiting of our democracy. The symptom has been presidential lying, the disease presidential ambition. It happened with Lyndon Johnson, Nixon, and Reagan, and it seemed close to happening now with Bush as policy-driven assertions about Iraq were presented as fact. The administration had actually argued that there was no need for congressional authorization for an attack on Iraq (because the authority was still available from 1991 as the Gulf War had never quite stopped) and no real need for a Security Council vote, either (because Iraq was already in material breach of its earlier commitments). Now, that pretty much just left the emperor, didn't it? The fundamental reality was that this man could take us to war tomorrow, and we would go. Or he could change his mind, and we wouldn't. And either way 280 million free Americans, 22 million Iraqis, and everyone else on the planet didn't have much of a say in the matter. That is an emperor.

Could we have any legitimacy as a nondemocratic empire? The United States really was conceived in liberty and dedicated to the proposition that all men are created equal. That is crucial to the state's legitimacy in our eyes. It is even more crucial to our legitimacy in the world's eyes. It is what, to others, makes our country great rather than just interesting and sometimes scary. President Bush, by making our stature in the world so dependent on our monopoly of violence, was in fact weakening us. He was trading in our legitimacy and democratic charisma for a respect based in fear. It was undignified; he was diminishing our national dignity.

V

IN THE INTERNATIONAL
COMMUNITY

The only alternative to my country's descent into imperial aggression that I could see—a weak alternative, I admit—was the international political system and in particular the outdated, cantankerous, clanking political machinery of the United Nations. It was interesting that much of the American elite had given up on UN structures, which are quite elitist, but the general public hadn't; over the past year every public in the world, including the American public, preferred that any action in Iraq be undertaken with a UN mandate. (They apparently didn't buy, or couldn't make sense of, the legalist hocus-pocus of Resolution 1441 already giving the United States an invasion mandate, either.) This support could not be attributed to abiding man-in-the-street affection for the United Nations. In the end, it seemed to me most explicable by the basic knowledge that absolute power corrupts—the powerful are often the last to remember this—and to the knowledge among some that, in the event of war, it was their kids who'd be doing the dying. These are the things Eisenhower knew. These are the things hundreds of millions of people know, and that should have counted for something, especially in democracies. Especially in our democracy.

If the United States, as a world power, was going to forget these things for a while, I wanted to watch the results unfold from a different vantage point. So I began to examine the career of Sergio Vieira de Mello, my potential new boss. He was a Brazilian who had spent his professional life in the United Nations, mainly in working with refugees. He was born in Rio de Janeiro in 1948; his father, a Brazilian diplomat, kept the family moving, with three different postings in Italy and one each in Lebanon and Brazil. As Sergio reached high school age his father continued to take European postings while the son remained with his mother and sister in Rio. He went to university in Europe, mainly in Paris. He was a passionate student of philosophy and a gifted linguist, moving easily among Spanish, French, Portuguese, Italian, and English. He was also politically passionate, in a leftist-student way. In 1969, his father was dismissed from the foreign service by Brazil's military government. The son turned, at the end of that same year, to the United Nations, at the age of twenty-one.

When I asked friends at the UN about him, they invariably called him Sergio. This meant something; the UN tended toward formality. One person I knew said he was "the most dynamic person at his level in the Organization." In the months ahead I would learn how to weigh each of those words, as well as grow accustomed to calling the UN "the Organization." Another friend described him as "probably the best-looking man in the UN," which I found interesting if also alarming.

Professionally, he was singled out for several qualities. He excelled at dropping into very serious conflicts and making a grim situation better. This required a rare combination of political attentiveness, negotiating skill, personal courage, belief in the UN, and a certain cowboy eagerness for a challenge. He was also frequently described as charming; and this was in turn linked to his ability to talk to all sorts of people, of high or low status, including some truly horrible individuals, and convince them to want to please him so he might come back and charm them again. Finally, he had that special ability to both delegate and keep control, even when his plans were unorthodox. This organizational skill had been honed in various humanitarian emergencies but reached its apex from December 1999 to the spring of 2002 in East Timor, a tiny region in Indonesia that he had overseen, on the UN's behalf, in its transition from war to independence.

The East Timor job was what had propelled Sergio to the level where he could be named high commissioner for human rights, so I paid particular attention to it. The Timor mission had been a military one, in part; the Australian Army was what guaranteed the peace there, such as it was, on behalf of the United Nations. It was also a substantial diplomatic mission, involving not just negotiations with a hostile Indonesian government over the likely loss of part of its territory but also very difficult talks with Australia on resource allocation. And it involved gaining an understanding of East Timorese society and nudging it toward legal and governmental forms that would both suit it and correspond adequately to the international norms that the UN was meant to propagate and uphold.

In the post–Cold War, internationalist context, Timor was a big deal. Looked at generously, it was the first instance of successful UN-led nation building. Earlier, Sergio had worked in Kosovo, with a generation of European and American internationalists animated by hopes for a rational, post-Soviet normalization led by a kind but firm international community. Kosovo was more of a standoff than a normalization, but Sergio brought those same hopes to Timor and there, under his leadership, they seemed to have been fulfilled. The idealist and the practical person had, for once, succeeded together.

The prospect of a vigorous United Nations, which Sergio seemed to embody for many people, made the world look brighter. For me, it offered political work bent on practical results in a nonnational context, which was precisely what I wanted to attempt. It also offered, or seemed to offer, an escape from the Iraq obsession and the general America obsession that accompanied it.

I couldn't altogether tell what entering this "international community" might really mean. Besides, there was considerable doubt as to whether Sergio was the right appointment for the job of high commissioner for human rights, and that was potentially a problem.

The human rights world he was entering—he took office as high commissioner on September 12, 2002—was one of bureaucratic institution building, legal standard setting, and moral exhortation, none of which were among Sergio's strengths. The previous high commissioner, Mary Robinson, had emphasized, on one hand, the building up of the international human rights community, which had grown immensely since its great surge in the 1970s. On the other hand, she had tried to act, through what was known as "naming and shaming," as a global conscience. She was a lawyer by profession, specializing in human rights and international law, and had also taught law before serving as president of Ireland and then as high commissioner.

This marriage of the legal and the political was characteristic of the international human rights world, particularly since the UN General Assembly adopted the Universal Declaration of Human Rights in 1948. The Universal Declaration provided the basis for subsequent treaties and conventions that together constitute the norms and standards for much of international human rights law. The bulk of this legal corpus was completed by 1970, after which states began, very unevenly, to ratify the treaties and undertake the legal obligation to enforce them on their own territory.

It was apparent (and expected) that this would often be a matter of the fox guarding the hens. With the standard setting largely accomplished, questions of investigation and enforcement loomed larger. How could the community of nations make states carry out their legal responsibilities to protect and promote human rights? And if the international community could not enforce compliance with its laws, then of what value or power was the word "legal"? Was international human rights "law" a mirage?

As often happens, the impulse for strengthening the law came from outside the law. In the 1970s and '80s, human rights became a popular movement. The main push came from uprisings that invoked human rights concepts in Central and South America (against military-authoritarian regimes), the Soviet bloc (against Communist governments), and sub-Saharan Africa (against colonial powers and rule by white minorities). There was also pressure, in the form of sanctions and condemnatory resolutions, brought by governments and intergovernmental bodies. Feeding this pressure was a newly powerful type of non-state political actor, the secular nongovernmental organization (NGO).

To a degree, NGOs were playing what were traditionally governmental roles—a possibility created by the fact that governments, in ratifying the various human rights treaties, had made solemn, public promises that they often did not want or intend to keep. NGOs' power in this quasi-governmental realm was only increased by the lack of strong, official investigative bodies, official courts, and so on.

The UN's human rights bodies played a very modest role in all this. But over time, some states began to see advantages in having the political energy of an international human rights movement channeled into UN institutions. For the United States and allied Western powers, this was a way to take the ideological fight with communism to a universal plane. For the growing number of former colonies, it offered the prospect of some protection against great-power interference and a means to press claims for economic rights (claims the rich countries steadily ignored). Many different countries also saw advantages in having some agreed universal language in which to talk to each other—a language other than war. Human rights provided such a language, and the United Nations was the obvious venue for an orderly conversation.

By the 1980s the significance of NGOs had grown enormously. White rule in Rhodesia had already ended late in 1979, and the eventual success of the antiapartheid movement in South Africa began to seem likely. At the same time, the Soviet empire and the very premises of state communism were collapsing. Western NGOs had had a direct hand in these developments; but more important was the continuity between the ideology of human rights and the decisive power of civil society.

Civil society put government power in brackets, so to speak, arguing that there were universal human norms of freedom and individual autonomy; governments would have to either uphold those norms or face dissolution; and the political actor that would judge those governments, and if necessary dissolve them, was civil society. But who or what was civil society, really, and where did its own legitimacy come from? Most of the answers were in the specific political alchemies of each uprising. But the clear ideological victor of the 1980s was the human rights movement, and the chief actors in that movement were the NGOs and the civil society they claimed to embody and guide.

With the fortieth anniversary of the Universal Declaration in 1988 came plans for a second international human rights conference. The resulting Vienna Conference, in June 1993, marked the human rights movement's coming of age as a global force. Along with a strong governmental presence, including heads of state, there were more than four thousand representatives of over eight hundred NGOs. Toward the end of the conference, a resolution was agreed upon to establish the position of a UN high commissioner for human rights.

The political exhilaration of the Vienna Conference coincided with a number of terrible lessons in the limits of power. The war in Bosnia and the siege of Sarajevo had begun in 1992 and were going at full strength during the Vienna Conference.

And in April 1993, Bacre Waly Ndiaye, an investigator sent by the UN Commission on Human Rights, submitted a report warning of the beginnings of a genocide against the ethnic Tutsis of Rwanda. The report contained concrete recommendations to head off the killings, but the Security Council and the international community were quite preoccupied with the Bosnian situation and with the gradual collapse of Somalia. (Twenty-four UN peacekeepers were killed there in early June.) Rwanda continued to deteriorate until April of the following year, when the three-monthlong slaughter of the Tutsis took place.

The excitement and optimism of the Vienna Conference formed a vivid contrast to these devouring battles. The emphasis of Vienna was on building human rights institutions—the UN "machinery," as it was called, and national human rights institutions to complement it—and extending the power of NGOs and international civil society. It was all about soft power.

At the same time, however, the human rights disasters in Bosnia, Somalia, and Rwanda were completely resistant to soft power. Whatever the root causes of these conflicts, it was too late to fix them by the gradual spread of what was called human rights culture. In such cases, the time for the promotion of human rights had passed; the time for forceful protection had arrived. And there was very little protection on offer from the much-referred-to international community.

This was the context in which the notion of humanitarian intervention began to evolve. (It was likewise the context for a revival of interest in an International Criminal Court [ICC].) The basic idea of humanitarian intervention had been around forever—ever since the first state, or coalition of states, explained an aggressive action abroad as a defense of the rights of the people whose country was being invaded. The most important modern variation on this, by far the most important, was European colonialism, in that its practitioners often considered invasion and conquest as part of a civilizing mission. Humanitarian intervention would not easily shed this imperial past. What was new in the 1990s was an international or universal theory of it. The post–Cold War world promised enough global unity of purpose and principle to imagine there could be an international consensus strong enough to generate truly international action.

The genocide in Rwanda in 1994 was held up as an example of a murderous nightmare that might have been prevented by humanitarian intervention. By 1995, calls for military intervention in Bosnia on humanitarian grounds grew steadily louder. The United States, in particular, under President Clinton, was being urged to use its vast military power to take out the Serbs' big guns and force Serbian president Slobodan Milosevic and his Bosnian allies to negotiate a peace.

NATO's bombardment of the Serbs began at the end of August 1995. In concert with several military offensives on the ground, and a very strong diplomatic push, the bombardment had the intended effect, and by November 1 the principals in the war had arrived in Dayton, Ohio, to negotiate a peace. The Dayton Agreement was formally signed in mid-December.

Advocates of humanitarian intervention took this to indicate the rightness of their idea. When conflict in the Serbian province of Kosovo resulted in heavy refugee flows, and a determined diplomatic process seemed to be utterly blocked, the second humanitarian intervention war began. NATO's bombardment of Serbia, including Serb positions in Kosovo, began on March 22, 1999. On April 22, Britain's prime minister, Tony Blair, gave a speech in Chicago called Doctrine of the International Community. Speaking of the Kosovo campaign, Blair said, "This is a just war, based not on any territorial ambitions but on values. . . . We have learned twice before in this century that appeasement does not work. If we let an evil dictator range unchallenged, we will have to spill infinitely more blood and treasure to stop him later."

In April 2000, Kofi Annan proposed that the international community formally come to grips with the idea of humanitarian intervention. The resulting paper, released in December 2001 under the title *The Responsibility to Protect*, held that the international community had the responsibility, chiefly through the United Nations, to infringe on the sovereignty of any nation that grievously failed to fulfill its responsibility to protect its own citizens. The concept certainly had its flaws and an excess of historical baggage. But to reject it entirely was almost to accept that any massive slaughter was somehow in the natural order of things and not something one could do anything about, and this idea, too, had baggage and grim implications of its own.

Such, roughly, was the state of things when I met Sergio's special assistant, Jonathan Prentice, for lunch in the fall of 2002. A nonviolent, law-oriented, activist human rights movement had pulled up alongside a violent, politics-oriented, state-based human rights movement advocating intervention. They both saw themselves as global and indeed universal, and they overlapped in many ways—they shared personnel—but they were on still quite distinct paths. And it seemed to me that, absent a strong centralizing pull, the two paths were likely to diverge, if only because the universal legitimacy of humanitarian interventions would come into further doubt as nations with wildly differing agendas undertook to intervene.

Jonathan was an extremely clever young Englishman (with a good deal of Irish in him) whose greatest joy seemed to be in laughing at pretension. He had seen plenty of it, having served at UN headquarters for several years in the Department of Political Affairs. He had also worked in Cambodia and as Sergio's executive assistant in Timor. His acute sense of fun took me off-guard, as did his physical presence, which was unusual among UN people: he seemed as though he might as soon be playing rugby as negotiating a treaty. He had written his undergraduate thesis on humanitarian intervention, arriving at the specific conclusion that Vietnam's invasion of Cambodia to unseat the Khmer Rouge was defensible. Like Sergio, he was not quite "a human rights person," as human rights people tended to put it. He liked action. He made it clear that Sergio liked action, too. Jonathan also did not have the anti-American reflexes common to the international civil service. That mattered for my prospective job, partly because I am American but mainly because a rote antipathy to the United States—or a passivity-inducing assumption of American hegemony, which amounted to much the same thing—would probably make him and Sergio ineffective, and I was not eager to join a doomed enterprise.

They were irritated by the incomprehensibility of the human-rights legal bureaucracy and impatient with conferences and roundtables, of which there seemed to be no end. They wanted the Office of the High Commissioner for Human Rights to become more like the office Sergio knew best, the Office of the High Commissioner for Refugees—that is, an operational office oriented toward projects in the field and away from important-sounding meetings in Geneva and New York.

They wanted to Do Something, and so did I. I suppose it was because of 9/11 and a certain midlife weariness with the limits of my journalistic trade; the job at the *Times* had seemed so wonderfully crucial after 9/11, but that had waned. I wanted to write the Op-Eds, not edit them. Besides, the international system in which Sergio now had a senior role was experiencing a crisis, and I liked dealing with crises, as he clearly did. He even appeared to have something of a plan for this one. At least it wouldn't be dull.

I was also taken with Jonathan's emphasis on information gathering. This seemed to me one method for creating that centralizing force that would keep the soft and hard paths of human rights from diverging. Humanitarian interventions had to be based on, and justified by, information. If states were the only sources of information on such matters, then information could not slow states' drift into antagonism. It would always be a case of one state's information against another's. (This had happened repeatedly during the Balkan conflicts, particularly in Kosovo.) There was some counterbalance in the alternative information provided by NGOs. The leading global NGO, Human Rights Watch, had integrated serious fact-finding standards into its work from the beginning, which was a chief reason for its success in the media and the wider world (including in diplomacy). But it was also a campaigning organization, similar to Amnesty International and less publicity-oriented groups like the Open Society Institute and Médecins Sans Frontières (Doctors without Borders). States often see these groups as antagonists (sometimes with good reason) and their information as tainted by antagonism. The private media were an important source of information generally, but on human rights matters they most often took their lead from NGOs—and to a lesser extent governments and UN field-workers—and in any case quality international news gathering had been in decline since the 1970s.

So it seemed here was an opportunity for the Office of the High Commissioner for Human Rights, which had hundreds of full-time employees, a budget in the tens of millions, significant project-based fund-raising potential, about twenty field offices, and the on-the-ground access that came with being part of the United Nations. This, in theory, made it competitive with the global NGOs. If it could gather and circulate credible and comprehensible information, it could create a political space where states would have to reckon with information other than that provided by their own intelligence services. The information basis for humanitarian interventions would become more subject to consensus and more objective, and so would the information basis for softer forms of human rights promotion.

I told Jonathan I would get back to him. I had to talk to my wife.

Becky was willing enough to go along. She was eager for a change, and Switzerland had a reputation as a nice place to live. The kids could learn French, a language we had both studied. We could get out from under our 9/11 cloud. Sometimes, in New York, leaving seemed like the only sure way to do that.

In the meantime I happened to meet Xanana Gusmão and José Ramos-Horta, who were then president and prime minister, respectively, of East Timor, as they had been since independence. I asked, without saying why, what they thought of Sergio, and they both spoke of him in the most glowing terms. That meant a lot. Soon I was heading over to UN headquarters on the East River to meet Sergio. Jonathan collected me at the elevator and bounced back through various corridors to a distant room. I hadn't been to this part of the building before. It was inordinately depressing. People seemed to wander about or camp at their desks in a state of forlorn abstraction. It was much too quiet. Gray light filtered through from windows on both sides of the building; the UN headquarters is long and thin and was designed so that light would shine through it in a display of institutional transparency. But in the intervening decades gray and beige desks and gray and beige partitions had silted up and the light had gotten clouded. This was a building far from the flush of youth.

Sergio was waiting in a cramped enclosure. He was beautifully dressed and, as billed, improbably handsome. We were all too big for the furniture. Jonathan rocked from side to side with occasional forward lunges, whereas Sergio looked as if he might at any moment pop vertically from his chair. These two had more energy than everyone else on that floor combined. Sergio was grinding his jaw. I asked most of the questions. I wanted to know where he got his information and what he wanted to do with it. He described the UN country teams and his old connections through the refugees' office and some of what he had learned in the humanitarian affairs department. He wanted to use this information in a very active diplomatic program, to intervene in particular situations, and to publicize human rights violations.

I said that if those were his goals he would need to get a different sort of work out of his current staff, unless he was willing to rely on other sources. From what I could tell, his office was mainly turning out highly specialized communications products by human rights professionals for human rights professionals and of interest only to that small world. The educational products were not bad, but there were too few, they weren't rationally organized, and they were technologically backward. As to the more popular products—basically general-audience speeches and press statements, as the office appeared to produce no video or audio, photos, or pamphlets, and the website limited itself to official UN documentation—they depended for their influence on the United Nations' stature, which seemed to me a fragile asset. I explained what I thought I had to offer, which was an ability to write whatever he needed and to train people in the office how to gather information, organize it, and present it in such a way as to maximize their audiences. I left signed copies of my books and soon enough was by myself out on the terrace on the north side of the building, smoking a small cigar and looking out over the East River at the crumbling masonry buildings on the southern tip of Roosevelt Island. I didn't think the meeting had gone very well.

Over the next days and weeks, I couldn't get the UN job out of my mind. Jonathan wanted to know when I could start, but I was uneasy about it. At the same time, it seemed the perfect moment to get into politics, given that the momentum continued to build toward an unwise war in Iraq and the United Nations seemed to be crumbling. What better time to hitch one's star to a charismatic, international human rights supremo with endless energy? But I still wanted to get a sense of what Sergio was like. I wanted to agree on a job description that would guarantee I wouldn't end up sitting in a corner, writing speeches. And I wanted to test how much he wanted me for the job.

We met at his New York apartment, which he had described on the phone as "a shithole." It was on a high floor of a building in the East Thirties. It didn't seem that bad, just a drab, modern room with a big view. It all looked fine once he, Jonathan, and I settled on the couches with glasses of Black Label on the rocks. I asked for and got an offer to head a policy planning unit they were going to start within the executive office (part of an attempt to strengthen the high commissioner vis-à-vis his senior managers). The new unit would, I hoped, give me the power to push through some policy innovations, particularly with regard to information gathering and communications, and to provide a place for ambitious staffers to bring new ideas and develop them. The job description would need to be written, though, and approved and posted. In the meantime, they would find a temporary salary line in the budget.

I sighed inwardly—I didn't particularly want to upend my professional and personal lives on a bet that this man could bend the bureaucracy to his will—then mentioned Gareth Evans and the International Crisis Group (ICG), and Sergio warmed to the topic. Gareth Evans had been Australia's foreign minister during the Timor years, then joined the ICG in 2000 as president. He was someone Sergio knew and who was his own age—someone he could be straightforwardly competitive with. The International Crisis Group got a good deal of its funding from governments, but it behaved more as an information-gathering and analytical NGO, paying analysts to live in countries of interest and write public reports about them, as well as to exert influence privately. The ICG had created a new, rigorous foreign-news product, not unlike what Human Rights Watch had done. Both governments and the media were starting to quote the group's reports as authoritative. I wondered what Sergio thought of this approach.

He said he admired the ICG and he admired Gareth for taking on something new. But Sergio believed any real change had to come through direct engagement with governments. So he had to keep working in the system; he couldn't go outside. "It has to be through the states," he said. "It has to be through the states." I suppose—maybe this was another 9/11 effect?—I didn't want anything too dreamy, and I really didn't want to waste my time. I was impatient. Sergio was impatient, but unlike me he also had a plan of action. Maybe this would be that new world, with international affairs reaching some balance of hard and soft powers! Maybe I could at least get beyond this year of sudden traumas, of debilitating hesitation and indecision everywhere—at the *Times*, in Congress, on the Security Council— except in the White House and the Pentagon, which were all too sure of themselves.

VI

GENEVA

January is not a great month in Geneva but I felt like a new man in a new world and was happy. I had a small, cheap room in the Hotel des Tourelles overlooking the Rhône River. (My family was to stay in New York until the job contract got sorted out.) I might have seen Mont Blanc from my window but it was never clear enough; instead, I saw the nearby Salève, an unexpected great wedge of earth that rose in a stolid mass to the southwest. Immediately before me was the Coulouvrenière bridge and, passing beneath it, a strip of land, with river on both sides, called the Promenade des Lavandières. I liked that I knew what *lavandières* meant and so could imagine the "washerwomen" on their promenade with the river rushing all around. I liked it as much, maybe even more, that I hadn't a clue what a *coulouvrenière* was, for that held the promise of future discoveries. On a Sunday morning I would jog up the Quai Turrettini—who or what was Turrettini?— followed by the Quai des Bergues, across the flag-lined Mont Blanc bridge, past the city's sweetly silly big clock made of earth, flowers, and shrubs, and up through an allée of pollarded plane trees.

New smells and new sounds, electric trams, the very curious, rather medieval hats of municipal workers. A new language, as in the phrase *affichage sauvage*. This was, per the frequent signs, what was *interdit*, "forbidden": *affichage* (the putting up of *affiches*, "posters" or "notices") *sauvage* (meaning "unregulated," but also, more commonly, meaning "wild" or even "savage"). Affichage sauvage, the wild and savage putting up of posters! I was delighted. I laughed out loud walking alone in the streets of Geneva. I hadn't done that in New York for a while. I wandered past the house where Jean-Jacques Rousseau was born and the house to which Jorge Luis Borges came to die. I pressed against the cool stone walls of the St. Pierre Cathedral and listened to the organist practice. And at night I'd look out at the lights and clatter of the quayside cafes; the building-top neon signs for Rolex and Inter Maritime Bank, stuck in a font from the 1950s; and the quiet river swelling past the lovers and the drug dealers on the Promenade des Lavandières.

The walk to work went along the bank of Lake Geneva, or Lac Léman, past a flurry of watch shops and watch advertisements. A narrow strip of park extended all along the embankment. The design was plain except for an inelegant statue of Elisabeth (Sisi), Empress of Austria and Queen of Hungary and an emblem of mid-nineteenth-century poetic female melancholy. She was walking here when she was stabbed on September 10, 1898, by the anarchist Luigi Lucheni. (It is said that he had wanted to kill a member of the Orleans family but couldn't locate one, so he killed her instead.) The statue is thin and distracted, like Elisabeth herself, who had a phobia of weight gain.

Just back from the lake was the sort of well-heeled, hideout neighborhood where mysterious assassinations still happened from time to time. But, in general, mildness ruled here. Out from the embankment an earthen pier took you to a beach where in the warm months people swam at lunchtime and after work. There would be a Ferris wheel, ice-cream stands and sandwich stands, people reclining on the grass with a beer or a glass of wine, and municipal gardeners changing the public flower arrangements every other week. Even the red-light district, which stood between the nice part of town and our office, seemed genially bawdy, with old-school matrons and half-curtained windows. It was sometimes said that Geneva was Paris frozen in the 1950s. I took that as a compliment and an invitation.

Our offices were in the Palais Wilson. It had been built as a hotel in 1873–75, in the French style of the time, with mansard roofs and two wings flanking a central tower. The hotel became headquarters for the new League of Nations in 1920 and was named for the league's founder, President Woodrow Wilson, in 1924. The league moved up the hill, to the new Palais des Nations, in 1936, and the Palais Wilson passed to the city and then to the Swiss federal government. In 1997, Kofi Annan asked if the United Nations might use the building for the Office of the

High Commissioner for Human Rights (OHCHR). Mary Robinson accepted the building at a ceremony the next year.

The wide staircases, with their elegant banisters and low risers, lighted by a wall of stained-glass windows, were unusually open and inviting. Given the office's mission, it was only right that one go about the day with some sense of urgency—all the more so in a building of such easeful opulence. So human rights workers could be seen rushing somewhat desperately up the elegant stairs rather than lingering by the elevators and appearing less than urgently committed. It was easier if you were young (as most of the staff were) or if you were Sergio, who, as one secretary explained to me, never took the elevator. Rather he would sprint up the stairs, most often, she said with a melting expression, "two steps at a time."

I had a corner room that overlooked the main entrance and, across the Rue des Pâquis, an elementary school. I settled into studying up on the high commissioner's office and preparing a speech for Sergio's next appearance in New York. The cold fact was that I had never written a speech. I had never concealed this. Neither had I emphasized it. I thought I could figure the thing out. Like any form of professional writing, speech writing follows fairly rigid norms that can be learned.

This was true in abundance for UN speech writing, as a look at some speeches showed, including many of those Sergio had had to give. In reading through them I was struck in particular by the combination of outrage and passive verbs: "It is appalling that impunity for gross violations of human rights and grave breaches of humanitarian law is so rampant." Of the two, the passivity—"Conflict often emerges where the rule of law collapses"—struck me as the more dangerous. There was also the question of high-commissioner grandiosity: "I am often concerned that distance serves to dull our senses as to the truly awful, destructive impact that conflict has on those caught in its maelstrom. We must not let that happen." And there were all the other tics of the *langue de bois*, the "wooden language," a phrase invented for Communist Party speeches but carried over to that of the United Nations: bottomless gratitude and admiration for the crucial work contributed by all panel members on the occasion of the fifteenth meeting of the commission's special committee, and so forth. I felt confident I could improve on this.

From these speeches several themes emerged. Sergio clearly saw the human rights movement as being at a turning point, with the optimism of the Vienna Conference in 1993 being replaced by pessimism. ("Our hopes collided head on with reality.") He always emphasized the rule of law, as embodied in the human rights treaties since 1945, and the responsibility of states: "We will work in partnership with States. I can never repeat it enough: the primary responsibility to promote and protect rights lies with them. . . . They have, in the words of one recent report, a 'responsibility to protect.'"

Sergio also showed, to some audiences, an interesting willingness to be confrontational. In the Third Annual BP World Civilization Lecture at the British Museum in November 2002, he said, "I hope you do not think me a coward, but civilisation is, I would suggest, a concept that eludes definition. You will not get one from me." He talked about:

> notions of cultural superiority, of elitism, of imperialism and—largely speaking—of Western idealism. If one considers oneself civilized, after all, then those who are different are not civilized: they are uncivilized. Indeed, it was only a few years ago that it was suggested the western concepts were so dominant, so incontrovertibly accepted, that what we were witnessing was an 'end of history' in the sense that there was no longer the fuel for a clash of civilizations. Who would really dare propound such hubristic notions now? . . .
>
> What I am suggesting is that we may be overreaching ourselves to talk of world civilisation. We also may be misleading ourselves. More important than striving to attain such a state (or even to define it) is the need to focus on, highlight and better appreciate the universality of human dignity. . . .

He also said that human rights are "dynamic," that they "move with the times" and "confront new challenges," and that they "are easy to understand." This boded ill, since the orthodoxy in most human rights circles was that human rights did not move with the times, they only expanded with the times, and while they might, in some elementary sense, be easily understood, they could only be interpreted by highly specialized legal professionals.

I was supposed to write Sergio's speech for a February 18 symposium at Columbia University marking the tenth anniversary of the office. The two previous high commissioners would be there, as would many eminent scholars and a sprinkling of NGO people. The relative lack of NGO people worried me but didn't surprise me. Before leaving for Geneva, I had had separate meetings with several heads of major national and international NGOs. They were kind and supportive, but the frankest of them spoke for the others when he said the UN human rights system did not strike him as worth much. They had expressed low opinions of the multilateral bodies, their committees, their staffs, the field offices, the publications, and even the poor website. The UN human rights system, including our office, had, according to one, "the most disorganized system of fact-gathering I can imagine." They were wary of Sergio, whose desire to intervene directly in conflicts was novel and risky. They knew, as everyone did, that his greatest achievements had been as a deal maker and consensus builder who tried to make the best out of bad situations—a best that was, by definition, far from perfect. It wasn't just that you could find fault with his solutions in Kosovo, Congo, Bosnia, Cambodia, Timor, and elsewhere. You couldn't help but find fault with them. Sergio himself couldn't help but find fault with them. This may have partly accounted for his angry energy and general agitation, which only seemed to be relieved when he was working toward a specific goal or when we were on the move. He had no way of truly knowing all the bad effects his actions had had over the years. What politician does?

He had suggested I write a speech around some questions. These should be questions that the human rights community as a whole ought to be asking, so they were not so much questions as challenges—issues that the community was neglecting. It amounted to an act of quiet aggression by a newcomer to a post that many in the room would have worked for years to create. I was happy to go along—I liked provoking discussion—but I wondered if it was such a good idea.

We arrived in New York just in time for Colin Powell's testimony before the Security Council on February 5, 2003. I was at UN headquarters and saw some of the testimony on the televisions that hung from the ceiling near the main entrance. Most of the information was familiar. The presentation struck me as a "best case": if all this were true, and their interpretations of it were all accurate, then the following conclusion could be reached . . . But if this was the best they had, then the case was likely not all that great. Powell, tellingly I thought, did not allude (as Rice and others habitually did) to darker realms of intelligence lying behind this presentation. He gave the information as it was and suggested a conclusion, as DCI George Tenet sat behind him in the role of guarantor. It seemed that you could perceive this cup as half full if you liked; to me it was more than half empty.

The most distressing fact was that it was Powell and Tenet up there. They had always been the brakes on the Iraq juggernaut. Powell's reluctance seemed to be a combination of distrust of his bureaucratic foes and a basic feeling that invading Iraq was just a bad strategic idea that would end in sorrow. Plenty of his fellow military men felt the same way. Tenet found himself in the uncomfortable position of being the director of central intelligence in the period prior to a declaration of war that would be based on intelligence. This gave him a level of responsibility that seemed to make him uneasy. He had consistently refrained from endorsing the administration's more extravagant claims, such as Vice President Cheney's assertion that Mohammed Atta met with an Iraqi intelligence officer in Prague prior to 9/11.

The Tenet statement that interested me most, however, came in an exchange with Senator Carl Levin during a meeting back in October 2002. If Saddam Hussein "did not feel threatened," Levin asked, "is it likely that he would initiate an attack using a weapon of mass destruction?"

Tenet replied: "My judgment would be that the probability of him initiating an attack—let me put a time frame on it—in the foreseeable future, given the conditions we understand now, the likelihood I think would be low."

"But what about his use of weapons of mass destruction?" Levin continued. "If we initiate an attack and he thought he was in extremis or otherwise, what's the likelihood in response to our attack that he would use chemical or biological weapons?"

"Pretty high, in my view," Tenet said. There may be several ways to read such an exchange, but it did seem as though Tenet was saying Hussein was unlikely to use weapons of mass destruction unless we pushed him to it—an excellent reason not to push him.

I took a few days off to see my family and reassure everyone of the bright future that awaited us in Switzerland. In one sense, the timing was good; on February 7, the government announced we would move to "code orange," the second highest of five alert levels. The country had been put on orange alert just once before. Attorney General John Ashcroft and Homeland Security Secretary Tom Ridge cited "specific intelligence" indicating a high risk of an attack by al Qaeda. They emphasized the possibility of a chemical, biological, or radioactive attack. This led to a particular emphasis on duct tape and plastic sheeting, which people immediately went out to buy. Why risk death just because you were too lazy to buy some duct tape? At the same time, the whole thing seemed laughable. Maybe it was the humble nature of tape. This was several steps down, sophistication-wise, from hoarding Cipro; we seemed rather to be in the realm of telephones made from tin cans and string. Was it really conceivable that tape might make such a difference?

Soon the late-night talk show hosts were making duct tape jokes. Tom Ridge, who after all was charged with our survival, became a figure of fun. The humor made our vulnerability both easier to bear (as it relieved tension) and much worse, in that the butt of the joke was our natural desire for safety.

Becky's mother half-seriously suggested she get a canoe. I told Becky that Geneva was not only a lovely town but one that I couldn't imagine anyone bothering to blow up.

The next week Jonathan and I went to D.C. for meetings with Deputy Secretary of State Richard Armitage and others. Sergio was in Madrid and supposed to meet us in D.C. In the meantime I went to lunch with Vince Cannistraro, the former CIA man who had written an Op-Ed for the *Times* in December 2001 urging that the United States keep its focus on fighting al Qaeda. ("If we divert our attention to Iraq now," he concluded, "we will diminish our ability to deter new rounds of violence against America—and we may create new threats rather than containing immediate ones.") He wrote a second piece in May 2002, also about the fight against al Qaeda, that didn't mention Iraq at all. Our lunch was depressing. In the past we had talked about "smart sanctions" against Iraq. Then that faded. Vince did some consulting for the Pentagon, and it was clear the Iraq war plan had developed great momentum. So then we looked to Powell and Tenet and others to slow the momentum until something—but what?—came along to halt the war process.

But Powell and Tenet did their UN presentation, and then, just a day later, they had both thrown caution to the wind before a Senate committee and decided that yes, after all, Iraq and al Qaeda were tightly connected. There was absolutely no new evidence beyond the very weak assertions of past intelligence, but the attitude had changed—and Osama bin Laden himself had weighed in with an audiotape, the existence of which Powell announced in his Senate testimony. Bin Laden, rather holding his nose at proposing anything that might aid the Baathist "socialist," Saddam Hussein, urged all Muslims to oppose the pending American aggression. "The fighting should be in the name of God only," he said, "not in the name of national ideologies, nor to seek victory for the ignorant governments that rule all Arab states, including Iraq." The statement, the *Times* reported, "offered little evidence of an alliance between Mr. Hussein and Mr. bin Laden, but it did seem to validate Arab leaders' warnings that Islamic extremists would exploit any assault on Baghdad to further inflame the region." Half empty? Half full? Vince and I tried to have a laugh or two, but it was a grim time.

It was snowing heavily in Madrid, so Sergio never showed up. His plane had been delayed. He only got as far as Paris. He seemed happily resigned to some free time in Paris. He had been less than excited about the Washington trip. I had tried to stir up some enthusiasm, pointing out that, looked at a certain way, the administration might be considered an ally. There were the Doha "development round" of World Trade Organization (WTO) negotiations, the development and anti-AIDS commitments made at the beginning of 2002, the innovations of the Millennium Challenge Account, the African development initiative of the Group of Eight (G-8)—all of these owing much to Bush's leadership. The National Security Strategy released in September, understood to be chiefly the expression of Condoleezza Rice channeling the president, made ample use of human rights language and could be construed as indicating a strategic direction roughly in line with our own objectives.

However, the resignation in the past few days of the State Department and the CIA to invading Iraq, come what may, put these more moderate initiatives, which had always seemed to hover at the administration's margins, deep into the background. War finally dominated everything.

Before returning to New York I went for an early run on the Mall. This was mid-February so of course it was bleak and cold, but I don't imagine that, under these political circumstances, it would have felt much better at cherry blossom time. The one lesson from September 11 everyone had seemed to agree on—that the United States is dependent on the rest of the world for its safety and prosperity—was being, from what I could see, unlearned. My feet crunched on the frosted ground alongside the reflecting pool, and then it was up the steps of the Lincoln Memorial, nearly empty at that hour. I never miss visiting the Lincoln Memorial when I'm in D.C. There were those words again, etched in cold stone: "Conceived in liberty, and dedicated to the proposition that all men are created equal." Down the steps and crunch-crunch through some trees; then down into the cold, shallow black *V* of the Vietnam Veterans Memorial, with all the names; and back up again, crunch-crunch across the grass. Maybe it was because of the lunch with Vince but I kept thinking of my old friend Dave, the optimist, with that gun in his hand at Qala Jangi. "The problem is, he needs to decide if he wants to live or die, and die here. . . . Gotta give him a chance, he got his chance." *Dave, what happened to us? Where are you now?* Crunch-crunch-crunch, then up off the lawn, and back to the hotel.

In the cab coming in from La Guardia all it took, still, was the mutilated skyline of Manhattan to make me go rigid with sadness. I could get away from this in Geneva, but not here. Most people I knew in New York had, somewhere in their apartments or houses, perhaps tucked away in a guest bathroom, a photograph of the World Trade Center, often just a postcard; and it was somehow impossible to put these pictures away. "But grief He created strong in its birth, / and weak in its growth," the Andalusian poet Shmuel HaNagid wrote, "and wherever it festers / in a thinking heart— / heart is lost." The 9/11 grief would have to go, somehow. But then what forms would memory take—or should memory take?

I didn't want to leave this question up to the official storytellers, with their mixture of revenge and desperation. They sometimes seemed to be saying: "It upsets you to see pictures of Saddam Hussein because you associate him with the World Trade Center, don't you? Don't you? If we eliminate Hussein, won't it ease your painful memory of that day?" This was, to me and many others, a gross misuse of the dead.

Another difficulty was that the public memory of September 11 was changing shape and separating from one's private memories. In those early months we really were, especially in New York, living something like a collective experience, reading the same papers, reaching for the same solaces (catastrophe sex! radios you can crank!), smelling the same smells, missing the same neighbors. Maybe even hating the same enemies. But now what remained as the public memory of September 11 kept getting smaller, more repetitive and controllable, more useful to the powerful and increasingly useless to the rest of us. As for us—our most real memories looked more and more private, personal, exceptional, and finally less interesting. That's just *your* memory; and it doesn't matter, because it isn't public, or shared. But then you looked around and realized that what was now public and shared was concocted by other people and you had no part in it. So what really happened? Is it significant at all, your memory? And if you were *there*, did that experience really transcend your ordinary isolation—was it really shared, as it had seemed to be in those first weeks, when we were all so good to each other, or was that an illusion, too?

An agreement seemed to have been reached, more or less, on rebuilding the World Trade Center's site. I had liked one of the plans last year—a building echoing that curving fragment that had stood for a while, alone in the destruction. It would be a tribute to our city's stubbornness, which was something to celebrate; and because it would be modeled on a ruin it seemed as though it would memorialize the people we had lost without giving anything up to their killers.

The plan now was for some large buildings with a pit, thirty feet deep, at the site itself. I didn't like the idea much because it didn't communicate the person-by-person intimacy of what had happened. The high spirits and smiles of that beautiful morning; the sudden, terrible, terrible falling; the scratching about for what was left of our friends. For bin Laden they were not people, they were roadkill on his path to power; and with this anonymous pit maybe we were starting to think of them that way, too, as an aspect of our war, the war they'd never heard of because they were already gone. Early casualties. No, no, no—we can't do that to them. That would be a great mistake.

Many months before, back at the *Times*, the Op-Ed page published a piece by Gabriella De Ferrari in which she proposed that each dead person be memorialized by a bench. Each bench would be situated at a place determined by the family, presumably a place that had been dear to the person they'd lost. I loved this idea. It was so right and so impractical. Because, of course, many families would want the same place. There are only so many commonly cherished places: nice picnic spots in parks, hillsides and stretches of shore with particularly good views. The benches would gather where happiness had been most concentrated. Benches would cluster where first kisses had been. There would be competition for these spots, followed by lawsuits: all just as it should be, because this is New York. There would also be eccentric spots and inexplicable choices where in the times to come you would be walking along and there would be, with no explanation, a bench with someone's name. You'd wonder: why here? And you would never, ever know. That would be part of the memorial too, the not knowing. Just about no idea what we had lost, whom we had lost, why. What that person might have been.

At least, on this trip to New York, I had even worse things than 9/11 to think about, namely, Congo's war. Sergio was to brief the Security Council on February 13 concerning conditions in the eastern half of the Democratic Republic of the Congo. I'd begun reading the draft of the briefing in Washington. I was still trying to make sense of it when I got to headquarters in New York. The problem was that I couldn't tell how we knew what we would be asserting to the Security Council. The report lurched from highly specific incidents to very broad characterizations of political actors and trends, and back again, without indicating on what basis one could say that the broad patterns could reasonably be extrapolated from the incidents. This is exactly what reporters do when they want to make a big story out of too little information. It doesn't mean the big story is wrong, but it does mean it isn't supported and so probably shouldn't be told. The other problem was that I couldn't tell what the sources were for the facts themselves.

This mattered more than it might have because Sergio, just as Mary Robinson before him, wanted to bring human rights issues to the Security Council more often than had been the case. The Rwanda disaster haunted everyone. Bacre Ndiaye's human rights report to the Commission on Human Rights had been delivered one year before that genocide, and it had not really had any influence at all on the Security Council, which had the power to intervene.

When I got to headquarters I pressed Jonathan about it and he put me on to our person for that area. We were in borrowed space again; it happened that I was using the desk of that same Bacre Ndiaye, who was out of town. I spent frantic hours on the phone, trying to track down the facts—and trying to discover the exact nature of our fact-gathering methods. It turned out that some of the facts were shaky and our methods were utterly opaque. It appeared that the bulk of the information was not derived from multiple independent sources; rather, it was mostly secondhand or even thirdhand, a cut or two above rumor. I couldn't quite believe it. We were going to present this to the Security Council? I trimmed and adjusted, and all too soon we were walking down to the council's chamber. We went past a crowd of photographers. "They're not here for me!" Sergio said cheerily. He was right. They were there for any statement having to do with Iraq. Hans Blix was due to discuss the state of weapons inspections in Iraq the next day, and France, in particular, was gearing up for a confrontation with the U.S. over the necessity of going to war.

We entered the chamber and Jonathan and I settled into the seats behind Sergio. Jean-Marie Guéhenno, the head of peacekeeping, was also there to give his own report on the Congo. When Sergio's turn came he spoke fluidly and passionately. He took questions from the various ambassadors, answering in their own languages when he could. We passed notes back and forth. It was very new to me and exciting, so much so that at times I let myself forget that we didn't really, by my standards, quite know what we were talking about.

Five days later we went to Columbia for the tenth-anniversary conference. Sergio spoke last and began with, "This is a lesson in humility." After four hours of hearing his predecessors and others speak of their visions of the office, he said he "felt intimidated by the high stakes that all of you have set for my job."

Soon he moved on to his five questions. The first had to do with terrorism. He had said many times before, and noted here again, that states should be extremely careful not to let the fight against terrorism lead them to abrogate human rights. Now he wanted to say something else: human rights doctrine might have to find better ways to deal with non-state terrorist actors. He said,

I was even approached by a very leading supporter of our office and of the human rights cause who told me that I should not use the expression "serious violation of human rights" when referring to terrorist acts because that was

limited to state practice. While I appreciate the reasons for such careful word-
ing, and they are strong reasons indeed, I also believe that most people would
find such locutions curious, if not evasive. I believe that governments intent
on repelling such attacks will not be impressed by such precision. These are
real problems. As human rights defenders, when faced with something new,
we must find new responses that are credible to states but also to human rights
activists, and people outside these two circles, that is to say, the vast majority
who may look to us for guidance.

His second question was, "What are the limits to the growth of human rights?"
He next went on to ask how the human rights community might come to better
terms with religion. ("Religion is, for example, often too aggressive and transformative to fit well in the category of cultural diversity.") His fourth question was, "Can
we improve our understanding of the self-interest of states?" What he meant was
that rights activists needed to think more about how to lure states into embracing
their responsibilities, and necessarily to emphasize some rights more with some
states than with others. "Human rights discourse," he said, "often seems to wish
for an eventual disappearance of states in favor of universal human rights. . . . By
analogy to religion, world government is the eschatology of human rights. But in
our field, as in theology, the end days are a long way away. We might as well speak
of this frankly." He ended by asking whether the human rights community couldn't
orient itself much more toward delivering practical results, a question he related to
the previous four. He spoke of "the daily lives of people who desperately need our
help and do not have time to wait. They almost certainly do not need workshops."
    The audience managed to squeeze out a clap or two. I spoke to a few people I
knew, and they strained to say something nice. I don't know what the audience had
expected or wanted. They couldn't have expected Sergio, who was new to the field,
to have more answers than they, who had spent their lives in it. This was perhaps
why he had thought to ask questions rather than give answers. But the questions
implied a need for significant rethinking, and the human rights community was
not at all in the mood for rethinking, certainly not at Sergio's suggestion. They were
in a defensive crouch, afraid of George W. Bush and the war he was bringing. (Blix
and the French had not turned things around earlier at the Security Council.) They
were worried about what seemed to be the dwindling momentum of their move-

ment in the Western states, and the increasing identification of it by politicians elsewhere as a cat's-paw of those same states. And finally they were worried that the treaty system built up so painstakingly since 1945 might lose its prestige and even, at some future point, its purpose.

I thought Sergio would be enraged by the poor reception, but he wasn't. He had said what he believed and that was enough for the day. Maybe he wasn't such a politician after all.

It wasn't long after we got back to Geneva that Jonathan came into my office, closed the door, and said that President Bush wanted to meet with Sergio. It made us laugh, because on our last trip to D.C. the president had not been on our list—their choice, not ours—and we suspected that Sergio's failure to turn up in Washington that time had been interpreted as a signal that we would only come if the meetings were at the highest level, whereas the truth was that Sergio really had been stuck in a snowstorm in Madrid and missed his connection in Paris. In any case, now Bush wanted to meet, and Sergio said yes.

Fate was toying with me. One of the reasons I had come to Geneva was to get away from American power, to put it to one side—to escape from the kind of power that made people want to attack you, the way we had been attacked on September 11. I also wanted to see if there wasn't some alternative global political structure, preferably one based on human rights, that might yet pull the world away from all this war. And yet here I was, in pretty Geneva, contemplating a trip to the White House.

We dusted off the February agenda and adjusted it for a presidential visit. These were getting-to-know-you meetings, and the agenda was modest; our strongest stance was on the treatment of prisoners in the antiterror war—in particular, against torture. Sergio argued publicly that America's prisoners had been put in a legal "black hole," as symbolized by Guantánamo, and that this had to end. We were also urging an easing of the rules on AIDS drug patents, a stronger U.S. push on Mideast peace, an American buy-in on the effort to reach agreement on an international treaty on the rights of the disabled, and a few other items. Mainly we wanted to get the doors open for more substantive work later. What the Americans wanted from us was hard to know. They would want to talk about the upcoming fifty-ninth session of the Commission on Human Rights, which would begin at the end of the month; they were sending the formidable Jeane Kirkpatrick as head of the delegation, which seemed to indicate something serious on their part, and they were in a twist about the nomination of Libya to head the commission. They would want to talk about the war on terror and about Iraq, but in what ways we could not foresee.

I busied myself preparing briefing papers on the various personalities and issues we were likely to encounter, and soon enough the three of us were checking into Washington's Mayflower Hotel. Sergio, Jonathan, and I worked out in the tiny windowless gym, with its relentless mirrored walls; Sergio and I lifted weights while Jonathan pounded the treadmill. We met later in the hotel bar, then went nearby for dinner. We were all preoccupied by the White House visit the next day; none of us had been there before, and of course it was thought to be rather hostile territory. But Sergio would go into the meetings as he always did, ready to talk to anyone.

Besides, the problem in Washington was not a lack of common ground, he told me, so much as "this obsession with Iraq." I think it was the obsessiveness that bothered him. It indicated a lack of balance, even an irrationality. We passed a somewhat solemn dinner, despite the red wine and steaks. The mood only really lightened when Jonathan and Sergio reminisced about Timor; despite a large gap in age, status, and experience, the two of them had become close friends. Partners in adventure: the kind of relationship that Sergio established so easily. We were on an adventure, all right, just a rather grim one, since we all knew that the invasion of Iraq wasn't far off.

Our first meeting the next morning was with a roundtable of State Department officials led by Paula Dobriansky, the undersecretary of state for global affairs. Their main interest was in Iraq. What were we planning to do there? I had sent Jonathan a memo on post-conflict Iraq the previous week, after hearing Harold Koh at the Columbia event—he had been assistant secretary of state for human rights under Clinton—urging that we have a post-conflict Iraq plan ready. At the State Department, Sergio began by explaining that there was no relevant Security Council resolution and so we had no mandate for Iraq. Nonetheless we had given, "hypothetically," some thought to post-conflict needs. Jonathan then gave a presentation about human rights monitors, training Iraqi law enforcement officers and judges in human rights law, starting a mass-communications program to disseminate news and educate people about their rights, and helping Iraqis to found national human rights institutions so that the promotion and protection of human rights could get on a solid footing after a war. Sergio repeatedly emphasized the need to get power and responsibility into the hands of Iraqis as quickly as possible.

The next few meetings, at the State Department and on Capitol Hill, were unexceptional and somewhat in the shadow of the meeting with the president. At 2:00 p.m. Sergio squared his shoulders and strode into the Oval Office, with Jonathan and me trailing behind. The press photographers, who were arrayed outside the room, looking in through windows, were allowed to tumble through for a minute and take pictures, then hustled back out to the yard, in a ritual that was disturbingly reminiscent of a visit from the family pets; they might have been allowed a bit more dignity. The president shook Sergio's hand and said, "You work out!" This seemed to throw Sergio off a bit. Heads of state didn't normally ask after his exercise program.

Two sofas faced each other across a coffee table, at one end of which were two chairs. Sergio sat in one, Bush in the other. Jonathan and I took one sofa. Across from us were National Security Adviser Condoleezza Rice (closest to the president), two staffers from the NSC (Tony Banbury and Courtney Nemroff), Lewis "Scooter" Libby of the vice president's office, and the assistant secretary of state for democracy and human rights, Lorne Craner. Just as we were starting, a phone rang. There was an exchange of glances. Rice explained to Bush that it was a special phone. The White House still had special phones! Rice indicated the caller was Tony Blair. The president decided he could take the call later. "Tony's always worrying," he said with a faint smile and a look of parental sufferance. I focused on taking notes. I had never felt sorry for Tony Blair before.

Sergio presented our issues politely and compactly, emphasizing detainee treatment and the necessity of not using torture. He told about a woman he had met recently in Pakistan who believed her husband had been detained by the United States but had no idea where he was. We'd discussed this story before; Sergio thought it might concretize certain realities for Bush.

The president asked Rice to look into the question of the Pakistani woman. He stressed that the United States did not torture people. There was no torture at Guantánamo Bay. He said, for example, that "KSM"—Khalid Sheikh Mohammed of al Qaeda, who had been captured in Pakistan over the weekend—"will be treated humanely." He stressed, "These were illegal combatants, trying to kill lives."

Bush said he had just had a meeting with the representative of the Pope, and they had discussed the concept of a "just war." Bush spoke of his duty to "protect my country. That is a sacred obligation." He considered Saddam Hussein a threat to his country. "Part of 'just war' is that the human condition improves," he said, adding with respect to Iraq, "when it's liberated, the human rights condition of the people will improve."

We had not asked President Bush to justify the likely invasion of Iraq, but he evidently wanted to for his own reasons. "Deep in my bosom is a great desire for freedom for people," he insisted. "At my core is a great desire for freedom and the human condition to improve." Bush said that a huge humanitarian relief effort was already planned for postwar Iraq, and that the existing network of registers, distribution points, and so forth created for the UN Oil-for-Food Program would be used to reach Iraqis across the country.

The conversation began to lose coherence. Bush said he didn't want war ("I really don't"). He said, "We want the UN to work." He also said, "I don't give a damn whether we get a [second] resolution or not"—that is, a new resolution by the Security Council backing a decision to go to war. This is what Tony Blair wanted.

Bush then reimposed coherence by turning to the idea of "a different kind of war," the kind that he had been fighting since September 11. In this war, he wanted to ensure that no one could "go back and fade into this shadowy network, then come back to kill us."

Bush urged us to bring issues to him, and there seemed to be hints of possible movement on Guantánamo and on torture. The president and the high commissioner talked a bit about the Middle East—Ariel Sharon, Bush confided, was "meaner than a snake"—and about AIDS, and that was that. I thought I had made it to the door when I heard Bush's voice from behind: "Where you from, big boy?" I turned around; we shook hands. "California," I said, and backed out of the Oval Office as quickly as good manners allowed.

We met Condoleezza Rice later that day in her small office in the West Wing. She, too, wanted to talk about Iraq. She wanted speed: rapid containment of the military theater within Iraq's borders, rapid humanitarian relief (she, too, emphasized the channels established for the Oil-for-Food Program), quick identification of Iraqi technocrats to run the civil administration. She emphasized that Iraq had long been under a "heavy" system, and "we don't know what's under there." We touched on other subjects, including torture. Rice said that the president had meant what he said when he pledged not to allow the torture of Khalid Sheikh Mohammed or anyone else. Sergio urged her to have the president make a strong and unequivocal statement against the use of torture and expressing his commitment to the decent treatment of detainees. He pressed for an easing of intellectual property rules for AIDS drugs. We talked about Chechnya and the Middle East. But mainly the topic was Iraq and terrorism. "We want to delegitimize terrorism," she said, "as we delegitimized slavery." There was a painting over her sofa that appeared to be a scene from the struggle against slavery.

I wouldn't deny her a metaphor, particularly one that so efficiently conveyed her commitment. And Rice was a personable, steady person, without Bush's unsettling combination of swagger and insecurity. (It sometimes seemed that when he was least coherent he was also at his most condescending, a combination I had never before encountered.) But slavery had next to nothing in common with terrorism, and I hoped they weren't planning on drawing lessons from the struggle against one to guide their fight against the other. The whole business of terrorism and metaphors had been a mess from the beginning. Was Saddam Hussein a Hitler, and was accommodating his regime the same as appeasing Hitler? Was fundamentalist Islam best understood as "medieval" or as a form of spiritualized modernism, or as fascist, or as postmodern? Did 2003 equal 1938? Whatever the United States (or Britain) failed to do in the 1930s, those failures did not come from using the wrong metaphors, so it struck me as extremely odd that so much energy was now going into finding the right ones. It suggested a lack of seriousness somehow.

The mood in the White House during our visits, and even at the State Department, was a mixture of gravity and high spirits. People were clearly excited about this war they were starting—stressed out, yes, but still excited. Jonathan and I had one meeting with third-tier State Department officers who were expecting to leave very soon for Iraq to undertake a mission of humanitarian and reconstruction assistance that, they assured us, would be of an extraordinary scope; they had already been spending tens of millions of dollars on pre-positioning aid supplies. Like Rice, they noted that the first push would have to be military—and for strictly security matters, the U.S. military might have to be there for a while—but they expected the

With Jonathan Prentice, center, and Sergio Vieira de Mello at the White House entrance.
Dawn Calabia

trend to shift pretty quickly to civil consolidation, rebuilding, and the construction of a post-Baathist, free Iraqi nation. That was why these young people at the State Department were anticipating shipping out so soon.

At the end of the meeting we went by Lorne Craner's office, which was nearby, and he escorted us back to the elevators. He asked how we thought the meeting had gone between Sergio and Bush. Jonathan said he thought it had gone well, and I agreed, a bit flippantly. "They're both boyish men's men," I said, "and they connected on that basis."

We left the next day, March 6, 2003. The American press had been overstuffed with bitter eulogies for the United Nations and dire thoughts on the collapse of the international system. On the tenth, President Bush's spokesman said, paraphrasing the president, that if the UN "fails to act, that means the United Nations will not be the international body that disarms Saddam Hussein. Another international body will disarm Saddam Hussein." The secretary-general stated, "If the U.S. and others were to go outside the Council and take military action it would not be in conformity with the Charter"—that is, it would be, in some sense, illegal. Russia's foreign minister and France's president both declared they would veto a Security Council resolution, sponsored by the United States, Britain, and Spain, authorizing the use of force against Iraq should Iraq fail to prove its disarmament by March 17.

In the meantime we had to get back to Geneva for the annual meeting of the Human Rights Commission. Sergio was to give a speech at the opening.

Given his determination to work within the state-based system, he had promised to spend a lot of time at the commission. I polled senior colleagues about what they wanted in the speech and spoke with Sergio. Apart from some policy points, he wanted passion in the speech. The commission was at a low ebb. An unpopular war was about to begin in Iraq, and it was highly unlikely that this commission would be able to say or do anything about it. Sergio worried that a cranky diplomatic listlessness would smother the proceedings. Besides, he was good at passion and came alive when he had a sense of emergency. He also wanted a less bureaucratic style in his speech than was the norm. Toward that end, he mentioned the gravestone of Jorge Luis Borges, which was in a cemetery in the Plainpalais neighborhood. The cemetery held a number of luminaries, most notably John Calvin. Sergio's recollection was that on Borges's gravestone there was a slogan, possibly in Old English, something along the lines of "and never be afraid." Maybe that could provide an ending note for the speech?

I was on deadline but managed to race over to Plainpalais in the late afternoon. I didn't yet know the neighborhood and looked somewhat desperately for the cemetery, only to arrive just as it had closed. I was walking along, dejected, when my cell phone rang. It was Sergio. He had left the office early and gone to the cemetery himself to find the quote. Soon I saw him ahead of me, talking to me on his phone. I savored the comedy of it and the delight of having a boss who was such an adventurer-pedant. *And ne forhtedon na*, Sergio had written down; the inscription ran beneath a carving of seven men crammed into a Norse-style boat and above the dates 1899–1986. We weren't sure what language it was and I was unable to get a reliable translation in time, so we didn't use the quote, though we did know what we wanted to convey, which was not to be afraid.

"Fear is a bad adviser," I wrote. The phrase seemed so obvious that I doubted it was original. But it captured something Sergio wanted to convey at a very troubled moment. It did occur to me that politics without fear was practically inconceivable. That idea, however, pointed down a dark road that was not where we wanted to go as the commission got under way.

After the opening speech we settled into trying to make the best of the commission meeting, which would go on for six weeks. Our office provided clerical and expert support for the commission. But we didn't appoint members or control the agenda; states did that. So we were reluctant to take the blame for the commission's failings, such as the election that year of Libya to chair the commission, and had been making some efforts already to distance our office from them. For despite its history as a crucial body for the setting of legal human rights standards and monitoring states' compliance, the Human Rights Commission had by now become a byword for dysfunction. The main reason was the continuation in this venue of the fight between the colonizers and the colonized. As a Palestinian colleague explained to me once the commission opened: This commission is not about the United States. This is about Europe and its former colonies.

Part of the explanation lay in simple numbers. The Commission on Human Rights reflected, in its apportioning of votes, the universal-membership model of the UN General Assembly. Once the formerly colonized countries became a majority of the world's independent nations in the 1970s, they could control the voting in any such institution, and with the breakdown of the Cold War order they were no longer hindered by an alliance to the West or to the Soviet Union. These countries were finally and truly "nonaligned." They tended to become either democracies or semi-authoritarian, and they tended to develop moderately open market economies. In short, the majority of the world's nations in the 1970s and 1980s were beginning to look more like Western democracies. But this was somewhat deceiving, for it seemed to imply (especially to Westerners) that the rest of the world was "catching up." Former colonies did not want to see their evolution as Westernization, as though they were still children to the Western parent, as in colonial days. They also did not want, on the whole, to receive any moral instruction from the former colonizers, who were, in their view, the real morally corrupt party, given the bloody, venal realities of colonialism.

The professionalization of human rights, and its exhaustive codification in treaty law, were intended to take the moralizing out of the equation and avert exactly this kind of political blockage—that is, quarrelling among nations over who did the first bad thing that led to all the bad things that succeeded it. Human rights were meant to be politically neutral. The bureaucratic language that evolved was therapeutic, infinitely patient. The commission "expressed concern," then "grave concern." It "noted" murders. It "urged" states to do something about them. It could send investigators to gather information (and the state in question could refuse to let them visit, as often happened). The commission did not compel states. The commission had no means to compel states, but beyond that, the whole system was designed by states not to allow compulsion of states. Allowing compulsion, or the use of force, would allow politics and history back into the system, and that might well destroy it, whether interventions were humanitarian or not. States would divide into compellers and the compelled, perhaps into good and bad, or modern and backward, but certainly into strong and weak. The goal of universal objectivity, which was at the heart of the UN human rights system and crucial to its legitimacy and stability as a legal structure, would be lost.

Unfortunately, the price of keeping this system intact as it was got higher and higher from the 1970s on. Mistakenly thinking that the spread of democracy and open markets, the growth of trade, and the globalization of communications constituted a decisive Western "victory," the West acted like a victor, seeing its own power and prosperity as a reward for virtue and feeling that the rest of the world would always, as it seemingly just had, come around to the Western position sooner or later. The Western states, therefore, thought it made excellent sense that the West would continue to dominate the international institutions.

The former colonies saw it differently. They saw Western power as partly derived from successful Western exploitation—of them. They saw Western prosperity as partly based on continuing exploitation of their poverty and weakness. Given that the international institutions depended, to a very considerable degree, on the West for their resources and power, they were seen as often advancing the interests of the West at a cost to the rest of the world. So the international institutions, most of them set up in the 1940s, looked increasingly sinister to much of the world and particularly to governing elites who did not want to be told how to run their states. These rest-of-the-world countries had no chance of reforming the international institutions. They could never be united enough to do something that positive. But individual states could withdraw from or ignore the international institutions. They could concentrate on their own regional groupings. And they could simply wreck international institutions, which was pretty much what was happening with the Commission on Human Rights.

Americans and Europeans often looked past the pattern, because they spent so much time just contemplating each other. It was another symptom of thinking like a victor. The United States and united Europe, having established that the great battles of history were over and everything pointed to their own shared triumph as the decisive holders of world power, had only each other left to argue with. So they would contend over whether the rule of law was more perfectly refined in Europe than it was in America. Which one is first in the world for wisdom, you or I? Which one is first in the plastic arts? Performing arts? Which one assimilates non-Western peoples better? Which one lives best?

Too often, American policymakers would begin and end their assessment of world opinion with European opinion; similarly, European policymakers, confronting a problem, would sound out the United States until they found some contradiction or obstacle, then throw up their hands and say, "We would like to save the world, and of course we know just how to do it, but the Americans probably won't go along, so what's the point?" This was the most perfectly narcotic and self-serving form of anti-Americanism, and it was gravely worsening under Bush, who tended to feed it.

Despite such epic self-absorption among the Western powers, it was pretty hard to miss the distinctly ex-colonial pattern at the Commission on Human Rights. The Western states no longer had the votes to get what they wanted, which was usually a more aggressive pursuit of political and civil rights in non-Western countries. The non-Western states did not have a rival positive agenda, although they were often interested in economic and cultural rights, which promised either wealth or technology transfers from the West or a possibility of protection from Western culture.

Led by a caucus called the Like-Minded Group, these states mainly aimed at reducing the scope of the commission's activities—in particular, its ability to pass censure motions against specific countries. Because the commission's membership of fifty-three countries was elected by a completely opaque system of regional caucuses, the non-Western states that got on the commission tended simply to be those that lobbied harder. They had to be of a certain size to have the necessary power, and they had to have a motivation. In many cases, their motivation was to defend themselves; so you frequently ended up with rights-violating countries making sure that they got on the Human Rights Commission. The other countries in the regional groups didn't care enough to keep it from happening. Thus you had a commission stocked with states whose main interest lay in blocking the commission's actions. Sergio had insisted that substantial change would come through the states if it were to come at all, but one had to wonder how many states were still willing to play the game.

The Commission on Human Rights opened on the seventeenth of March, a Monday. The U.S.-led invasion of Iraq began at first light on that Thursday. Most countries with permanent representation in Geneva hosted a cocktail party during the commission, and soon Sergio, Jonathan, and I were driving to the U.S. mission for drinks. The subject of Iraq came up often there, as you would expect, although I was struck that no one seemed enthusiastic about either the war or its prospects. There was a generic war excitement, but that was all. I stood around with the senior U.S. representatives, and one of them, smiling, said after some awkwardness, "Here's to a short war!" I didn't want to toast this war, short or long, but I raised my glass anyway and drained it.

It was getting late when Sergio and I got into his BMW sedan—Jonathan had since left—and headed back to the Old City, where Sergio lived by himself in a small apartment. We chatted about the commission and the war, the various personalities. We brought no vigor to it; the scene before us was just too depressing. The Security Council wasn't working, the commission wasn't working. It was hard to see, within the system, what action to take. Sergio's personal life was a mess; he was separated from his wife, closing in on divorce, and did not see enough of his two sons, who were now young men. His girlfriend was still living in New York. Somehow his life had hit this pitch of loneliness—personal, political, and professional. He parked by his apartment, and we sat there for quite a while, sometimes discussing the war but mostly staying silent. Finally I asked him if he was going to be all right. He said yes, and I left him there for my own walk home through the silent Old City.

The commission trundled along. Big talk about a special Iraq war session quickly died down. The Like-Minded Group, led by Cuba and Algeria, chipped away, with impressive bureaucratic dedication and thoroughness, at the commission's authority. Back home, the government of Fidel Castro actually imprisoned dozens of political opponents even as the commission sat, an event that caused only a slight hiccup in the proceedings. Near the end of March, a Sudanese official had announced that his government was choosing the military option in response to a breakdown in negotiations with rebel groups in a then-obscure region called Darfur. On March 28, the commission's investigator for Sudan, Gerhart Baum, reported in Geneva, "The country remains under the iron-tight grip of the omnipresent security apparatus, which continues to enjoy virtual impunity." He drew special attention to the new situation in Darfur. We considered making a statement, though there were a million other things to do. At one point Jonathan was racing down a hallway, and he looked over his shoulder at me and shouted, "Imagine what would happen if there were a real genocide!" I shouted back, "We already know!" I was thinking about Rwanda again.

Sergio seemed to be keeping his head above water by following a breathless schedule of meetings with foreign ministers, heads of state, and ambassadors. For my own sanity, I tried hard to gin up some Europhilia. The Palais des Nations, where the commission met, was an interesting place for this sort of exercise. It was in a large park up above the lake and the city, a bequest from the Revillod de Rive family to the city of Geneva. One condition of the gift was that peacocks be allowed to walk freely on the grounds, a charming idea although you had to watch where you sat and the birds emitted harsh squawks throughout the workday.

It is a huge building, and even during the commission there were meetings elsewhere in the palais on such things as standards for marine mining. This was the great temple of rule making; elsewhere around the city were the World Health Organization, the WTO, the World Meteorological Organization, the International Telecommunications Union, the International Organization for Standardization. From the Palais des Nations, I contemplated the history and excellence of this European project of standard setting and the expectation, which was its underpinning, of a constant expansion of the rule of law from here outward. That was the measured Europe I wanted to groove on, with its eco-friendly washing machines, small food portions, health care and long vacations, safe streets, eighteenth-century music, tremendous attention to the details of good living, and this wonderful weight of all the European past, with its refinement and thorough disasters—a weight that had, as part of the relatively recent European economic miracle, become light and comfortable because in Europe the European past didn't really weigh anything anymore. The darkness of 1914–45 had slowly but surely been dispelled, leaving behind only its wise lesson of limits.

To my mind, the one lesson still unlearned in Europe was that of humility. I often thought that this lack of humility was what would push Europe, against its will, into its next fateful encounter with the rest of the world. I was reading a book by Peter Sloterdijk called *Si l'Europe s'éveille* (If Europe wakes up). Writing in the early 1990s, he saw Europe as a mythic entity that depended for its survival on a diet of visions and grandeur. Europe's driving myths "must be constructed like luminous dreams, and developed to become the inner life of new generations."

He didn't mean to, but he nonetheless seemed to view Europe as the culmination of history, a view shared by many other European writers of a less transcendent and speculative temperament (who tended to present Europe as the model for a global "rules-based order"). What was striking to me, in post–Cold War Europe, was how this type of self-love could coexist so happily with a feeling that Europe had no particular responsibilities in the rest of the world and had achieved, through the purging of its own nationalisms, a durable innocence everywhere. What would it do when its blamelessness and innocence were affronted? It would blame the United States, of course; Europeans had got into the habit of blaming Americans, a habit that might prove hard to break. But beyond that, how would Europeans look at themselves differently, when their post–Cold War "normality"—that was the European version of the end of history—started to change?

It was a question I tried not to ask too often. I wanted, while I could, to leave the world's problems aside at the end of the day, to make informed use of my leisure time—to have, in short, a perfect middle age, a goal for which Europe, in this historical moment, seemed suited like nowhere else on earth. And sensing that the moment wouldn't, couldn't last made it that much sweeter.

As the war got under way, and the fears at home continued to rattle her, Becky set her morning alarm, back in Brooklyn, to a French radio station. Hannah and Ben were being tutored in the language. They were planning their escape into another language. But the process of my gaining a permanent UN post seemed to go on and on. My calls to Becky began to acquire a desperate edge. Often I'd ring from the cell phone as I made my way home in the evening, arguing and fretting with Becky, then turning to happy talk with the children. I would describe to them the swans that patrolled the passage where Lac Léman turned into the Rhône, and the men who played chess in the park below the Old City using plastic chess pieces that were as big as Ben.

In that same period in late March, as the commission dragged on, Sergio began to think about speaking out on Iraq. The French foreign minister, Dominique de Villepin, had promised him that he would try to convince other Europeans to bring human rights considerations more firmly into Security Council debates. Sergio argued at one of our office's regular morning meetings that it was strange that the Security Council had focused on the question of Iraqi weapons of mass destruction to the exclusion of human rights considerations. And now that there was war in Iraq this exclusion seemed, in a sense, even stranger.

This discussion led to my drafting an article, which Sergio, Jonathan, and I then worked over before sending it on to the secretariat in New York for advice and approval. It appeared in the *Wall Street Journal* on April 21, two days before the commission ended, and was republished in about twenty countries in subsequent weeks. "The military preponderance of the U.S. and Britain must not lead us to think international stability can be ensured by force," the piece began. "If the international system is to be based on something other than might, states will have to return to the institution they built: the U.N."

Sergio went on to point out that the Security Council before the Iraq War had focused on weapons of mass destruction but was "unable to talk about a wider subject, which was how to deal with the security dangers posed by a regime that flagrantly violated the human rights of its citizens and, given the tendency brutality has of pushing beyond its borders, went on to attack its neighbors." Since the war began, the council had been unable to pass a resolution of any kind about Iraq. Meanwhile, the Commission on Human Rights had also been unable to discuss Iraq, with many states passing the buck back to the Security Council. He wrote,

> Both venues lacked a way to conceptualize security in human-rights terms and to recognize that gross violations of human rights are very often at the core of domestic and international insecurity. This is not a new problem. Consider the list of the U.N.'s recent failures, most notably its inability to prevent genocide in Rwanda and massacre in Srebrenica. . . .
>
> This is the signal political failure of our era: the failure to understand the security threat posed by gross violations of human rights, and the failure to achieve practical consensus in acting against such a threat. Surely we can now see, as we contemplate the loss of thousands of lives in Iraq, that the price of our failure is getting higher. . . .

He urged the permanent five members of the Security Council in particular—the United States, Britain, France, China, and Russia—"to grapple with this failure and to overcome it in a way that is based on responsibilities . . . Power rightly rests with member states. They must find a way to use it in addressing human rights as a core factor in domestic and international security. . . . Only then will responsible states, rather than the merely strong powers, be able to bring lasting stability to our world."

It was an attempt to salvage some positive direction out of what, institutionally, looked like a complete debacle. On April 16, the commission had voted not to pass a resolution on Sudan. The Like-Minded Group was in full cry, with a barrage of accusations from Algeria, Syria, Sudan, and Cuba that the commission was giving in to "politicization," whereas human rights should be "objective." Libya spoke of extending its hand to Zimbabwe, which was still suffering the "effects of colonialism." Cuba said Sudan's hard work for human rights really had not been appreciated enough while Sudan urged more recognition of Myanmar's "great progress."

Cuba, inevitably, got the final performance, taking the discussion away from colonialism and into the island's special quarrel with the United States. Cuba's representative said the commission was undergoing a "profound crisis of credibility," its members terrorized by the "fascist" power of the United States and its "equally

disgusting lackeys" in Latin America. In a performance of Leninist cliché and spit-
ting anger, the Cuban representative spoke of "a fifth column of US-paid merce-
naries" and "scores of agents of the US subversion." The session was like a revival
meeting for third-tier diplomats. Even some who disagreed with Cuba began, as
its representative spoke ever more loudly and his rage spun ever further away from
reason, to let their expressions of irritation and exhaustion give way to faint smiles.
Cuba, a curiosity and an orphan, was placing itself now, through will and declama-
tory stamina, at the very center of world events, and what ambassador couldn't, at
some level, envy that? China's representatives, habitually reserved to the point of
muteness, were not clapping so much as pounding their palms together in some
purgative frenzy. Syria and South Africa, too, were beside themselves. And when at
long last the commission ended, we all went to a party hosted by the Cubans, drank
mojitos, and grabbed free Churchill cigars until they were all gone.

———

At this moment, in late April 2003, the United States was nearly certain that
the Iraq War was over—a second victory, to be placed alongside the one in Afghanistan, which was felt to be well secured. The American approach to Saddam Hussein
had been vindicated; Tony could stop worrying. This was more or less consensus
opinion, and in the Op-Ed we had spoken of the Iraq War's "aftermath" and "a
contested and contentious peace."

Nonetheless, victory or no victory, we couldn't help thinking that the apparent breakdown of the existing international architecture was regrettable. What we
were going to do about it was unclear. The commission had finished to a chorus of
derision, mostly. The NGOs pitched their expectations ever lower. We still had our
office and its programs, but unfortunately Sergio's concentration on them was no
better now than ever. The "operational" emphasis was still just a promise. He would
say he was waiting for his executive office team to fill in. Yet it was clearly also the
case that Sergio had no intention of himself filling the void. He spent very little
time with his senior managers, who were, as they told me, losing faith in him. The
several hundred people beneath them fared no better. The office was adrift when it
could not afford to be.

Sergio was infinitely better when in motion, whether intellectual or physical. The Op-Ed, however minor, was at least something, a form of action and an attempt to reason our way out of this crisis. We wanted to keep that slight momentum, and the week after the commission we attended a small meeting in Geneva at something called the Center for Security Policy. It was not a human rights venue; there would be a number of military people present. I had written a speech up quickly and gave it to Sergio on our way to the car.

It was fun to make trips like this. The normally languid driver would become animated. The guards liked to give Sergio a slightly mocking salute when he came and went—all the more intimate and comradely for its staginess. He had a manner that didn't appeal only to men but did appeal to most of them, the manner of a charming boy gathering up friends for a lark.

In the car he put on his glasses, which age was forcing on him and which he hated. (I was just learning to print out his speeches in large type.) He read the speech and wrote fresh passages in the margins: on the "responsibility to protect," on his disappointment with the Security Council, on the risks of holding elections too soon in a post-conflict situation, on the challenge of the Security Council facing up to human rights violations by its own members. When we arrived at the center he turned the energy on: leading with the jaw, the trim suit jacket buttoned, the immense smile, the gray hair at the temples, and the deep voice. Lots of handshakes, a few canapés, an effusive introduction, and there he was, looking almost happy, banging on about human rights and security and how complementary the two were.

On May 1, President Bush flew onto an aircraft carrier and declared an end to major combat operations in Iraq. It seemed premature, though not by much. So we began to think in more practical terms about Iraq—somewhat reluctantly, since helping to fix up Iraq felt an awful lot as if we were helping to validate the unilateral approach of the Bush administration, if not the actual invasion of Iraq. For now, the action was in New York, with the negotiations over a post-conflict Security Council resolution that would aim at defining a UN role in the occupied country.

Sergio had some fairly developed ideas about this, and we put them into a speech he gave in Lausanne on May 7. "Many states want to be certain that the Security Council not do anything that could look like approval of the Coalition's war," he said.

This raises the always interesting question of legitimacy. It is a question the UN has faced before. My own feelings are rather ambivalent with regard to the role of the United Nations in the construction of a nation. Some believe that the UN should not assume such a role. They believe that the era of colonialism—and by extension, neocolonialism—is over and the UN has no business reviving it. . . . And besides, who are the international community or the UN to give lessons for the edification of a nation or a state?

I feel a natural sympathy for this line of argument. But it is in the order of things that one will continue to make appeals to the UN. . . .

The alternative, as he saw it, was collapse, the rule of the strong, and the irrelevance of the United Nations and its principles. "If we are not there to offer our support in situations where the state has collapsed, then what are we for?" Tellingly, the speech was built from an earlier text he had written about East Timor, using Timor examples—ten points about the construction and reconstruction of states, from warnings about holding elections too early to his belief in gender parity as part of reconstruction.

His final point was to emphasize that the UN, in reconstruction efforts,

must have the will to cede power as early as possible. Which brings us back to the question of legitimacy I referred to above. The UN, ardent partisan of decolonization, was, in East Timor as in Kosovo, seen as having something like neocolonial powers. This was, from the beginning, pretty disturbing. We were not, however, neo-colonialists. Probably one should not be overly abstract about these things. Making history and judging it are two different activities. When the United Nations finds itself faced with a state that needs construction or reconstruction, it does not, in my opinion, have a choice other than to act when it can and do the best that it can.

As the other Iraq shoe slowly dropped we did manage one interesting and forward-looking meeting with Luis Moreno-Ocampo, the new chief prosecutor of the brand-new International Criminal Court. The court had been inaugurated on March 11; Moreno-Ocampo was named on April 22. Everyone wanted to greet this as a bright moment in an otherwise darkening institutional landscape. There had, in recent years, been a number of ad hoc tribunals—for Rwanda, Sierra Leone, the former Yugoslavia, and others—each of which had tried something new and experienced its own successes and failures. But it wasn't clear that these varied efforts would accumulate into some firmer jurisprudence and codification of best practices. That was the practical promise of the ICC.

The founding of the court had other meanings as well. All the processes that went into identifying, condemning, and trying to prevent gross human rights crimes had been weakened by the lack of a permanent court to judge them. And now here it was, in a time that seemed so set against such things! Given its nature as an international tribunal, the ICC even reached back to the emotional core of the international system, the resolve to prevent forever, through institutions, any revival of aggressive nationalism, fascism, imperialism—for the ICC's lineage was quite explicitly traced to the Nuremberg trials, such that it felt as though a long-lost sibling of the post–World War II settlement had come home. The concept of the court had been revived in the 1980s, and so, for the human rights world, the court also evoked that optimistic period that had culminated in 1993 in Vienna.

The meeting itself was suffused with good feeling. Moreno-Ocampo indeed seemed new to his job; he acknowledged no obstacles yet, just areas of potential cooperation between his office and ours. Soon he would need to look at which cases to take on, a complicated task that we might help with by giving advice. The ICC also had two glaring weaknesses: no fact-gathering capacity and a lack of arrest power. The chance to help address these weaknesses, and the political questions involved in case selection, appealed deeply to Sergio's particular brand of diplomatic athleticism. As the small group in the meeting celebrated with glasses of wine—something we almost never did—Sergio and Luis looked set to accomplish great things together.

It had been rumored since the beginning of April that Sergio was being considered for the post of Annan's special representative in Iraq. I never asked him about it. Some sort of involvement in Iraq had seemed inevitable and had, of course, been a central topic during our Washington meetings. When we had returned to Geneva Sergio asked me for a memo on Ahmad Chalabi, the Iraqi exile leader, and now he had me prepare one on L. Paul Bremer, the new American administrator for Iraq.

Early in May a colleague in the secretariat phoned to ask if Sergio was happy in his job: was he finding it all just too legalistic? I tried to paint a rosy picture; I couldn't see how this line of inquiry would lead anywhere good. Soon it was widely reported that Sergio was indeed being seriously considered for the job of the secretary-general's special representative for Iraq. I called Jonathan, who assured me it wouldn't happen. I wanted the rumors not to be true, for many reasons, including what such an appointment might say about the priority of human rights in the UN system (not as high as I had thought) and the appalling lack of talent in the Organization such that you would have to vacate a senior position in order to get the right person for Iraq.

The final version of the Security Council resolution on Iraq (1483) passed on May 22. By that Saturday, the twenty-fourth, it was being reported that Sergio was the choice for special representative. He had agreed to serve for four months.

I next saw him jogging down the path along the Arve River as I was jogging up. He had taken the overnight SwissAir flight and was, he said, hoping to run off the jet lag. It was very hot that day.

"Congratulations on the new post," I said.

"I don't know if 'congratulations' is the right fucking word," he said. "But thank you."

We chatted a little, I promised to brief some Iraq issues for him—he had very little idea what to do in Iraq —and Sergio took off downstream, toward town, while I continued upward, past some tennis courts and an old mill, up a steep and rocky path, through some village streets, and across the border into France. I was getting to love this place, getting to know it through runs in the morning and long walks at night, through history books and writers like Jacques Chessex and painters like Ferdinand Hodler. I was also—this was perhaps another 9/11 effect—beginning to think of my new little world as vulnerable, so I had mixed feelings, as I jogged back into Switzerland and back down along the Arve, about the hundreds of anti-globalization protesters who had just set up camp in a great field on the river bank.

Instinctively, I wanted to be on their side, and it was strange to realize that I wasn't. Mass antiglobalization protest had its good qualities but it was a blunt instrument; besides, the objects of this protest—the governments assembling for the G-8 summit down the lakeshore, in Evian—were all making pledges about relieving third world debt and getting aid for Africa. Most parts of the international system had already converted, if incompletely, to the fight against inequity and poverty. So, in the logic of these things, the antiglobalization movement had fragmented into smaller causes, retrenched into a purist rejection of the progress that had been made, and taken another look at the romance of violence.

As I walked past the tents, taking in the sights and scents of radical style, I noticed Sergio again, at the far edge of the camp-field. He was pacing, his head down. He had his shirt off and was a picture of admirable fitness and utter dejection. His own background had been left wing, in the Parisian fashion, circa 1968. There was an anecdote somewhere about a barricade and some stones and a battle with police. (A truncheon blow was said to have caused the droop of his right eye.) But his orientation was no longer toward political ideologies and parties. In any case he was neither French nor European and had never found a place on the political scene of his native Brazil. Sergio had poured his idealism into the UN mold. I didn't know him well enough to say what that choice was doing to him right now, on this hot day, as he paced along a low rise above the tents of the sons and daughters of his fellow '68ers and contemplated a tour in Iraq.

With Sergio back and an expedition in the offing, there was a welcome bustle in the halls of Palais Wilson. Old friends from the refugees' office were coming around. Some from our office were going to Baghdad as well: Jonathan, Mona Rishmawi, Sergio's wonderful secretary Carole Ray. They all chattered animatedly about flight plans and who else was going with the team. Sergio was able to bring out the best the UN had. I doubted any one of them supported the invasion of Iraq, but they did want to be where the action was. Since I had come to the UN, I was constantly told that the Organization only proved its worth in "the field," as the phrase went, not in Geneva or New York. UN people loved to describe themselves as "on mission." There was a romance to it. Once Sergio had accepted his fate the depression lifted and he became quite the whirlwind, assembling an impressive team in about a week. He was bringing along people from the IMF and the World Bank—an innovation on a mission of this sort, and one he was proud of. Some very successful people were dropping everything to follow Sergio to Baghdad.

I was outside this charmed circle of adventurers and felt it keenly. There were promises I could get to Iraq later. For the moment I was to busy myself writing Iraq issue briefs until Sergio left. He had told me plainly that he did not know what he was going to do in Iraq and welcomed any suggestions. Colin Powell, he said, had told him he should interpret his mandate liberally, which sounded nice but was in fact not, as all it did was increase the number of possibilities for failure. The Secretary-General apparently hadn't been much more helpful. At the morning meeting when Sergio formally told his Geneva managers of his appointment as special representative, he said that his *Wall Street Journal* Op-Ed was largely to blame, in that it had led people in the secretariat and elsewhere to say: OK, Sergio, if you're so clever let's see you fix this.

To the extent that he had a plan, it was to make a strong display of respect for Iraqis and do everything to encourage dialogue among them and with their neighbors—a simple plan. And if the Americans had been less high-handed, self-absorbed, and generally pleased with themselves than they were, Sergio's strategy might even have been redundant. As matters stood, it was ambitious.

The Iraq briefing papers were an initial attempt at a plan and had six main points. First, I suggested he focus on the short period of his appointment: the four-month mark would give the mission some focus in an unfocused situation. I suggested he concentrate in particular on civil society, which the occupying powers, with their emphasis on obedience, would be poor at cultivating, and which might have some chance of holding Iraqi society together. My second point was that he should get some small economic projects going, and I attached a list of Baghdadi capitalist families.

The third suggestion was to try to bring some political coherence to the place. I prepared briefing papers on the different parties and personalities and a time line of the unsuccessful efforts to date. I suggested he pay special attention to Muqtada al-Sadr, who I thought was being underestimated. (According to some reports, he had survived underground in Saddam Hussein's Iraq, which was a striking achievement in itself and politically suggestive. Then again, I had no sound way of judging the accuracy of such reports and was basically winging it.) Fourth, I urged him not to forget the demobilized Iraqi military. Jerry Bremer had ordered the disbanding of the Iraqi military at almost the very moment that Sergio got this job. "You need something to reach these young men," I wrote, "a jobs program or employment bank. Something. They will be the foot soldiers of division otherwise." The final recommendations were to focus a project on mothers, perhaps obstetric care, which had reached a terrible state; and to get some decent media going.

In the brief, I saw the mission as having a small window of time. The White House was, it seemed to me,

> nervous . . . The missing weapons of mass destruction are not a small issue (for Blair either). For that reason and many others, the Americans are looking to you and the SG [the secretary-general] for legitimacy. It happens that you and the SG (and others) are also looking to this Iraq mission for the Organisation's own legitimacy—for the legitimacy of multilateral politics. As you said Friday, this is the game we're in now. You laid down your marker in the Op-Ed (sorry about that). The SG needs a way out of this impasse, the Security Council impasse, all the stuff we've been talking about. The US needs a way out, too—not as badly, but it still needs it.

Finally I wrote remarks for delivery on arrival in Baghdad, mostly stuff about the glory of the Mesopotamian past and other flattering declarations of respect. I made one set of briefings for Sergio and one for Jonathan, putting them all into neatly labeled file folders. Too soon, the cars were packed. On Sunday, June 2, from my corner window, I watched them all drive away from Palais Wilson. They waved to the guards at the gate, spirits high.

After a few weeks Sergio asked me from Baghdad to serve as the front-office coordinator for Iraqi matters. I was thrilled and threw myself into seeing what there was, or should be, to coordinate. It was a bit thin. There were human rights projects being cooked up in Baghdad, and there were Iraq-related human rights projects being thought about in Geneva, but the twain were not meeting. Thus the need for a coordinator.

Not long after Sergio left, Eric Schwartz arrived from Washington to serve as chief of staff for the no-longer-there high commissioner. Eric decided to undertake a top-to-bottom review of the office's many programs. Each project manager would present and defend his or her project. The idea was to weed out the weakest, shore up what needed shoring, and have a comprehensive assessment ready when Sergio returned so that the renovation of the office could begin at last. Eric had years of government experience; he had served for most of the Clinton administration in various posts on the National Security Council and before that at Human Rights Watch and its predecessors. He seemed to have limitless patience and an iron stomach for meetings and jargon. He was able to blend reformist energy with sheer bureaucratic endurance in a way that maximized his effectiveness—a weird sort of miracle, to my mind, but still a miracle.

Some of the office's projects were perfectly sensible, but others, too many, were almost inexplicable. It was as though the jargon of human rights had metastasized and killed off all the real-life cells, leaving only the langue de bois itself. "We're providing technical assistance," a project manager would say, confidently or warily. But what kind? To what end? "To strengthen capacity building and enhance human rights protection." Enhance how? "Through technical assistance." And so forth. This could go on for quite a while. As part of the process, we tried to determine what a project's "outputs" were, but that did not always help. Attendance at a conference or meeting, for example, was sometimes considered an "output," which came close to saying that the existence of our official presence somewhere constituted the result of that presence. The culmination, for me, arrived when a senior manager reported on his attendance at the inaugural meeting of a coordinating committee. The question at hand was whether we should seek regular membership on this new committee. The manager said that the committee's bureaucratic positioning and vague brief suggested to him that it would do no work of concern to our office and possibly no work at all. His recommendation? We should join the committee in order to monitor it; otherwise, we could not be certain that it was continuing to do nothing.

Eric's effort was widely resented but necessary if the high commissioner's front office was ever to have much influence over what were, in theory, its own programs. The same turned out to be true, on a smaller scale, for my Iraq coordination. The office's customary torpor was exacerbated by the staff's thorough hostility to the Iraq War and its ambivalent feelings about Sergio. Beyond these, no one wanted to support, in any way, the Bush administration's assertion of its absolute power in the world. And finally, Eric's and my being American made our positions still more difficult; but our nationality was inescapable.

I found coordination of the Geneva people and those in Iraq to be a tricky business. At some point late in June I heard from Baghdad that Sergio was almost decided on having one of the UN's more operational agencies take on much of the initial human rights project's work.

I pleaded and I begged. It seemed the worst possible message to send to our staff: their erstwhile high commissioner didn't feel he could rely on them to handle what was arguably the most important (and politically the most hazardous) human rights operation in the world at that moment. It would further undermine morale and deepen the paranoia about Sergio's relationship with the Americans. I begged and I got a reprieve. If I could get the project together, including funding, we could keep the Iraq file. But I only had a few weeks.

It was the emergency I had longed for. I set about educating myself on the various bureaucratic processes of project design and approval. I didn't tell colleagues that we faced an ultimatum; I felt that would either depress them or make them dig their heels in, or both. I also lacked power in the usual sense—power over salaries and status. But I had energy and a willingness to embarrass myself, in the bureaucratic context, and to show up again and again at the door to ask what progress was being made, never pushing too hard but never backing down, either. Such a willingness can be powerful in a social environment where others are oriented toward self-protection and risk avoidance. Anyway, it was what I had.

Gradually the project came together. In Baghdad, Mona Rishmawi and her colleagues were working closely with Iraqis on projects to advance human rights education for judges. There was a rudimentary human rights–monitoring presence that our office could enhance. A small human rights office was being set up in Baghdad, along with a system for organizing the information coming in from all over about abuses under Saddam Hussein. We were translating human rights materials into Arabic and printing them. Various personalities had to agree on the details of these projects; getting them to agree, quickly, was much of my job. Then there was the matter of funding. It took a while, but the budget people eventually helped me find around $2 million, which would take our programs through to the end of the year.

While I worked on all this I was in frequent contact with Baghdad and developed some sense of how things were going. The security situation was uneven, at best. Coalition soldiers and private contractors were being attacked—not all that effectively, but still, it was clear that the road to stability in Iraq would not be as short as had been hoped. The brusque demobilization of the Iraqi military was now more widely perceived to be an error. The looting of armories boded ill. Worse still, Iraqi political forces remained seriously at odds, with no group or coalition able to bring the others along in anything resembling national unity. Relatedly, Iraq's neighbors remained very ambivalent about the occupation. Under such conditions, the American instinct seemed to be to gather yet more power into American hands and to resist devolving power to Iraqis.

Sergio's main activity, then, was to broaden participation by seeking out and consulting as many Iraqi political actors as possible and trying to bring them into Iraqi political life as it was evolving under occupation, with an emphasis also on tangibly increasing Iraqi power within the occupation framework. In practice, this required a particular focus on those Iraqi actors who were reluctant to participate or with whom the occupying powers—essentially, the Americans, as the British and any others were kept at a distance from this kind of decision making—were unable to talk. So he met with the Communists, the pro-Iran Shiite leaders, Ayatollah Ali al-Sistani, Muqtada al-Sadr, and listened to them, and tried to find ways for them to take their appropriate place in the evolving political scene. By the same token, he met with Iraq's neighbors—Saudis, Iranians, Kuwaitis, Jordanians, Syrians, Turks—to assess their fears, needs, and ambitions and to find ways to balance them with Iraq's right to stable self-government. He met with civil-society groups, particularly human rights and women's groups. Finally, he tried to bring the Americans along to this broader view of political participation and away from their focus on friends and enemies and on their own success.

228 — GENERATION'S END

There was considerable debate within the Baghdad mission on these strategies. One group of senior UN advisers tended to argue that Sergio shouldn't do anything in Baghdad. Four months was too little time. He didn't know the region, the language, or the players. The Americans would simply use him when they could and ignore him when they couldn't: he would be their tool, whether he liked it or not. So he should sit on his hands, and listen, and run down the clock. Ideally, it was sometimes said, he and the mission shouldn't have been there at all.

Others felt that the risks of inaction were also high. It would underscore the popular impression of UN uselessness, for one thing, and it would mean missing a chance to further the political empowerment of Iraqis and thus speed the withdrawal of the Americans.

Not surprisingly, given his character, Sergio chose the active role. His position was more and less scrupulous than that of the Americans; or you might say he was operating with a different set of scruples, based on a different assessment of human and political possibilities. One of the apparent reasons the Bush administration had invaded Iraq, at least in the case of the president, was a wish to prove a point about human nature: that human nature is good. Iraqis were, just as all (good) people are, freedom loving, and when they had freedom they would do good things with it. This was the point of the analogy with Eastern Europe under communism; when people were governed by a tyrant, all you had to do was keep pushing and eventually their society would pivot from perversity to normality, thanks to your benevolent insistence on universal rights. The natural love of freedom was also part of the point of Rice's analogy with slavery, although that analogy, I had come to believe, had a second point: to justify the use of force by a vanguard to engineer an anti–status quo outcome that could be vindicated only in the long term. (This was rather a Leninist view of abolitionism. It had had a direct application to Eastern Europe, during the formative years of Rice and others in the administration when they had worked for James Baker on the reunification of Germany. In that effort, the Baker team had pressed hard for reunification against the wishes of many Germans and a great many Europeans.) After 9/11, President Bush had replaced his (traditionally conservative) skepticism about the use of power to force change with optimism about American power and the receptivity of people everywhere to its assertion. This optimism about human nature and human freedom was so strong that it could only understand opposition to it as springing from ignorance or something worse.

By contrast, Sergio, while impressively optimistic about some things, held no special regard for Americans in their use of power, nor, as far as I could tell, did he believe that human beings were destined by their nature to use freedom wisely, given the chance. He had witnessed, by this point in his career, numberless instances of people using their newfound freedom to slaughter, rape, expel, and degrade other human beings. Freedom was an aspect of power, not an antidote for it. Freedom lay in channeling power in ways whose value had been proved by experience.

For Sergio—oddly enough, for a UN man—effective power was always local. This was more wisdom than morality, and in the worst situations his characteristic approach could seem accommodationist and even immoral. (There were reasons why, in the Balkans, he'd been given the nickname Serbio.) Yet if his judgments were sometimes dubious, they were not cynical. He seemed always to feel that if he could get that one more meeting with one more political player he might turn the key and make things better—slow the conflict, get more refugees out, get more food in. Something. For him, this was the constant in a changeable world; and this persistent, ground-level betterment was, for him, the existential condition of the United Nations and the international civil service.

The United Nations, in this view, was what lasted. He told reporters at various points that the American occupation of Iraq was temporary while the UN's commitment to the Iraqis was permanent. In Iraq, he worked on the assumption that after the United States was gone the UN would still be there, and everywhere; it was the United Nations that endured. In his experience this made sense, in that powers would come and go, muck things up or make them better, but the UN was there regardless, and Sergio was there, in the wreckage of colonialism and of anticolonialism.

But was this idea of the UN really viable any longer? The way in which the United States, in the case of Iraq, had dealt with the UN—with its particular notions of law and legitimacy, its structures, its rules—had gravely reinforced the impression that the UN could not act forcefully unless it was serving American interests, and therefore that when it did act forcefully it must have been serving American interests. This made the UN politically problematic at best and led some of Annan's advisers to advocate a simple declaration that the invasion was illegal.

In Iraq, the difficulties were if anything increased, because the United States was so overwhelmingly the main actor, with only skittish allies; because the American motives in invading Iraq were so fundamentally opaque; because the concept of a benevolent invader, or a reluctant occupier, made so little sense to many people, such that they were unable to believe it even if it was true; and, finally, because the great act that set off this historical chain, the attack of 9/11, was an American trauma that had precious little to do with Iraq. The one could not be resolved by addressing the other. An American trauma was not a universal trauma, and to try to make it one, as the Bush administration did, was, among other things, to belittle the traumas of every other nation in the world. This belittling effect was worsened by the president's tendency to claim special insight into man's fate as a result of his own experience of 9/11. Having experienced 9/11 (he seemed, increasingly, to say), having assessed it and given it its true weight, he could now see further into the human future than others of less grim experience.

In among the daily challenges of diplomacy and management, Sergio was thinking about these problems and what they might mean for the United Nations. In mid-summer he reported to the Security Council about Iraq, and while he was in New York he had Jonathan call and see if I could write an Op-Ed about the legitimacy or illegitimacy of occupation.

Later that day I sent in a draft that began:

Can there ever be a good foreign occupation? One rarely finds complete clarity in politics, but I do not believe there can be a good occupation. Can an occupation be legitimate? Only if it aims openly and effectively at its own disappearance and replacement by the one power that is always legitimate: that of the people who make up the occupied nation. That is what we are aiming at in Iraq.

The rest of the piece analyzed the current situation in Iraq; the narrative structure was chronological and otherwise held together by variations on the concept of political legitimacy. The article was intended to act as timely support for Sergio's main political project, the new Iraqi Governing Council (IGC): to bolster its legitimacy in the eyes of the international community, the occupying powers, and the Iraqi people, and to correspondingly quicken the pace of the occupiers' withdrawal.

Soon Sergio and Jonathan were back in Baghdad, and the Op-Ed went to a back burner. Now that Sergio had given his Security Council presentation and per-

formed as well as possible in helping form a representative Iraqi Governing Council, he was close to being a lame duck. His mandate would end soon. Both the Iraqi
politicians and Bremer were losing interest in him. They needed UN expertise in
holding elections and got it. But the political forces did not really want the UN for
anything else; they were engaged in an increasingly bitter fight over political legitimacy in which their one point of agreement was that legitimacy was not something
for the United Nations to bestow. The Iraqis believed this as much as the Americans
did. Sergio was perhaps incapable of believing it. In the event, he slipped into an
uncharacteristic sort of depression and tried to do something he was no good at,
namely, waiting.

In succeeding drafts of the Op-Ed, the phrase "over a week ago," in reference
to the IGC, was replaced by "last month" as July gave way to August. Eventually we
settled on a version to send to the secretariat in New York. It was twice as long as
my original, with more detail and texture from Baghdad and a more extended ad-
vocacy of the governing council ("as representative an institution of governance as
one could imagine in the Iraq of today"). The piece now began with a defense of the
international community's responsibility to protect. This doctrine was, of course,
central to Kofi Annan's vision of the post–Cold War world. I would have preferred
not to bring it up in the Iraqi context; given the strength of opinion against the
invasion, it seemed to me that defending a responsibility to protect doctrine in the
Iraqi case could only weaken the doctrine's appeal. But there was a logic to it from
an institutional point of view. It also made this article more congruent with our
earlier Op-Ed on the Security Council and human rights.

Having established these doctrinal points, the article shifted to a more modest
tone. "While history will sit in judgment on the decision to invade," Sergio wrote,
"what we must all wrestle with now—Iraqis more than anyone—is the fact of Iraq's
occupation. We, the enigmatic international community, would do well to display
humility in addressing the question of Iraq for we have greatly contributed, by act
and omission, to the suffering of its people and the turbulence that now prevails." I
noted the lack of examples and wondered what ones he would give at some future
press conference. The Op-Ed continued:

In the short time I have been in Iraq, and witnessed the reality of occupation,
I have come to question whether such a state of affairs can ever truly be le-

gitimate. Certainly, occupation can be legally supported. Occupation can also certainly be carried out benignly, grounded in nothing but good intentions. But morally, and practically, I doubt it can ever be legitimate: its time, if it ever had one, has passed.

This, I believe, is the uncomfortable truth that the United States, the United Kingdom and others in the Coalition Provisional Authority [CPA] face in Iraq today. No matter how constructive their presence, no matter what went before, indeed, no matter how arguably necessary it might be, the people of Iraq currently view their lives through the humiliating prism of being under foreign occupation. Victor Hugo could well have been speaking of Iraq today when he suggested that liberation is not deliverance. The people of Iraq would, I am sure, agree with him. . . . [Therefore the occupying powers] must aim openly and effectively at their own disappearance and replacement by the one power that is always legitimate, namely the power of the Iraqi people. This, I would argue, they are trying hard to do and the United Nations is playing its part in assisting both the people of Iraq and the coalition to make this transition both smoothly and quickly.

The grammar had broken down in the sentence that began, "No matter how constructive"—evidence of a thought process under strain. Sergio was saying clearly that the United States and the United Kingdom were in the grip of a structural error. It didn't matter how good their intentions were. The historical period for occupations had passed. Yet this was too mechanistic and absolute for someone with Sergio's cast of mind. An anti-occupation doctrine would relieve the various parties in Iraq of their responsibilities. Look at how the sentence lifts its clauses up to the narrow peak of "it" in "no matter how arguably necessary it might be"—what is "it"? The presence of the CPA? The humiliating prism of being under foreign occupation? Or viewing one's life as an Iraqi through that prism? From this vague summit the sentence advances hopefully toward the necessary subject, the sovereign actor that made sense to Sergio and clarified his thinking: "the people of Iraq." To him, how they viewed their own lives was a fact, not an opinion or disposition; this reality gives shape to the responsibilities of the occupiers, the politicians, the UN, and the neighboring countries. From what Sergio could tell, having traveled widely and listened, the Iraqis felt humiliated by the occupation. So the occupation had to end, not for doctrinal reasons, but to give the Iraqis a way to restore their own pride and dignity before each other.

A second difficulty with an anti-occupation doctrine was that it endangered the doctrine of a "responsibility to protect." Perhaps that was another reason why he had begun with a preamble defending that very responsibility. Sergio needed to uphold the principle of foreign powers intervening in a nation that had failed in its responsibility to protect its own citizens. But how such interventions would actually take place without leading to occupations was, to say the least, not obvious. Invaders with justice on their minds may not want to be occupiers, but they become occupiers anyway, as had just been demonstrated, yet again, in Iraq. Besides, a humanitarian intervention that removed or greatly altered a government, but did not involve a subsequent occupation, would be very hard to distinguish from a coup. As Sergio knew, good intentions mattered remarkably little in how acts of force played themselves out.

The wisdom and the determination and the contradictions were all there on the page. We would have to see what New York thought. I was going on vacation but promised to stay in touch if they needed me. I wanted to see my family. The office in Geneva was back in the Iraqi human rights picture now, with financing and a detailed action plan, after the close call earlier in the summer. We had this strong anti-occupation, pro-Iraqi article ready for the fall. Sergio had convinced Jerry Bremer and the CPA to give the Iraqi Governing Council more authority and broader membership. He expected to be back in Geneva, or at least out of Baghdad, by some point in September. I thought I'd take the kids up to Quebec, where they could hear French and get more comfortable with the idea of being in a foreign country with a strange language.

Becky was involved with a trial, so I took the kids, borrowed my brother-in-law's car and a canoe, and headed north. We went to amusement parks in small Québécois towns near the St. Lawrence River. We stayed in cheap, damp motels and huddled on the bed to watch cartoon shows in French, which I justified as an educational project. As we made it farther north we began to camp next to lakes. The farther north, it seemed, the bigger the lake. The earth flattened and stretched itself up closer to the sky and we grew taller. We spent days in the water pretending to be fish. The cell phone signal back to New York got weaker; every evening we'd drive to the highest point we could find and try to reach Becky. Finally, she reported that she had "prevailed," a lawyerly term that gave us a lot of laughs, and we turned back south toward Quebec City to meet her there.

I had stayed in infrequent touch with Jonathan to see how things were going in Baghdad. He was heading off for a holiday the week of the thirteenth. It happened that the thirteenth was also the day George Packer had a good sit-down with Sergio in the UN mission's offices in the Canal Hotel. Sergio talked about what a good working relationship he had built up with John Sawers (the UK representative in Baghdad), Ryan Crocker (the U.S. ambassador there), and Jerry Bremer. The problematic one had been Bremer. Sergio had mentioned to me before that Bremer had what Sergio called a neoconservative side, which seemed to mean mainly that he didn't like to work with UN people and UN processes, and was very reluctant to allow someone who might disagree with him to have power. But Crocker and Sawers, in Sergio's view, had been able to bring Bremer along in achieving what were Sergio's main goals: greater Iraqi authority and broader Iraqi participation. However, Sawers and Crocker had recently left. The situation was declining as Bremer's "neocon" side came out, along with the exclusivist self-assurance of many of his senior American advisers. Sergio told George that he was waiting impatiently for Jeremy Greenstock, Sawers's replacement as UK representative, to arrive.

Sergio said he was looking toward spring 2004 as a point that "would be excellent in terms of a shorter timetable for the U.S. to turn things over." He and the team were closely involved in election planning. He was well aware of the shortcomings of the Iraqi Governing Council he had worked so hard to empower, but he said, characteristically, "There's no alternative. So, rather than criticizing them, we need to help them identify their weaknesses and resolve them, and we are trying to do that in our own discreet way here." Sergio and George hashed over the various players, including the Communist Party, whose legitimacy Sergio had done so much to promote. "Why? Not because they're communist," Sergio said. "That's out of date anyway. But because they're secular, and there aren't many secular parties in this country with a national vision for the country."

George said, "They may well end up being something of a social democratic party."

"Exactly," Sergio said. "Exactly. I've used that argument. And they won't be defending the interests of Shiites, of Kurds, of Turkomans, they will be defending national interests, which is what this country needs, no?"

"Did the Americans resist that, by the way?" George asked.

"At the beginning. Not at the end."

This had, he said, been true of many groups (such as the more radical Shiites) now represented on the IGC. He described in considerable detail all that he had done, in his view, to democratize the council. It made him angry that the council was still being described as "American-picked." How many on the council, George asked, were "not original American picks"? "Many. Many. Many," Sergio said. "Over half would not have been there if Jerry could have had it his own way in the first half of June."

The interview gradually wound down. Sergio had talked about how he felt "irritated and, uh, and, uh, embarrassed by the very low profile the UN has here." The work so far had been mainly political, aimed at ensuring that the IGC would not be "vulnerable to the 'U.S.-appointed, U.S.-friendly' accusation that this council, in my view, does not deserve. . . . Incidentally, I wouldn't be touring countries in the region trying to sell the governing council if I didn't believe what I'm saying—because the last thing I need and the Organization needs is to be marketing the interests of the United States." He wished—and George agreed with him—that the United States had been able earlier on to share power and accept multilateralism, with its attendant limits on American power. It might have made everything easier. As it was, George pointed out, Iraq was in a shambles, and parts of it were already reaching a third world state of collapse, leading people to say it was looking like parts of Africa.

Sergio said,

And it shouldn't. That is also part of the humiliation. And they tell you, "This is not a failed state! This is not Rwanda!" They keep referring to Rwanda. Why the hell do they refer to Rwanda? In summary, yes, we could have helped, and we would have been only too happy to do so, also pointing to our own mistakes, because unless you admit why things went wrong and why it is you are now offering a lesson, you won't be heard. You see? And we could probably have done that. We still can. There's still time.

That was on Monday. George left Baghdad soon afterward, and Jonathan did too, as I learned on the Friday when I rang from Quebec and Rick Hooper answered Jonathan's phone. Hooper was someone I'd heard a lot about. He was the Arab specialist for the Department of Political Affairs, and a northern Californian, about my age. He had a considerable reputation within the Organization. He was on that unwritten list of still-somewhat-youngish people who were likely to lead the Organization's renewal, should there be one. I was looking forward to meeting him, perhaps in Baghdad, which I was hoping to visit before the end of the year to have a look at our human rights projects.

But for now I was going to maximize the time I had left with my children in Quebec City. We had a room in a modest place called the Hotel des Bastions, in the old city, looking eastward down the St. Lawrence as it flowed toward the Ile d'Orléans. This old quarter is still surrounded by the high defensive walls that went up when France and England were competing for domination of North America. Although the French lost, the Québécois have kept up their defensiveness, and as long as the stakes aren't too high there's a distinct truculent charm to it. Here they make their stand, safe behind these walls. It was great for the kids. We could noodle around the streets in tranquility. On our last night as a threesome we were doing just that—wandering, resting on a stoop or bench when we got tired—when we heard singing. Because the *vieille ville* was such an open place once you were inside, we let nothing more than curiosity push us through the dark streets, and the music got louder and louder until finally we turned into a courtyard, where there were rows of folding chairs and a little stage.

A few dollars bought us entrance. There were perhaps two hundred people there, with room for many more. The band was local, and after a few pop numbers the emcee announced he wanted to play some songs he thought everyone would recognize—songs of their childhood and youth. Songs that maybe some in the audience had forgotten. Was there anyone here tonight from France? (A number of hands went up.) Well, he didn't want to suggest that life over there had gotten maybe too "modern," or that people had lost track of what really matters, but here in Quebec they still knew the old songs, like this one for example . . . And they played what sounded like songs your mother would have sung to you in the 1920s. The crowd, including the slightly insulted French visitors, sang along with great pleasure, even when a light rain fell. I couldn't keep from grinning. Hannah (the six-year-old) asked me to explain what was happening. It should have been easy. But the background—the fight for territory, the building of city walls, the battles to defend them, the decisive confrontations, the receding into whatever remains, the assessment of what it means, the sometimes desperate assertion of its significance— was hard even to sketch. Yet, on the face of it, it should have been easy. Grownups sing lullabies for themselves, too.

Once Becky joined us I felt I could leave the cell phone off and relax. She fell easily into our slow pace of carriage rides and long dinners. All along the wall outside our hotel there were black cannons, plugged, huge iron things pointing at the river far below. The kids couldn't believe their luck. They would climb all over one, begin getting bored, then see the next one, ten or twenty feet away, and dash for it, and start clambering again. It was a miracle of distraction.

On the morning of Wednesday, August 20, I saw that everyone was still sleeping away and slipped out to go downstairs for some coffee. The banner headline on the cover of the *Globe and Mail* read, "IRAQI BOMB RIPS INTO UN: CANADIAN AID WORKER, TOP UN ENVOY AMONG 17 DEAD IN MASSIVE EXPLOSION." The *National Post* had little else on its cover: "BAGHDAD BOMB SHAKES UN," with a huge picture of the rubble. "Chief Envoy Likely Target of Deadly Truck Bombing," read one headline; another, "UN 'Star' Cried Out from Rubble." That second headline was above a piece by Isabel Vincent that went:

> Moments after a powerful blast ripped through his third-floor office in Baghdad yesterday afternoon, UN envoy Sergio Vieira de Mello managed to call for help on his cell phone.
>
> In a shaky voice, Mr. Vieira de Mello, who was seen by many as a possible secretary-general of the United Nations, told his top aide he was buried in rubble and an iron bar had fallen across his legs. He could not move. . . .
>
> [A]s several hours passed with rescue workers frantically digging by hand to reach the victims of the bomb blast, the badly injured Mr. Vieira de Mello, who was bleeding profusely from his legs, grew increasingly weak. He no longer answered his cell phone, which rang under the rubble where he was trapped.

A witness, who refused to give his name, told journalists in Baghdad Mr. Vieira de Mello's final words were "water, water" uttered in a barely audible whisper. By the time rescue workers reached him, his body was cold.

I gathered the papers, went upstairs to our room, sat on the edge of the bed by the window. I told Becky, "Sergio's dead"; showed her the papers; and cried and cried. "All he was doing was trying to help," I said. I couldn't think of anything else to say as my body clenched and shook. The tears flowed.

After a while I began a frantic search for my cell phone. I found it and went outside—I didn't want the kids to hear all this—and sat on a bench among the black cannons. I finally reached Carole Ray, then Jonathan. So they were alive. Mona, I could not reach; she was badly wounded. Rick Hooper was dead, Nadia Younes, Sergio's chief of staff, was dead. I got the list.

It would not be even remotely true to say I don't remember what happened after that. I remember everything: the long drive south through Maine, the place we stopped at for lobsters, the aquarium where you could pet little sharks, the fenced-in pool at another motel, and phoning in quotes to an obit writer in London. Reading Kofi Annan's abject line, "I only had one Sergio," and mumbling to myself, "Me too," while I sobbed. The SwissAir flight back to Geneva, crowded with UN people. My first sight of Mona, her face gray and askew from her wounds. The funeral service put together by Sergio's doughty sons, the two handsome young men whom I had only seen before in a photo on Sergio's desk of them posed on the Brooklyn Bridge. They had his and their mother's self-possession: for the service they had selected a Coldplay song, "The Scientist," with the laconic refrain, "Nobody said it was easy / It's such a shame for us to part / Nobody said it was easy / No one ever said it would be this hard."

I remember it all too well. How some rose to the occasion of grief and others didn't. How quick people were to blame the dead for all that went wrong. How shrines went up; there were flowers and notes and pictures all politely piled by a drinking fountain in the Place du Bourg-de-Four. Of course this reminded me of September 11, which I had taken this job partly to forget.

I went by the cemetery in Plainpalais soon after Sergio was buried there. I had failed to find the Borges quote on my first visit; I had lacked the resolve to jump the fence and get the job done. This time I climbed over and wandered back among the stones. Soon it began to grow dark and cool and of course very quiet because the cemetery was closed and I was alone. Borges's grave was very near Sergio's. He would have liked that. *And ne forhtedon na*: the quote was taken from a tenth-century poem recounting a battle of the Saxons against the Vikings and had been addressed by the hero Byrhtnoth to his soldiers. We thought it meant "and not to be afraid," although in the tenth century the word "forhtedon" probably represented not the feeling of fear but the thing that caused it: disaster, calamity, danger, ambush, and treachery are all associated with the old word. The things we fear, the fear we feel—the differences in meaning grow indistinct. The soil over Sergio's body was still loose and mounded. There was a cross with his name and dates. "I don't know what to do now," I told him. "What should I do?" Then I sat down on the grass at the foot of his grave as night fell.

EPILOGUE

Lessons in Power

The years after Sergio's death were . . . less full. The Organization didn't handle the survivors very well, or the families of the dead. Publicly, Sergio was memorialized as a fallen hero. Privately it was a different matter. The anti-occupation Op-Ed, his last major statement, was looked at in the secretariat and quietly filed away; I suppose that should have told me what I needed to know. I returned to New York and the *Times*, to edit the foreign coverage at the Sunday magazine. I was a wreck and stayed that way for quite a while.

My unhappy protagonists, the United States and the United Nations, continued to cling to old forms of power as the actual substance of their respective powers shrank. The destruction of the UN offices in Baghdad broke a spell. The objectivity of the UN and the global centrality of American power might have been recovered afterward, I suppose. There were many strong efforts in both those directions: to reform the UN, to internationalize the Iraq mission, to universalize the American view of the relationship between power and freedom. But none of these efforts worked very well.

It was hard to say whether the UN and the Bush administration caused this failure or the failure was a symptom of larger shifts. I leaned toward the latter interpretation. America has its own unique political charisma, and that charisma has its moments of resurgence. One of them was at the end of the Cold War. President Bush tried to bring on another. The shock of 9/11 seemed, in a way, as though it ought to issue in such a resurgence, and President Bush tried to make it happen. Yet the effect of his efforts was the opposite, and it only seemed to get worse with time.

The president's rhetoric about the new American-led era reached a height of grandiosity in his second inaugural speech in January 2005. "By our efforts, we have lit a fire as well—a fire in the minds of men," he said. "It warms those who feel its power, it burns those who fight its progress, and one day this untamed fire of freedom will reach the darkest corners of the world." Because it was the United States, everyone was listening; but practically no one was following. He had declared victory too often already. The clear triumphs of Afghanistan 2001 and Iraq 2003 became the disasters of Iraq 2006 and Afghanistan 2007, and then . . . whatever they became, it was bloody, and it was not obviously victory. The Bush administration and the Pentagon did slowly learn from their many mistakes, but the fundamental, geopolitical problem remained: the rest of the world refused to accept the leadership of the United States.

At the same time, as American power and charisma weakened, other nations were unable to seize the resulting opportunity in anything but selfish ways. No alternative principle emerged. No alternative institutions grew up. On the contrary, existing institutions became still weaker. The more time passed, the further away 1945 was—and the more helplessly the institutions of that postwar era foundered. The UN and global civil society made one more big push, with international panels and salvoes from the think tanks. Kofi Annan's intellectual legacy, the doctrine of the global "responsibility to protect," was, in 2005, accepted by the General Assembly as a new dogma to be enforced by all states. Yet as with President Bush's own, more colorful effusions earlier that year, it led to very little. And on those few occasions when the responsibility to protect was effectively invoked, it was outside the UN's purview.

Matters might have limped along like this, with both the United States and the United Nations dwindling in significance, except that two new things appeared in the world: Barack Obama and the weakening of globalization. Irony was certainly not dead! A black first-term senator with no executive experience emerged and somehow managed to revive America's image both abroad and to a great many Americans; and the sudden collapse of a system of global financial interdependence made states begin to realize how crucially they relied on each other. Obama, coming from a minority within a minority (as a half-white person who looked black), could not represent America in the way the forty-three white men who had preceded him represented it. He was biologically unable to represent just a single strand of the American experience. His appeal then was necessarily collective and a bit abstract. Yet because Americans' emotions concerning race are often intense, and our collective experience of race is basic to our nature as a nation, this was an advantage for him, one he brilliantly, consistently identified and used. As a candidate, he said: We have a past together, but we aren't trapped by it. Look at me. I am the proof. And when he became president, he used this same biography, with a few tweaks, to tell the world that American leadership was back, but in a minor, more cooperative key—that American leadership was no longer white leadership, and thus in some way it wasn't Western leadership, either. With his biography, Obama promised to return America to its role as a nonimperial third party to the ancient quarrel between the colonizers and the colonized (something Bush had also attempted but failed to achieve).

At just this same moment, as fate would have it, some dynamic nonwhite parts of the world—China, India, Brazil, Indonesia—were surging forward, and saying: We are not trapped. We are growing and becoming stronger and wealthier. The dominance of the white, Western world is not going to last.

The UN and the other 1945 institutions were not, however, geared to deal with such a development. The shift demanded a mature, negotiated, flexible, and innovative redistribution of power—an impossibility without extraordinary leadership, extraordinary stress, or perhaps both. In 2008 the stress came. Financial collapse brought on a deep recession. The institutional response was fascinating: the UN was unable to do anything more than commission studies, but the leading rich nations' grouping, the G-8, was likewise immobilized. You just never know. A previously humble bureaucratic backwater, the Group of Twenty (G-20, essentially the G-8 plus the next tier down of countries), became the forum of choice, slowly under the outgoing Bush administration and with greater speed under Obama. Western leadership was collaborating, willy-nilly, in its own institutional weakening and absorption into a (somewhat) more democratic, and significantly less Western, structure. The G-20 began to look for ways to blend its powers with those of the International Monetary Fund, until recently the most hated of international capitalist institutions but now a venue for, of all things, power sharing between West and East, North and South. Maybe that would last, or maybe the G-20's early momentum would shift to other institutions, old or new. But the basic trajectory seemed clear.

American leadership in this necessary recalibration has been uneven. Obama's biography, in itself, was merely a literary solution to what were durable geopolitical problems. Yet he was also shepherding a genuine shift—in particular, a generational shift to an age group that was not overwhelmed by World War II or by Vietnam (or even by the civil rights movement), one that preferred, more as a matter of taste than conviction, a humbler American role abroad. Whether this will be good for the world is left for us to determine and discover.

A NOTE ON SOURCES

The source material for this book consists of newspaper and magazine clippings, books, printed e-mails, drafts of speeches and memos and Op-Eds, all lugged about among several homes over a period of years. I hope the reader will forgive me for no more elaborate sourcing. Public statements and published articles can be found online, for the most part; and the rest is in that other, non-Web place where so much of historical interest resides. Within quoted material, all emphases are in the original texts.

ACKNOWLEDGMENTS

In the course of writing this book I made the strange discovery that my friends had more faith in me than I did; they pushed me to keep scribbling when I thought I should be doing other, more sensible things. In this respect I have to thank, in particular, Caryl Phillips, Bruce Robbins, and David Rieff. If not for their persistence over a period of years, this book would not exist. Other friends (and family), too, kept me going, often with comments on the manuscript as it took shape: Salman Ahmed, Tina Bennet, Derek Chollet, Semezdin Mehmedinovic, Christi Malcomson, William Malcomson, Rebecca Martin, Pankaj Mishra, George Packer, Orhan Pamuk, Jonathan Prentice, Clive Priddle, Laura Secor, Adam Shatz, Terry Tang, Geri Thoma, and Minky Worden. Thank you.

INDEX

ABOUT THE AUTHOR

Since leaving the United Nations in early 2004, Scott L. Malcomson has been foreign editor at the *New York Times Magazine*. Articles he assigned and edited there have won the magazine wide acclaim for its foreign coverage and have earned many awards, including the Pulitzer Prize and the National Magazine Award. He is a longtime member of PEN American Center and a life member of the Council on Foreign Relations. He is the author of three previous books, including *One Drop of Blood: The American Misadventure of Race* (2000).